Mary Kingsley

TRAVELS
IN WEST AFRICA

Abridged and
introduced by
ELSPETH HUXLEY

EVERYMAN
J. M. DENT · LONDON
CHARLES E. TUTTLE
VERMONT

First published as an Everyman Classic, 1987
Reissued 1992
This edition first published in Everyman in 1993

J. M. Dent
Orion Publishing Group
Orion House, 5 Upper St Martin's Lane,
London WC2H 9EA
and
Charles E. Tuttle Co. Inc.
28 South Main Street, Rutland, Vermont
05701, USA

Printed in Great Britain by
The Guernsey Press Co. Ltd, Guernsey, C.I.

British Library Cataloguing-in-Publication Data
is available upon request.

ISBN 0 460 87394 6

CONTENTS

NOTE ON THE AUTHOR AND EDITOR

MARY KINGSLEY, niece of Charles Kingsley, was born on 13 October 1862 in Islington, London. Her father, George Kingsley, qualified as a doctor but spent most of his life as an adventurer-explorer. Mary and her younger brother were lucky if they saw their father more than once every two years, but during the brief periods he spent at home, their lonely life was transformed by the talk of his travels. They were all keen naturalists but Mary had no formal education, except for a little tutoring in German. When his health failed, and he had to give up travelling, George Kingsley began the task of preparing for publication the enormous amount of material he had amassed during his travels, and Mary assisted him with this work. Mary's mother was already an invalid and the burden of caring for her parents fell on Mary's shoulders. When they both died within six weeks of one another in 1892, Mary found her freedom but her narrow life meant that she had few friends or outside interests. Her decision to continue her father's studies in West Africa is therefore all the more remarkable.

She made two journeys: the first in 1893, the second in 1894–5. News of her exploits reached home, and her account of her travels, published in 1897, was an immediate success, not least because of the lively and witty style in which it was written. When the Boer War broke out, she went to Cape Town to help nurse the Boer prisoners-of-war, but within a few months she caught enteric fever and died on 3 June 1900.

ELSPETH HUXLEY was born in London in 1907, but spent her childhood in East Africa where her parents ran a coffee farm at Thika, just outside Nairobi. She married Gervas Huxley, a cousin of Aldous, and with him travelled the world. She has written crime stories, travel books, and novels, many with an African background. Her autobiographical novel, *The Flame Trees of Thika* (1959) was dramatised for television, and in 1986 *The African Poison Murders* was reissued in paperback in Dent's Mastercrime series.

CHRONOLOGY OF MARY KINGSLEY'S LIFE

Year	Age	Life
1862		Born Islington, London, 13 October
1863		Family move to Highgate

CHRONOLOGY OF HER TIMES

Year	Artistic Events	Historical Events
1862	Flaubert, *Salammbo* Victor Hugo, Les Miserables Birth of Edith Wharton	Bismarck appointed Prussian Prime Minister
1863	Charles Kingsley, *The Water Babies* Sir Richard Burton, *Wanderings in West Africa* and *Mission to Gelele, King of Dahomey*	Ashanti war with British in Gold Coast Birth of David Lloyd George
1864	Dickens, *Our Mutual Friend* Tolstoy, *War and Peace* J. H. Newman, *Apologia pro Vita Sua*	Gen. Grant becomes Commander-in-Chief of Union armies Sir Samuel Baker reaches Lake Albert Nyanza
1865	Lewis Carroll, *Alice in Wonderland* Death of Elizabeth Gaskell Birth of Kipling and Yeats	American Civil War ends (begun 1861) Abraham Lincoln assassinated Leopold II succeeds to Belgian throne
1866	George Eliot, *Felix Holt* Dostoevsky, *Crime and Punishment* Birth of H. G. Wells	First Barnardo home opened Atlantic telegraph cable laid Alfred Nobel invents dynamite
1867	Matthew Arnold, *Culture and Anarchy* Ibsen, *Peer Gynt* Trollope, *The Last Chronicle of Barset*	Second Reform Act Marx, *Das Kapital I* Alaska sold by Russia to USA Garibaldi begins march on Rome
1868	Wilkie Collins, *The Moonstone* Birth of Maxim Gorky and Edmond Rostand	Grant elected President of USA Gladstone replaces Disraeli as Prime Minister

Year	Age	Life
1879	16	Family move to Bexley, Kent

Year	Artistic Events	Historical Events
1869	Flaubert, *L'Education sentimentale* R. D. Blackmore, *Lorna Doone*	Suez Canal opened Birth of Mahatma Gandhi
1870	Jules Verne, *Twenty Thousand Leagues under the Sea* Death of Dickens and Alexander Dumas *père*	Franco-Prussian War Italians enter Rome, which is declared capital Birth of J. C. Smuts
1871	George Eliot, *Middlemarch* Darwin, *The Descent of Man* Birth of Marcel Proust	Stanley meets Livingstone at Ujiji Wilhelm I becomes first German Emperor
1872	Samuel Butler, *Erewhon* Thomas Hardy, *Under the Greenwood Tree* Jules Verne, *Around the World in Eighty Days*	Birth of Leon Blum and Calvin Coolidge Death of Giuseppe Mazzini First soccer international (England and Scotland)
1873	Tolstoy, *Anna Karenina* Birth of Ford Madox Ford	Ashanti War begins Death of Livingstone
1874	Hardy, *Far From the Madding Crowd* Birth of Robert Frost, W. Somerset Maugham and Gertrude Stein	End of Ashanti War General Gordon arrives in Khartoum
1875	George Eliot, *Daniel Deronda* Mark Twain, *Tom Sawyer* Birth of Thomas Mann Death of Hans Christian Andersen	Suez Canal purchased Telephone invented Captain Webb first swims English Channel
1876	Henry James, *Roderick Hudson* Sir Richard Burton, *Two Trips to Gorillaland and the Cataracts of the Congo*	Queen Victoria proclaimed Empress of India Ethiopians defeat Egyptians at Gura
1877	Ibsen, *The Pillars of Society* Zola, *L'Assommoir*	Russo-Turkish War First Kaffir War
1878	Hardy, *The Return of the Native* H. M. Stanley, *Through the Dark Continent*	Greco-Turkish War Electric street lighting in London CID formed in London (Scotland Yard) Birth of Trotsky and Stalin
1879	George Meredith, *The Egoist* Strindberg, *The Red Room* Birth of E. M. Forster	Zulu War begins: Battle of Isandhlwana Tewfik succeeds Ismail as Khedive of Egypt

Year   *Age*   *Life*

1886   24   Family move to Cambridge (brother at Christ's College)

Year	Artistic Events	Historical Events
1880	Dostoevsky, *The Brothers Karamazov* Zola, *Nana* Death of George Eliot and Flaubert	Boers declare independent Transvaal republic Garfield elected President of USA
1881	Henry James, *Portrait of a Lady* R. L. Stevenson, *Virginibus Puerisque* Birth of P. G. Wodehouse Death of Thomas Carlyle	First Boer War begins Alexander III crowned Tsar Death of Disraeli
1882	Ibsen, *An Enemy of the People* Birth of James Joyce and Virginia Woolf Death of Trollope, Darwin, Longfellow and D. G. Rossetti	British occupy Cairo First Boer War ends Triple Alliance formed (Italy, Austria, Germany)
1883	Olive Schreiner, *The Story of an African Farm* R. L. Stevenson, *Treasure Island* Birth of Compton Mackenzie Death of Ivan Turgenev	Kruger becomes President of South African Republic British evacuate Sudan Birth of Benito Mussolini
1884	Mark Twain, *Huckleberry Finn* *Oxford English Dictionary* begins publication Birth of Sean O'Casey	Gordon reaches Khartoum Third Reform Act London Convention on Transvaal South-West Africa proclaimed German protectorate
1885	Rider Haggard, *King Solomon's Mines* Maupassant, *Bel Ami* Birth of D. H. Lawrence and Ezra Pound Death of Victor Hugo	Gordon killed in Khartoum Death of Ulysses S. Grant Congo taken over by Leopold II British protectorate over N. Bechuanaland and Niger River region
1886	Henry James, *The Bostonians* R. L. Stevenson, *Dr Jekyll and Mr Hyde* Death of Emily Dickinson	Indian National Congress first meets Gladstone introduces Irish Home Rule Bill
1887	Sir Arthur Conan Doyle's first Sherlock Holmes story ('A Study in Scarlet') Hardy, *The Woodlanders*	Queen Victoria's Golden Jubilee First Colonial Conference (London) Birth of Chiang Kai-shek

Year	Age	Life
1888	26	First trip abroad, to Paris with friend
1892	30	Death of father (February) and mother (April)
		Trip to Canaries
		Moves with brother to Addison Road, London
1893	30-1	Sails for West Africa. Travels to Ambriz, Kabinda and Matadi on Congo and Old Calabar
1894	32	Returns to England
		Second trip to West Africa. Ascends Mungo Mah Lobeh
		Trades in rubber and oil. Collects insects, shells, plants, reptiles and fish for British Museum
1895	33	Returns to England

Year	Artistic Events	Historical Events
1888	Kipling, Plain Tales from the Hills Strindberg, Miss Julie Zola, La Terre Birth of T. S. Eliot	Matabele King Lobengula under British protection Jack the Ripper murders in London Wilhelm II German Emperor
1889	Jerome K. Jerome, Three Men in a Boat R. L. Stevenson, The Master of Ballantrae Death of Browning, Hopkins and Wilkie Collins	British South Africa Company granted royal charter Archduke Rudolf of Austria commits suicide Birth of Adolf Hitler
1890	Ibsen, Hedda Gabler Oscar Wilde, The Picture of Dorian Gray Knut Hamsun, Hunger	Bismark dismissed First underground railway in London Cecil Rhodes becomes Prime Minister of Cape Colony Birth of Dwight D. Eisenhower and Charles de Gaulle
1891	Hardy, Tess of the D'Urbervilles Kipling, The Light that Failed Gissing, New Grub Street	Wilhelm II visits London Triple Alliance renewed Young Turk movement founded
1892	Ibsen, The Master Builder Oscar Wilde, Lady Windermere's Fan Death of Tennyson	Agreement between Britain and Germany on Cameroons Death of Tewfik; succeeded as Khedive by Abbas II Grover Cleveland elected President of USA
1893	Wilde, A Woman of No Importance Sir Arthur Wing Pinero, The Second Mrs Tanqueray	Self-government in Natal Transvaal annexes Swaziland Matabele rising against British South Africa Company
1894	Kipling, The Jungle Book (First) Shaw, Arms and the Man Birth of Aldous Huxley Death of R. L. Stevenson	Uganda becomes British protectorate Dreyfus arrested and deported Dahomey proclaimed French colony
1895	Conrad, Almayer's Folly Hardy, Jude the Obscure Wilde, The Importance of Being Earnest	Rhodesia formed Jameson raid into Transvaal Marconi invents wireless telegraphy

Year	Artistic Events	Historical Events
1896	Chekhov, *The Seagull* Housman, *A Shropshire Lad* Death of Harriet Beecher Stowe and Edmond de Goncourt	Klondike gold rush France annexes Madagascar Kitchener's campaign in Sudan
1897	H. G. Wells, *The Invisible Man* Conrad, *The Nigger of the Narcissus* Rostand, *Cyrano de Bergerac*	McKinley inaugurated US President Port Arthur occupied by Russia Queen Victoria's Diamond Jubilee
1898	Henry James, *The Turn of the Screw* Oscar Wilde, *The Ballad of Reading Gaol* Shaw, *Caesar and Cleopatra* and *Arms and the Man*	Kruger reelected President of Transvaal Battle of Omdurman Curies discover radium
1899	Ibsen, *When We Dead Awaken* Kipling, *Stalky and Co.* Birth of Garcia Lorca and Noel Coward	First Hague Peace Conference Anglo-Egyptian Sudan Convention Boer War begins (ends 1902)
1900	Colette, *Claudine à l'école* Conrad, *Lord Jim* Chekhov, *Uncle Vanya* Death of Oscar Wilde	Roberts appointed C. in C. South Africa Boxer Rising in China Australian Commonwealth formed King Umberto I of Italy murdered

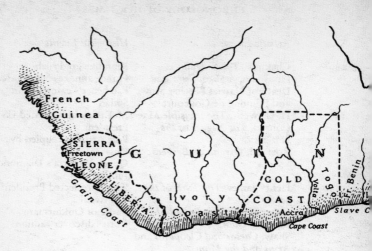

French
Guinea

SIERRA
Freetown
LEONE

G   U   I   N

GOLD
COAST

Togo

Fr. Benin

LIBERIA

Grain Coast

Ivory
Coast

Accra

Slave C

Cape Coast

GULF OF GUINEA

S O U T H

A T L A N T

O C E A N

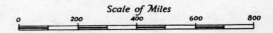

Scale of Miles

0   200   400   600   800

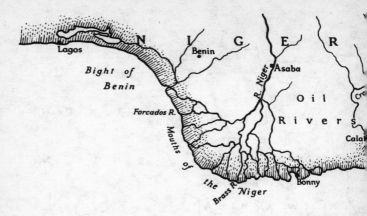

N I G E R

Lagos

Benin

Asaba

R. Niger

O i l

R i v e r s

Cro

Bight of
Benin

Forcados R.

Cala

Mouths

of

the

Brass R.

Niger

Bonny

Fernand

G U L F   O F

Big

B i

G U I N E A

Princes I.

N

St. Thomas I.
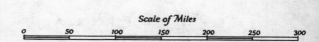

Scale of Miles

0   50   100   150   200   250   300

Editor's Introduction

Of the five sons born to the Rev. Charles Kingsley between 1819 and 1830, two died young and the other three took to the pen. Only the youngest, Henry, became a professional writer. The eldest and most famous, Charles (1819–75) achieved his main distinction as a clergyman but also kept up a prodigious output of novels, social tracts, historical romances, poems and essays on natural history. George Kingsley, Mary's father, was born in 1826 and qualified as a doctor, but was too idle and too footloose either to practise regularly in his profession or to organise and publish the great quantity of material he collected during his travels. Most of his life was spent roaming the world in the *entourage* of various noblemen, keeping diaries and notes, collecting curios and shooting an enormous number of wild animals.

His daughter Mary, born in 1862, had an unusual, solitary and possibly not very happy childhood, spent mainly in a small house in Highgate with her mother, who was lucky if she saw her husband once every couple of years or so, and with a younger brother. None of the Kingsleys was well off and George seems to have made little effort to provide more than bare subsistence for his family. For the whole of her childhood, Mary wrote, she was confined to house and garden. 'The living outside world I saw little of, and cared less for, for I felt myself out of place at the few parties I ever had the chance of going to, and I deservedly was unpopular with my own generation.' But she had 'a great amusing world of my own other people did not know, or care about—that was in the books in my father's library'.

She idolised her father. During his sojourns with his family, the drabness of a straitened life in Highgate was transformed into a kind of picnic. The house filled suddenly with talk, activity, tobacco smoke and souvenirs of the doctor's travels. All the Kingsleys were keen naturalists and it was from her father that Mary learnt the rudiments of natural history, as it was then called. George was an excellent, if spasmodic, letter writer, and his descriptions of distant places and strange adventures fired her imagination, as his eclectic library fed her alert and receptive mind.

Her reading was quite unsupervised and she was never taught;

she had to pick up knowledge for herself, as one of the fighting-cocks she kept in the garden doubtless picked up his corn. The only money ever spent on her education, she wrote, was on a little tutoring in German—and this was to make her useful to her father in translating scientific papers; whereas £2,000 was spent on her brother's education, 'I still hope not in vain'. French was ignored, and she found the lack of it a great handicap in her subsequent travels. Her passion to learn could be ruthless. Her father extolled a book called *Solar Physics*, and promised to lend it to a friend; despite his wrath she hid it away and 'the book returned to civilised society when I had got right through it—not before'. She managed to scrape together enough money to subscribe to *The English Mechanic* and 'what I would have done without its companionship between sixteen and twenty I do not care to think'.

Life cannot have been easy in the Highgate household. George was given to outbursts of rage when inconvenienced, and would hurl a book at his daughter when her fighting-cocks crowed under his window, or something was lost. There was an unfortunate occasion when, in an attempt to fathom the workings of military mines, she ignited a tin of gunpowder that he had brought back from his travels and a tub of liquid manure exploded over the 'great spring blanket wash' hanging on the line.

When her father's health obliged him to give up travelling, the family moved to Cambridge. Mrs Kingsley had herself been an invalid for some time, and the ordering of the household, and most of its actual work, had increasingly devolved upon the only daughter. In Cambridge, George set about the task of classifying and preparing for publication his enormous collection of notes and translations. A comparative study of sacrificial rites all over the world was a topic that had especially engaged him. Mary was for many years his 'underworker on that subject', and it was the hope of completing it that turned her thoughts to West Africa when she was released from her domestic bondage. That release did not come until after several years of 'work and watching and anxiety, a narrower life in home interests than ever, and a more hopelessly depressing one, for it was a losing fight with death all the time'.

The fight was lost in 1892 when her parents died within six weeks of one another. She was nearly thirty. Her whole life had been devoted to them; she had no outside interests, few friends. Now, suddenly, she was free. It was at first a hollow freedom. The purpose of her life had been knocked away; she had no one

to love and no one to be loved by either; there were 'no more odd jobs anyone wanted me to do at home'. She sought 'something to do that my my father had cared for, something for which I had been taught German, so that I could do for him odd jobs in it'. She decided to continue his 'study of early religion and law, and for it I had to go to West Africa, and I went there, proceeding on the even tenour of my way, doing odd jobs and trying to understand things, pursuing knowledge under difficulties with unbroken devotion'.

Mary Kingsley belonged to an age and generation when women's subjugation was so complete that even the death of both parents did not really set her free. There was still her brother Charles. So long as he needed her services, she felt in duty bound to postpone her own plans. The young Charles Kingsley was as selfish as his father but without his father's vitality or charm. After shilly-shallying for some time he at last, in 1893, departed on a journey to China, and Mary began the preparations she describes in her Preface to this book for the first of her two African journeys.

These journeys were remarkable not for any geographical discoveries—the days of West African exploration were over by then—or even scientific ones, although she did bring back 'one absolutely new fish' which was named after her, several new subspecies, 'one absolutely new snake, and one lizard the B.M. has been waiting for for ten years'. Rather they were remarkable because the traveller, a sheltered, middle-class, Victorian spinster lady of no unusual physique, without experience, without protection, without (to start with) any knowledge of African languages, who had probably never even slept in a tent on the lawn, went entirely alone into regions that were lethally unhealthy and primitive in the extreme, the territory of known cannibals, where a solitary, unprotected female, without possessions, travelling on foot, was an open invitation to be chopped and eaten like any stray wild beast. To the reader it seems almost a miracle that she emerged alive—and not only alive but, so far as one can tell, in excellent health. A bad cold caught on the heights of the Cameroon mountain in a tornado seems to have been almost the only ailment she considered worth mentioning, apart from sore feet.

The proviso, 'so far as one can tell', is necessary because no traveller has ever made light of hardship and danger with greater determination than Mary Kingsley. It was the essence of her brand of humour to convey an impression that to hack a

way through the densest rain-forests of the Congo, to be fired at
by hostile savages or charged by wild beasts, was scarcely more
arduous than a stroll through Hyde Park on a wet afternoon: a
brand of humour that, to modern readers, can seem at times
over-facetious, over-sprightly, too discursive and even verging
on the arch. But this was the way her mind worked, and she let
her mind run free and her thoughts flow from mind to pen and
pen to paper with a spontaneity that allowed little room for reflection, and none for the craftsman's shaping, paring and
carpentering together. 'I am convinced that I have somehow
strayed out of the 18th century into modern life,' she wrote to
her publisher George Macmillan. 'My style and that of the early
navigators is one and the same.' They would not, she added, take
themselves seriously, but 'would yarn for an hour at a time on a
dead whale they found, or an "exceeding merry Droll" they
played on their companions'.

Few women of her time and background have displayed
greater independence of mind, originality of thought or disregard for the accepted conventions; and yet, paradoxically, some
of those conventions—the outward rather than the inner ones—
she not only accepted and observed, but actively defended: notably in the matter of dress. The clothes she had worn in Cambridge seemed to her no less suitable for the Congo, and she
rejected with asperity any suggestion that she might adopt male
attire. When, arriving at an outpost soaked to the skin, coated
with mud and exhausted by wading rivers and struggling through
swamps, the young official in charge suggested a bath, she refused out of hand because his guest-house lacked proper doors
and windows and someone might have looked in. How she can
have toiled through bush and undergrowth, clambered in and
out of dug-outs canoes, in those long, black, trailing skirts, tight
waists, high collars and the little tocque-like fur cap she custo-
marily wore, baffles the imagination. But clamber, tramp, wade
and climb she did, stoutly maintaining that her clothes were not
only lady-like but advantageous; when she fell into a game-pit,
she was saved by her petticoats from impalement on the stakes
below; and when, on returning to her moored canoe, she found
a hippopotamus standing over it, she 'scratched him behind the
ear with my umbrella and we parted on good terms'.

In the period of which she wrote, only three types of European, generally speaking, were to be found in West Africa, all
three to some extent protected by the organisations to which
they belonged. There were Government officials, who had behind

them the strength of whichever *raj* they served with its flag, its soldiers and its punitive expeditions if things went wrong. There were the traders, most of whom belonged to well-established firms possessing a chain of factories, or depots, a fleet of river-boats and a network of African sub-traders who served their interests and kept them well informed. Finally there were the missionaries, who also operated, for the most part, from settled bases, had their sub-stations and African colleagues, and enjoyed the special protection of God.

Mary Kingsley travelled as a lone she-wolf. She had no base, no armed guards, no network of African agents, no means of transport, no equipment beyond a black bag, a small portmanteau and some collecting boxes, and practically no money. 'I started on the Coast with £300,' she told Macmillan, 'and by doing a little in rubber and ivory, I made that capital do.' It meant travelling hard, 'tentless and living on native food and so on', but this very austerity gave her the key to the African mind and way of life. Officials and missionaries lacked this key because they did not live and eat and sleep and learn to think as Africans did, uninsulated, without European skills and tools for subduing the environment. Like Africans she lived with the environment without attempting to change it, or to avoid its rigours.

Moreover she believed that to come among the 'unadulterated Africans' as a trader provided an immediate and recognisable link between her world and their own. If a strange, utterly alien being were suddenly to appear for no apparent reason, he (or she in this case) would almost certainly have been regarded as a kind of devil and almost as certainly put to death. Whereas if 'you want to buy and sell from them, they recognise there is something human and reasonable about you, and then, if you show yourself an intelligent trader who knows the price of things, they regard you with respect'. Mary Kingsley taught herself the ins and outs of commerce conducted with trade goods and tobacco, and became a very intelligent trader indeed.

Above all, she was a woman of extraordinary courage: not only physical courage, though that too in full measure, but a moral courage that took her alone into these lonely places with no one to turn to and no one, when it came to fundamentals, to care deeply whether she lived or died. And death was much more likely than survival. Her brother was indifferent, consistently denigrated her achievements and was no help at all. With the rest of her relations she seems to have had no deep relationships.

She had many friends but no intimates, and despite her gaiety, wit and vitality, she was at heart a solitary, confined in her reserve. In a letter to Stephen Gwynne, her first biographer, she wrote: 'I make the confession humbly quite as I would make the confession of being deaf or blind, I know nothing myself of love. I have read about it. I see from men and women's actions that the thing exists just like I read about it in books, but I have never been in love, nor has anyone ever been in love with me.'

When she was thirty-seven it is possible that she did fall in love, with an able and intelligent officer in the Royal Engineers, Matthew Nathan, who became Governor of Sierra Leone. To him, in probably the most revealing letter she ever wrote, she confided: 'The fact is I am no more a human being than a gust of wind is. I have never had a human individual life. I have always been the doer of odd jobs—and lived in the joys, sorrows and worries of other people. It never occurs to me that I have any right to do anything more than now and then sit and warm myself at the fires of real human beings. . . . It is the non-human world I belong to myself. My people are mangroves, swamps, rivers and the sea and so on—we understand each other.' It was in this letter that she made the statement: 'I went down to West Africa to die.' She added: 'West Africa amused me and was kind to me and was scientifically interesting—and did not want to kill me just then. I am in no hurry. I don't care one way or the other, for a year or so.' Within a year of writing that, she was dead.

Yet in 1893, at the age of thirty-one, she set out in high spirits on her first West African journey. In Captain Murray, skipper of the cargo boat in which she sailed, she found a staunch friend, and learned from him the elements of seamanship which she was later to apply to the navigation of West African rivers. The sea was in her blood, she said, and she took readily to the art of navigation. When a scientist friend to whom she sent the draft of her *Travels* attempted to correct her style and tampered with some nautical expressions, she exploded. As a scientist, she wrote, she had no reputation to lose, but as a seaman she had, having three times taken a vessel of two thousand tons over the Forcados bar and up the creeks with the critical approval of Captains Murray and Heldt. 'I don't mention half my picnics in the *Travels*,' she admitted, and this was one she left out. Another was an incident when she was shot in the ankle by a muzzle-loader and it took several months to get the bits of iron cooking-pot out of the wound.

At San Paul da Loanda she disembarked and travelled through parts of the Congo Free State to the Congo Français, thence to Old Calabar in the (British) Oil Rivers Protectorate, and so home. She kept a diary, and incorporated parts of it into her *Travels* written after a second journey made between December 1894 and November 1895. The object of both journeys she summed up as the pursuit of fish and fetish: fish for Dr Günther of the British Museum and fetish to enable her to complete her father's study of primitive religion and law.

Fish and fetish, she soon found, were not enough. More and more did she get drawn into the life and problems of West Africa: the customs and beliefs of its great diversity of peoples, the geography and natural history, systems of trade, the effects of missionary endeavour and all the topics of the day. She had no axe to grind, she was beholden to no one and she formed her own opinions which were often totally at variance with the accepted gospels of the day. She found herself, for example, championing the traders, 'palm oil ruffians' who in her opinion were serving their country, and often dying for it, rather than disgracing it as was generally believed. Missionaries, on the other hand, in her view did more harm than good, much as she respected some individuals; she defended polygamy, extolled the virtues of cannibal tribes and even spoke out in support of the liquor trade; you could see more drunkenness, she wrote, in the Vauxhall Road on a Saturday night than in the whole of West Africa in a week; if Africans wanted to get drunk they would do so on their own brews, and gin was an excellent article of trade that did not lose its value from mildew or rust.

On her return home in November 1895 Mary Kingsley settled with her brother in a flat in London and wrote the book which, in an abridged form, is presented here. News of her exploits had by this time reached her native land and she found herself a public figure, much in demand as a lecturer and soon caught up in various controversial matters. The contrast between her lady-like, conventional appearance and her adventures among primitive tribes and savage beasts produced a bizarre effect; 'she might have been dressed up to look like a duke's housekeeper', Stephen Gwynne observed. Her little round black hat had a tendency to slip to the back of her head, imparting a rakish look; and the suggestion that it might have been this very hat into which she shook the contents of a bag hanging up inside the hut of a chief who was her host for the night, and which proved to consist of several fresh human fingers, toes, ears and

eyes, no doubt added piquancy to lectures delivered to such
appreciative audiences as the Cheltenham Ladies College.
'Slender, upright, carrying her body with a curious stiffness,'
Mrs St Loe Strachey wrote, 'she looked, with her blue eyes,
humorous mouth, and hair parted in the middle ... less
like an explorer than anyone I ever saw ... She had a brain
masculine in its strength and the breadth of its outlook, but she
had also an unequalled sense of humour and was quite the most
amusing person I ever met.'

Travels in West Africa, published early in 1897, was an immediate success. She had intended to return to West Africa as
soon as she had seen it through the press, but found herself
drawn into an ever-growing correspondence with people eminent
in science, politics and trade, and her opinions sought on many
questions of the day, such as the ethics of the liquor trade, the
rôle of Christian missions, the aims of British colonial policy and,
in particular, the question of the imposition of a hut tax in
Sierra Leone. Early in 1898 she caught influenza which turned
to congestion of the lungs and affected her heart. She recovered,
and embarked on a second book, almost as long as the first,
published in January 1899 as *West African Studies*. Into it went
material that had been squeezed out of the *Travels*, disserta-
tions on trade and on African skills such as fishing, and her
personal, and far from favourable, opinions on British colonial
policy and on the objectives of the Christian missions. African
pantheism was 'I confess, a form of my own religion'. Perhaps it
was fortunate that by this time her famous uncle, the Canon of
Westminster, was in his grave and so undisturbed by her views.

'I come of a generation of Danes,' she wrote in *West African
Studies*, 'who when the sun went down on the Wulpensand were
the men to make light enough to fight by with their Morning
Stars; and who, later on, were soldiers in the Low Countries and
slave-owners in the West Indies, and I am proud of my ancestors; for whatever else they were, they were not humbugs: and
the generation that is round me now seems to me in its utter-
ances at any rate tainted with humbug.' The romanticism in-
herent in the whole Kingsley family glints through this passage.
No one could have been more down-to-earth, more of a realist
than this defender of trade gin, polygamy and (very nearly)
human sacrifice, yet she was a romantic too; no one could have
been more critical, on occasion, of British colonial policy, yet
she was an ardent believer in the imperialist ideal. When the
Boer War broke out she did not share the pro-Boer sympathies

of many of her liberal and intellectual friends. Nor did she succumb to jingo-istic fervour; she wanted to go where help might be needed; clearly in South Africa there would be 'odd jobs' to be done. 'I am not walking about the streets yet in a cockalory hat and khaki small clothes,' she wrote, 'but . . . I am going out the first week in March.'

Ostensibly, she went out to collect fresh-water fishes in the Orange River for Dr Günther. On arrival in Cape Town she went straight to the Principal Medical Officer of the army and offered to help in any way he pleased. He suggested nursing Boer prisoners of war in camp at Simonstown—'evidently expecting I wouldn't'. He did not know his Mary Kingsley. If ever there was an odd job asking to be done, this was it.

Typhoid and dysentery had broken out in the camp and overwhelmed the medical resources. The shortage of doctors and nurses was desperate. 'Killing work,' she wrote. 'Delirious, fretting strong men, every third man wanting a nurse to himself.' It was the work she wanted. 'I am down in the ruck of life again,' she wrote to a friend. 'I who was and am and never shall be anything else but a muddler. All this work here, the stench, the washing, the enemas, the bed-pans, the blood, is my world. Not London society, politics, that gateway into which I so strangely wandered—into which I don't care a hairpin if I ever wander again.' Back in her own world again she met the hardships and perils in her own way. She was 'the one bright spot for us,' a fellow nurse recorded, 'always with some amusing tale when we were at our lowest ebb.' To keep off infection she took to smoking, and instead of water drank wine.

These precautions were of no avail. At first she dismissed her symptoms as a touch of West Coast fever which she had had before. Soon there could be no pretence, and when she knew that she was finished she asked to be left alone to die, as animals do. 'It was hard for us to do this,' wrote the nurse in charge, 'but we left the door ajar, and when we saw that she was beyond knowledge went to her.'

She died on 3 June 1900, aged thirty-eight, leaving a last request that she should be buried at sea. 'This was, I believe,' wrote Stephen Gwynne, 'the only favour and distinction that she ever asked for herself.' It was granted. The coffin was drawn on a gun-carriage to the pier by a detachment of the West Yorkshire Regiment, taken out to sea in a torpedo-boat and committed to the deep that she had always felt to be her true home.

ELSPETH HUXLEY

Author's Preface

It was in 1893 that, for the first time in my life, I found myself in possession of five or six months which were not heavily fore-stalled, and feeling like a boy with a new half-crown, I lay about in my mind, as Mr Bunyan would say, as to what to do with them. 'Go and learn your tropics,' said Science. Where on earth am I to go, I wondered, for tropics are tropics wherever found, so I got down an atlas and saw that either South America or West Africa must be my destination, for the Malayan region was too far off and too expensive. Then I got Wallace's *Geographical Distribution* and after reading that master's article on the Ethiopian region I hardened my heart and closed with West Africa. I did this the more readily because while I knew nothing of the practical condition of it, I knew a good deal both by tradition and report of South East America, and remembered that Yellow Jack was endemic, and that a certain naturalist, my superior physically and mentally, had come very near getting starved to death in the depressing society of an expedition slowly perishing of want and miscellaneous fevers up the Parana.

My ignorance regarding West Africa was soon removed. And although the vast cavity in my mind that it occupied is not even yet half filled up, there is a great deal of very curious information in its place. I use the word curious advisedly, for I think many seemed to translate my request for practical hints and advice into an advertisement that 'Rubbish may be shot here'. This same information is in a state of great confusion still, although I have made heroic efforts to codify it. I find, however, that it can almost all be got in under the following different headings, namely and to wit:

The dangers of West Africa.
The disagreeables of West Africa.
The diseases of West Africa.
The things you must take to West Africa.
The things you find most handy in West Africa.
The worst possible things you can do in West Africa.

I inquired of all my friends as a beginning what they knew of West Africa. The majority knew nothing. A percentage said,

'Oh, you can't possibly go there; that's where Sierra Leone is, the white man's grave, you know'. If these were pressed further, one occasionally found that they had had relations who had gone out there after having been 'sad trials', but, on consideration of their having left not only West Africa, but this world, were now forgiven and forgotten. One lady, however, kindly remembered a case of a gentleman who had resided some few years at Fernando Po, but when he returned an aged wreck of forty he shook so violently with ague as to dislodge a chandelier, thereby destroying a valuable tea-service and flattening the silver teapot in its midst.

No; there was no doubt about it, the place was not healthy, and although I had not been 'a sad trial', yet neither had the chandelier-dislodging Fernando Po gentleman. So I next turned my attention to cross-examining the doctors. 'Deadliest spot on earth', they said cheerfully, and showed me maps of the geographical distribution of disease. Now I do not say that a country looks inviting when it is coloured in Scheele's green or a bilious yellow, but these colours may arise from lack of artistic gift in the cartographer. There is no mistaking what he means by black, however, and black you'll find they colour West Africa from above Sierra Leone to below the Congo. 'I wouldn't go there if I were you,' said my medical friends, 'you'll catch something; but if you must go, and you're as obstinate as a mule, just bring me——' And then followed a list of commissions from here to New York, any one of which—but I only found that out afterwards.

All my informants referred me to the missionaries. 'There were,' they said, in an airy way, 'lots of them down there, and had been for years.' So to missionary literature I addressed myself with great ardour; alas! only to find that these good people wrote their reports not to tell you how the country they resided in was, but how it was getting on towards being what it ought to be, and how necessary it was that their readers should subscribe more freely, and not get any foolishness into their heads about obtaining an inadequate supply of souls for their money. I also found fearful confirmation of my medical friends' statements about its unhealthiness, and various details of the distribution of cotton shirts over which I did not linger.

From the missionaries it was, however, that I got my first idea about the social condition of West Africa. I gathered that there existed there, firstly the native human beings—the raw material, as it were—and that these were led either to good or

bad respectively by the missionary and the trader. There were also the Government representatives, whose chief business it was to strengthen and consolidate the missionary's work, a function they carried on but indifferently well. But as for those traders! well, I put them down under the dangers of West Africa at once. Subsequently I came across the good old coast yarn of how, when a trader from that region went thence, it goes without saying where, the Fallen Angel without a moment's hesitation vacated the infernal throne (Milton) in his favour. This, I beg to note, is the marine form of the legend. When it occurs terrestrially the trader becomes a Liverpool mate. But of course no one need believe it either way—it is not a missionary's story.

Naturally, while my higher intelligence was taken up with attending to these statements, my mind got set on going, and I had to go. Fortunately I could number among my acquaintances one individual who had lived on the Coast for seven years. Not, it is true, on that part of it which I was bound for. Still his advice was pre-eminently worth attention, because, in spite of his long residence in the deadliest spot of the region, he was still in fair going order. I told him I intended going to West Africa and he said, 'When you have made up your mind to go to West Africa the very best thing you can do is to get it unmade again, and go to Scotland instead; but if your intelligence is not strong enough to do so, abstain from exposing yourself to the direct rays of the sun, take 4 grains of quinine every day for a fortnight before you reach the Rivers, and get some introductions to the Wesleyans; they are the only people on the Coast who have got a hearse with feathers.'

My attention was next turned to getting ready things to take with me. Having opened upon myself the sluice gates of advice, I rapidly became distracted. My friends and their friends alike seemed to labour under the delusion that I intended to charter a steamer and was a person of wealth beyond the dreams of avarice. The only thing to do in this state of affairs was to gratefully listen and let things drift. They showered on me various preparations of quinine and other so-called medical comforts, mustard leaves, a patent filter, a hot-water bottle, and last but not least a large square bottle purporting to be malt and cod-liver oil, which, rebelling against an African temperature, arose in its wrath, ejected its cork, and proclaimed itself an efficient but not too savoury glue.

Not only do the things you have got to take, but the things you have got to take them in, present a fine series of problems

to the young traveller. Crowds of witnesses testified to the forms of baggage holders they had found invaluable, and these, it is unnecessary to say, were all different in form and material.

With all this *embarras de choix* I was too distracted to buy anything new in the way of baggage except a long waterproof sack neatly closed at the top with a bar and handle. Into this I put blankets, boots, books, in fact anything that would not go into my portmanteau or black bag. From the first I was haunted by a conviction that its bottom would come out, but it never did, and in spite of the fact that it had ideas of its own about the arrangement of its contents, it served me well throughout my voyage.

It was the beginning of August '93 when I first left England for 'the Coast'. Preparations of quinine with postage partially paid arrived up to the last moment, and a friend hastily sent two newspaper clippings, one entitled 'A Week in a Palm-oil Tub', which was supposed to describe the sort of accommodation, companions, and fauna likely to be met with on a steamer going to West Africa, and on which I was to spend seven to *The Graphic* contributor's one; the other from *The Daily Telegraph*, reviewing a French book of 'Phrases in common use' in Dahomey. The opening sentence in the latter was, 'Help, I am drowning.' Then came the inquiry, 'If a man is not a thief?' and then another cry, 'The boat is upset.' 'Get up, you lazy scamps,' is the next exclamation, followed almost immediately by the question, 'Why has not this man been buried?' 'It is fetish that has killed him, and he must lie here exposed with nothing on him until only the bones remain,' is the cheerful answer. This sounded discouraging to a person whose occupation would necessitate going about considerably in boats, and whose fixed desire was to study fetish. So with a feeling of foreboding gloom I left London for Liverpool—none the more cheerful for the matter-of-fact manner in which the steamboat agents had informed me that they did not issue return tickets by the West African lines of steamers.

I will not go into the details of that voyage here, much as I am given to discursiveness. They are more amusing than instructive, for on my first voyage out I did not know the Coast, and the Coast did not know me, and we mutually terrified each other. I fully expected to get killed by the local nobility and gentry; they thought I was connected with the World's Women's Temperance Association, and collecting shocking details for subsequent magic-lantern lectures on the liquor traffic; so fearful

misunderstandings arose, but we gradually educated each other, and I had the best of the affair; for all I had got to teach them was that I was only a beetle and fetish hunter, and so forth, while they had to teach me a new world, and a very fascinating course of study I found it. And whatever the Coast may have to say against me—for my continual desire for hair-pins, and other pins, my intolerable habit of getting into water, the abominations full of ants, that I brought into their houses, or things emitting at unexpectedly short notice vivid and awful stenches—they cannot but say that I was a diligent pupil, who honestly tried to learn the lessons they taught me so kindly, though some of those lessons were hard to a person who had never previously been even in a tame bit of tropics, and whose life for many years had been an entirely domestic one in a University town.

One by one I took my old ideas derived from books and thoughts based on imperfect knowledge and weighed them against the real life around me, and found them either worthless or wanting. The greatest recantation I had to make I made humbly before I had been three months on the Coast in 1893. It was of my idea of the traders. What I had expected to find them was a very different thing to what I did find them; and of their kindness to me I can never sufficiently speak, for on that voyage I was utterly out of touch with the governmental circles, and utterly dependent on the traders, and the most useful lesson of all the lessons I learnt on the West Coast in 1893 was that I could trust them. Had I not learnt this very thoroughly I could never have gone out again and carried out the voyage I give you a sketch of in this book.

Thanks to 'the Agent', I have visited places I could never otherwise have seen; and to the respect and affection in which he is held by the native, I owe it that I have done so in safety. When I have arrived off his factory in a steamer or canoe, unexpected, unintroduced or turned up equally unheralded out of the bush in a dilapidated state, he has always received me with that gracious hospitality which must have given him, under Coast conditions, very real trouble and inconvenience—things he could have so readily found logical excuses against entailing upon himself for the sake of an individual whom he had never seen before—whom he most likely would never see again—and whom it was no earthly profit to him to see then. He has be-stowed himself—Allah only knows where—on his small trading vessels so that I might have his one cabin. He has fished me out

of sea and fresh water with boat-hooks; he has continually given me good advice, which if I had only followed would have enabled me to keep out of water and any other sort of affliction; and although he holds the meanest opinion of my intellect for going to such a place as West Africa for beetles, fishes and fetish, he has given me the greatest assistance in my work. The value of that work I pray you withhold judgment on, until I lay it before you in some ten volumes or so mostly in Latin. All I know that is true regarding West African facts, I owe to the traders; the errors are my own.

To Dr Günther, of the British Museum, I am deeply grateful for the kindness and interest he has always shown regarding all the specimens of natural history that I have been able to lay before him; the majority of which must have had very old tales to tell him. Yet his courtesy and attention gave me the thing a worker in any work most wants—the sense that the work was worth doing—and sent me back to work again with the knowledge that if these things interested a man like him, it was a more than sufficient reason for me to go on collecting them.*

It is impossible for me even to catalogue my debts of gratitude still outstanding to the West Coast. Chiefly am I indebted to Mr C. G. Hudson, whose kindness and influence enabled me to go up the Ogowé and to see as much of Congo Français as I have seen, and his efforts to take care of me were most ably seconded by Mr Fildes. The French officials in 'Congo Français' never hindered me, and always treated me with the greatest kindness. You may say there was no reason why they should not, for there is nothing in this fine colony of France that they need be ashamed of any one seeing; but I find it is customary for travellers to say the French officials throw obstacles in the way of any one visiting their possessions, so I merely beg to state this was decidedly not my experience; although my deplorable ignorance of French prevented me from explaining my humble intentions to them.

I owe my ability to have profited by the kindness of these gentlemen on land, to a gentleman of the sea—Captain Murray. He was captain of the vessel I went out on in 1893, and he saw then that my mind was full of errors that must be eradicated if I

---

* Despite the difficulties, Dr Günther wrote, which included the frequent upsetting of her canoe, 'She succeeded in bringing home in excellent condition a collection of eighteen species of Reptiles and about sixty-five species of Fishes', as well as a number of entomological specimens. (EH)

was going to deal with the Coast successfully; and so he eradicated those errors and replaced them with sound knowledge from his own stores collected during an acquaintance with the West Coast of over thirty years. The education he has given me has been of the greatest value to me, and I sincerely hope to make many more voyages under him, for I well know he has still much to teach and I to learn.

When in the Canaries in 1892, I used to smile, I regretfully own, at the conversation of a gentleman from the Gold Coast who was up there recruiting after a bad fever. His conversation consisted largely of anecdotes of friends of his, and nine times in ten he used to say, 'He's dead now'. Alas! my own conversation may be smiled at now for the same cause. Many of my friends mentioned even in this very recent account of the Coast 'are dead now'. Most of those I learnt to know in 1893; chief among these is my old friend Captain Boler, of Bonny, from whom I first learnt a certain power of comprehending the African and his form of thought.

I have great reason to be grateful to the Africans themselves —to cultured men and women among them like Charles Owoo, M'bo, Sanga Glass, Jane Harrington and her sister at Gaboon, and to the bush natives; but of my experience with them I give further details, so I need not dwell on them here.

I apologise to the general reader for giving so much detail on matters that really only affect myself, and I know that the indebtedness which all African travellers have to the white residents in Africa is a matter usually very lightly touched on. No doubt my voyage would seem a grander thing if I omitted mention of the help I received, but—well, there was a German gentleman once who evolved a camel out of his inner consciousness. It was a wonderful thing; still, you know, it was not a good camel, only a thing which people personally unacquainted with camels could believe in. Now I am ambitious to make a picture, if I make one at all, that people who do know the original can believe in—even if they criticise its points—and so I give you details a more showy artist would omit.

CHAPTER ONE

The Taking Habits of
West Coast Rivers

Mary Kingsley left Liverpool in the Batanga *on 23 December 1894 and reached Freetown, Sierra Leone, on 7 January 1895. The next calls were at Cape Coast and Accra in the Gold Coast (now Ghana) and, after calling at Calabar, she accompanied the Governor, Sir Claude MacDonald, and his wife to Fernando Po. She then went on to Old Calabar in the Oil Rivers Protectorate, now part of Nigeria, where she paid a visit to Miss Mary Slessor.*

This very wonderful lady has been eighteen years in Calabar; for the last six or seven living entirely alone, as far as white folks go, in a clearing in the forest near to one of the principal villages of the Okÿon district, and ruling as a veritable white chief over the entire Okÿon district. Her great abilities, both physical and intellectual, have given her among the savage tribe an unique position, and won her, from white and black who know her, a profound esteem. Her knowledge of the native, his language, his ways of thought, his diseases, his difficulties, and all that is his, is extraordinary, and the amount of good she has done, no man can fully estimate. Okÿon, when she went there alone—living in the native houses while she built, with the assistance of the natives, her present house—was a district regarded with fear by the Duke and Creek Town natives, and practically unknown to Europeans. It was given, as most of the surrounding districts still are, to killing at funerals, ordeal by poison, and perpetual internecine wars. Many of these evil customs she has stamped out, and Okÿon rarely gives trouble to its nominal rulers, the Consuls in Old Calabar, and trade passes freely through it down to the sea-ports.

This instance of what one white can do would give many important lessons in West Coast administration and development. Only the sort of man Miss Slessor represents is rare. There are but few who have the same power of resisting the malarial climate, and of acquiring the language, and an insight into the Negro mind, so perhaps after all it is no

great wonder that Miss Slessor stands alone, as she certainly does.

After returning down river, I just waited until the *Batanga*, my old friend, came into the river again, and then started for my beloved South West Coast. The various divisions of the West Coast of Africa are very perplexing to a new comer. Starting from Sierra Leone coming south you first pass the Grain Coast, which is also called the Pepper or Kru Coast, or the Liberian Coast. Next comes the Ivory Coast, also known as the Half Jack Coast, or the Bristol Coast. Then comes the Gold Coast; then the old Slave Coast, now called the Popos; then Lagos, and then the Rivers, and below the Rivers the South West Coast. In addition to these names you will hear the Timber Ports, and the Win'ard and Leeward Ports referred to, and it perplexes one when one finds a port, say Axim, referred to by one competent authority, *i.e.* a sea-captain, as a Win'ard port, by the next as a Timber, by the next as a Gold Coast port. It is just as well to get the matter up if you intend frequenting the Bights of Biafra and Benin. I will just give you, as a hint to facilitate your researches, the information that the Bight of Benin commences at Cape St Paul and ends at Cape Formosa; and the Bight of Biafra commences at Cape Formosa and ends at Cape Lopez. The Windward Coast is that portion between Cape Apollonia and the Secum River, just west of Accra. At this river the Leeward Coast begins, and terminates at the Volta.

When I was on the coast in 1893, Cameroons River was regarded in nautical circles as a River. Now, alas for me! it is not, and getting from Calabar to Cameroons is a thing you ought to get a medal for, for the line of vessels that run from Liverpool to Calabar goes no further than the latter place. I had to go on a homeward bound boat up as far as Lagos Bar and then catch a South Wester outward bound, and I assure you changing at Lagos Bar throws changing at Clapham Junction into the shade.

The town of Lagos is situated on an island in the Lagos River, a river which is much given to going into lagoons and mud, and which has its bar about two miles out. The entire breadth of the channel through this bar is half a mile, at least on paper. On each side of this channel are the worst set of breakers in West Africa, and its resident population consists of sharks, whose annual toll of human life is said by some authorities to be fourteen, by others forty, but like everything else connected

with Lagos Bar, it is uncertain, but bad. This entrance channel, however, at the best of times has not more than thirteen feet of water on it, and so although the British African and Royal African lines of steamers are noble pedestrians, thinking nothing of walking a mile or so when occasion requires, and as capable of going over a grass-plot with the dew on it as any ocean vessels ever built, I am bound to own they do require a certain amount of water to get on with. They can sit high and dry on a sand or mud-bank—they prefer mud I may remark—with any vessel. I have often been on them when engaged in this pastime, but it does undoubtedly cause delay, and this being the case they do not go alongside at Lagos, but lie outside the bar.

Now such is the pestilential nature of Lagos Bar that even the carefully built branch boats, the noble *Dodo* and *Qwarra*, to say nothing of the *Forcados* and others, although drawing only ten feet, are liable to stick. For the channel, instead of sticking to its governmentally reported thirteen feet, is prone to be nine feet, and exceeding prone also to change its position; and moreover, even supposing the branch boat to get across all right, the heavy swell outside with its great rollers lounging along, intent on breaking on the bar, looking like coiling snakes under a blanket, make the vessels lying broadside on to them play pendulum to an extent that precludes the discharging or taking on of heavy cargo; and heavy cargo has to come on and off for Lagos to the value of £1,566,243 a year. So as the West African trading vessels are enterprising and determined, particularly where palm oil is concerned, they arrange the matter by going and lying up Forcados River. This river, which is 120 miles below Lagos, is a mouth of the Niger, and has a bar you can cross (if you don't mind a little walking), drawing seventeen feet nine inches. This being the case they run just inside Forcados River and then wait for the branch boat from Lagos to come and bring them their heavy cargo. When they have got this on board, they proceed up coast and call off Lagos Bar, and another unfortunate branch boat brings off mails and passengers to them.

Well, the *Batanga* after leaving Calabar and calling at Bonny had duly waited for the branch boat in Forcados and ultimately got her and her cargo, with its attendant uproar; and an account of the latest iniquities of Lagos Bar which had one of its bad fits on just then and was capturing and wrecking branch boats galore; and we had the usual scene with Mrs S. Mrs S., I may remark, is a comely and large black lady, an old acquaintance of

mine, hailing from Opobo and frequently going up and down to Lagos, in connection with trading affairs of her own, and another lady with whom Mrs S. is in a sort of partnership. This trade usually consists of extensive operations in chickens. She goes up to Lagos and buys chickens, brings them on board in crates, and takes them to Opobo and there sells them. It is not for me as a fellow woman to say what Mrs S. makes on the transaction, nor does it interest the general public, but what does interest the general public (at least that portion of it that goes down to the sea in ships and for its sins wanders into Forcados River) is Mrs S.'s return trip to Lagos with those empty crates and the determination in her heart not to pay freight for them.

Wise and experienced chief officers never see Mrs S.'s crates, but young and truculent ones do, and determine, in their hearts, she shall pay for them, advertising this resolve of theirs openly all the way from Opobo, which is foolish. When it comes to sending heavy goods overside into the branch boat at Forcados, the wise chief officer lets those crates go, but the truculent one says,

'Here, Mrs S., *now* you have got to pay for these crates.'

'Lor' mussy me, sar,' says Mrs S., 'what you talk about?'

'These here chicken crates of yours, Mrs S.'

'Lor' mussy me,' says Mrs. S., 'those crates no 'long to me, sar.'

'Then,' says the truculent one, 'heave 'em over side! We don't want that stuff lumbering up our deck.'

Mrs S. then expostulates and explains they are the property of a lone lorn lady in Lagos to whom Mrs S. is taking them from the highest motives; motives 'such a nice gentleman' as the first officer must understand, and which it will be a pleasure to him to share in, and she cites instances of other chief officers who according to her have felt, as it were, a ray of sunlight come into their lives when they saw those chicken crates and felt it was in their power to share in the noble work of returning them to Lagos freight free. The truculent one then loses his head and some of his temper and avows himself a heartless villain, totally indifferent to the sex, and says all sorts of things, but my faith in the ultimate victory of Mrs S. never wavers. My money is on her all the time, and she has never disappointed me, and when I am quite rich some day, I will give Mrs S. purses of gold in the eastern manner for the many delicious scenes she has played before me with those crates in dreary Forcados.

Transferring at Forcados to the steamer Benguella, *Mary Kingsley continued her journey down the south-west coast to the mouth of the Ogowé river in the Congo Français (now the Republic of Gabon).*

My main aim in going to Congo Français was to get up above the tide line of the Ogowé River and there collect fishes; for my object on this voyage was to collect fish from a river north of the Congo. I had hoped this river would have been the Niger, for Sir George Goldie had placed at my disposal great facilities for carrying on work there in comfort; but for certain private reasons I was disinclined to go from the Royal Niger Protectorate into the Royal Niger Company's territory; and the Calabar, where Sir Claude MacDonald did everything he possibly could to assist me, I did not find a good river for me to collect fishes in. These two rivers failing me, from no fault of either of their own presiding genii, my only hope of doing anything now lay on the South West Coast river, the Ogowé, and everything there depended on Mr Hudson's * attitude towards scientific research in the domain of ichthyology. Fortunately for me that gentleman elected to take a favourable view of this affair, and in every way in his power assisted me during my entire stay in Congo Français. But before I enter into a detailed description of this wonderful bit of West Africa, I must give you a brief notice of the manners, habits and customs of West Coast rivers in general, to make the thing more intelligible.

There is an uniformity in the habits of West Coast rivers, from the Volta to the Coanza, which is, when you get used to it, very taking. Excepting the Congo, the really great river comes out to sea with as much mystery as possible; lounging lazily along among its mangrove swamps in a what's-it-matter-when-one-comes-out and where's-the-hurry style, through quantities of channels inter-communicating with each other. Each channel, at first sight as like the other as peas in a pod, is bordered on either side by green-black walls of mangroves, which Captain Lugard graphically described as seeming 'as if they had lost all count of the vegetable proprieties, and were standing on stilts with their branches tucked up out of the wet, leaving their gaunt roots exposed in mid-air'. High-tide or low-tide, there is little difference in the water; the river, be it broad or narrow,

* C. G. Hudson, Agent-General of Cookson and Hatton in West Africa. (EH)

deep or shallow, looks like a pathway of polished metal; for it
is as heavy weighted with stinking mud as water e'er can be,
ebb or flow, year out and year in. But the difference in the banks,
though an unending alternation between two appearances, is
weird.

At high-water you do not see the mangroves displaying their
ankles in the way that shocked Captain Lugard. They look
most respectable, their foliage rising densely in a wall irregularly
striped here and there by the white line of an aërial root, coming
straight down into the water from some upper branch as
straight as a plummet, in the strange, knowing way an aërial
root of a mangrove does, keeping the hard straight line
until it gets some two feet above water-level, and then
spreading out into blunt fingers with which to dip into the
water and grasp the mud. Banks indeed at high water can
hardly be said to exist, the water stretching away into the
mangrove swamps for miles and miles, and you can then go, in
a suitable small canoe, away among these swamps as far as you
please.

This is a fascinating pursuit. For people who like that sort of
thing it is just the sort of thing they like, as the art critic of a
provincial town wisely observed anent an impressionist picture
recently acquired for the municipal gallery. But it is a pleasure
to be indulged in with caution; for one thing, you are certain to
come across crocodiles. Now a crocodile drifting down in deep
water, or lying asleep with its jaws open on a sand-bank in the
sun, is a picturesque adornment to the landscape when you are
on the deck of a steamer, and you can write home about it and
frighten your relations on your behalf; but when you are away
among the swamps in a small dug-out canoe, and that crocodile
and his relations are awake—a thing he makes a point of being
at flood tide because of fish coming along—and when he has got
his foot upon his native heath—that is to say, his tail within
holding reach of his native mud—he is highly interesting, and
you may not be able to write home about him—and you get
frightened on your own behalf. For crocodiles can, and often
do, in such places, grab at people in small canoes. I have known
of several natives losing their lives in this way; some native
villages are approachable from the main river by a short cut, as
it were, through the mangrove swamps, and the inhabitants of
such villages will now and then go across this way with small
canoes instead of by the constant channel to the village, which
is almost always winding.

In addition to this unpleasantness you are liable to get tide-trapped away in the swamps, the water falling round you when you are away in some deep pool or lagoon, and you find you cannot get back to the main river. For you cannot get out and drag your canoe across the stretches of mud that separate you from it, because the mud is of too unstable a nature and too deep, and sinking into it means staying in it, at any rate until some geologist of the remote future may come across you, in a fossilised state, when that mangrove swamp shall have become dry land. Of course if you really want a truly safe investment in Fame, and really care about Posterity, and Posterity's Science, you will jump over into the black batter-like, stinking slime cheered by the thought of the terrific sensation you will produce 20,000 years hence, and the care you will be taken of then by your fellow-creatures, in a museum. But if you are a mere ordinary person of a retiring nature, like me, you stop in your lagoon until the tide rises again; most of your attention is directed to dealing with an 'at home' to crocodiles and mangrove flies, and with the fearful stench of the slime round you. What little time you have over you will employ in wondering why you came to West Africa, and why, after having reached this point of absurdity, you need have gone and painted the lily and adorned the rose, by being such a colossal ass as to come fooling about in mangrove swamps.

Twice this chatty little incident, as Lady MacDonald would call it, has happened to me, but never again if I can help it. On one occasion, the last, a mighty Silurian, as *The Daily Telegraph* would call him, chose to get his front paws over the stern of my canoe, and endeavoured to improve our acquaintance. I had to retire to the bows, to keep the balance right, and fetch him a clip on the snout with a paddle, when he withdrew, and I paddled into the very middle of the lagoon, hoping the water there was too deep for him or any of his friends to repeat the performance. Presumably it was, for no one did it again. I should think that crocodile was eight feet long; but don't go and say I measured him, or that this is my outside measurement for crocodiles. I have measured them when they have been killed by other people, fifteen, eighteen, and twenty-one feet odd. This was only a pushing young creature who had not learnt manners.

Still, even if your own peculiar tastes and avocations do not take you in small dug-out canoes into the heart of the swamps, you can observe the difference in the local scenery made by the

flowing of the tide when you are on a vessel stuck on a sand-bank, in the Rio del Rey for example. Moreover, as you will have little else to attend to, save mosquitoes and mangrove flies, when in such a situation, you may as well pursue the study. At the ebb gradually the foliage of the lower branches of the mangroves grows wet and muddy, until there is a great black band about three feet deep above the surface of the water in all directions; gradually a network of gray-white roots rises up, and below this again, gradually, a slope of smooth and lead-brown slime. The effect is not in the least as if the water had fallen, but as if the mangroves had, with one accord, risen up out of it, and into it again they seem silently to sink when the flood comes.

At corners here and there from the river face you can see the land being made from the waters. A mud-bank forms off it, a mangrove seed lights on it, and the thing's done. Well! not done, perhaps, but begun; for if the bank is high enough to get exposed at low water, this pioneer mangrove grows. He has a wretched existence though. You have only got to look at his dwarfed attenuated form to see this. He gets joined by a few more bold spirits and they struggle on together, their network of roots stopping abundance of mud, and by good chance now and then a consignment of miscellaneous *débris* of palm leaves, or a floating tree-trunk, but they always die before they attain any considerable height. Still even in death they collect. Their bare white sticks remaining like a net gripped in the mud, so that these pioneer mangrove heroes may be said to have laid down their lives to make that mud-bank fit for colonisation, for the time gradually comes when other mangroves can and do colonise on it, and flourish, extending their territory steadily; and the mud-bank joins up with, and becomes a part of, Africa.

Right away on the inland fringe of the swamp—you may go some hundreds of miles before you get there—you can see the rest of the process. The mangroves there have risen up, and dried the mud to an extent that is more than good for them-selves, have over civilised that mud in fact, and so the brackish waters of the tide—which, although their enemy when too deep or too strong in salt, is essential to their existence—cannot get to their roots. They have done this gradually, as a mangrove does all things, but they have done it, and down on to that mud comes a whole set of palms from the old mainland, who in their early colonisation days go through similarly trying experiences.

First the screw-pines come and live among them; then the wine-palm and various creepers, and then the oil-palm; and the *débris* of these plants being greater and making better soil than dead mangroves, they work quicker and the mangrove is doomed. Soon the salt waters are shut right out, the mangrove dies, and that bit of Africa is made.

It is very interesting to get into these regions; you see along the river-bank a rich, thick, lovely wall of soft-wooded plants, and behind this you find great stretches of death;—miles and miles sometimes of gaunt white mangrove skeletons standing on gray stuff that is not yet earth and is no longer slime, and through the crust of which you can sink into rotting putrefaction. Yet, long after you are dead, buried, and forgotten, this will become a forest of soft-wooded plants and palms; and finally of hard-wooded trees. Districts of this description you will find in great sweeps of Kama country for example, and in the rich low regions up to the base of the Sierra del Cristal and the Rumby range.

You often hear the utter lifelessness of mangrove-swamps commented on; why I do not know, for they are fairly heavily stocked with fauna, though the species are comparatively few. There are the crocodiles, more of them than any one wants; there are quantities of flies, particularly the big silent mangrove-fly which lays an egg in you under the skin; the egg becomes a maggot and stays there until it feels fit to enter into external life. Then there are 'slimy things that crawl with legs upon a slimy sea', and any quantity of hopping mud-fish, and crabs, and a certain mollusc, and in the water various kinds of cat-fish.

Birdless they are save for the flocks of gray parrots that pass over them at evening, hoarsely squarking; and save for this squarking of the parrots the swamps are silent all the day, at least during the dry season; in the wet season there is no silence night or day in West Africa, but that roar of the descending deluge of rain that is more monotonous and more gloomy than any silence can be. In the morning you do not hear the long, low, mellow whistle of the plantain-eaters calling up the dawn, nor in the evening the clock-bird nor the Handel-Festival-sized choruses of frogs, or the crickets, that carry on their vesper controversy of 'she did'—'she didn't' so fiercely on hard land.

But the mangrove-swamp follows the general rule for West Africa, and night in it is noisier than the day. After dark it is

full of noises; grunts from I know not what, splashes from jumping fish, the peculiar whirr of rushing crabs, and quaint creaking and groaning sounds from the trees; and—above all in eeriness—the strange whine and sighing cough of crocodiles. I shall never forget one moonlight night I spent in a mangrove-swamp. I was not lost, but we had gone away into the swamp from the main river, so that the natives of a village with an evil reputation should not come across us when they were out fishing. We got well in, on to a long pool or lagoon; and dozed off and woke, and saw the same scene around us twenty times in the night, which thereby grew into an æon, until I dreamily felt that I had somehow got into a world that was all like this, and always had been, and was always going to be so.

Now and again the strong musky smell came that meant a crocodile close by, and one had to rouse up and see if all the crews' legs were on board, for Africans are reckless, and regardless of their legs during sleep. On one examination I found the leg of one of my most precious men ostentatiously sticking out over the side of the canoe. I woke him with a paddle, and said a few words regarding the inadvisability of wearing his leg like this in our situation; and he agreed with me, saying he had lost a valued uncle, who had been taken out of a canoe in this same swamp by a crocodile. His uncle's ghost had become, he said, a sort of devil which had been a trial to the family ever since; and he thought it must have pulled his leg out in the way I complained of, in order to get him to join him by means of another crocodile. I thanked him for the information and said it quite explained the affair, and I should do my best to prevent another member of the family from entering the state of devildom by aiming blows in the direction of any leg or arm I saw that uncle devil pulling out to place within reach of the crocodiles.

Great regions of mangrove-swamps are a characteristic feature of the West African Coast. The first of these lies north of Sierra Leone; then they occur, but of smaller dimensions—just fringes of river-outfalls—until you get to Lagos, when you strike the greatest of them all. The whole of this great stretch of coast is a mangrove-swamp, each river silently rolling down its great mass of mud-laden waters and constituting each in itself a very pretty problem to the navigator by its network of intercommunicating creeks, and the sand and mud bar which it forms off its entrance by dropping its heaviest mud; its lighter mud is carried out

beyond its bar and makes the nasty-smelling brown soup of the South Atlantic Ocean, with froth floating in lines and patches on it, for miles to seaward.

In this great region of swamps every mile appears like every other mile until you get well used to it, and are able to distinguish the little local peculiarities at the entrance of the rivers and in the winding of the creeks, a thing difficult even for the most experienced navigator to do during those thick wool-like mists called smokes, which hang about the whole Bight from November till May (the dry season), sometimes lasting all day, sometimes clearing off three hours after sunrise.

The upper or north-westerly part of the swamp is round the mouths of the Niger, and it successfully concealed this fact from geographers down to 1830, when the series of heroic journeys made by Mungo Park, Clapperton, and the two Landers finally solved the problem—a problem that was as great and which cost more men's lives than even the discovery of the sources of the Nile.

That this should have been so may seem very strange to us who now have been told the answer to the riddle; for the upper waters of this great river were known of before Christ and spoken of by Herodotus, Pliny and Ptolemy, and its mouths navigated continuously along by the seaboard by trading vessels since the fifteenth century, but they were not recognised as belonging to the Niger. Some geographers held that the Senegal or the Gambia was its outfall; others that it was the Zaire (Congo); others that it did not come out on the West Coast at all, but got mixed up with the Nile in the middle of the continent, and so on.

Yet when you come to know the swamps this is not so strange. You find on going up what looks like a big river—say Forcados, two and a half miles wide at the entrance and a real bit of the Niger. Before you are up it far great, broad, business-like-looking river entrances open on either side, showing wide rivers, mangrove-walled, but two-thirds of them are utter frauds which will ground you within half an hour of your entering them. Some few of them do communicate with other main channels to the great upper river, and others are main channels themselves; but most of them intercommunicate with each other and lead nowhere in particular, and you can't even get there because of their shallowness. It is small wonder that the earlier navigators did not get far up them in sailing ships, and that the problem had to be solved by men descending the main stream of the

Niger before it commences to what we in Devonshire should call 'squander itself about' in all these channels.

And in addition it must be remembered that the natives with whom these trading vessels dealt, first for slaves, afterwards for palm-oil, were not, and are not now, members of the Lo family of savages. Far from it: they do not go in for 'gentle smiles', but for murdering any unprotected boat's crew they happen to come across, not only for a love of sport but to keep white traders from penetrating to the trade-producing interior, and spoiling prices. And the region is practically foodless.

I believe the great swamp region of the Bight of Biafra is the greatest in the world, and that in its immensity and gloom it has a grandeur equal to that of the Himalayas. I am not saying a beauty; I own I see a great beauty in it sometimes, but it is evidently not of a popular type. But Bonny! Well, come inside the bar and anchor off the factories: seaward there is the foam of the bar gleaming and wicked—white against a leaden sky and what there is left of Breaker Island. In every other direction you will see the apparently endless walls of mangrove, unvarying in colour, unvarying in form, unvarying in height, save from perspective. Beneath and between you and them lie the rotting mud waters of Bonny River, and away up and down river, miles of rotting mud waters fringed with walls of rotting mud mangrove-swamp. The only break in them—one can hardly call it a relief to the scenery—are the gaunt black ribs of the old hulks, once used as trading stations, which lie exposed at low water near the shore, protruding like the skeletons of great unclean beasts who have died because Bonny water was too strong even for them.

Raised on piles from the mud shore you will see the white-painted factories and their great store-houses for oil; each factory likely enough with its flag at half-mast, which does not enliven the scenery either, for you know it is because somebody is 'dead again'. Throughout and over all is the torrential downpour of the wet-season rain, coming down night and day with its dull roar. I have known it rain six mortal weeks in Bonny River, just for all the world as if it were done by machinery, and the interval that came then was only a few wet days, whereafter it settled itself down to work again in the good West Coast waterspout pour for more weeks. I fancy junior clerks of the weather-department must be entrusted with the Bight of Biafra's weather, on account of its extreme simplicity; their duty is just to turn on so many months' wet, and then a tornado season—

one tornado administered every forty-eight hours; then stop all
water supply and turn on sun; then a tornado season as before,
and back again to the water tap.

While your eyes are drinking in the characteristics of Bonny
scenery you notice a peculiar smell—an intensification of that
smell you noticed when nearing Bonny, in the evening, out at
sea. That's the breath of the malarial mud, laden with fever, and
the chances are you will be down to-morrow. If it is near evening
time now, you can watch it becoming incarnate, creeping and
crawling and gliding out from the side creeks and between the
mangrove-roots, laying itself upon the river, stretching and
rolling in a kind of grim play, and finally crawling up the side of
the ship to come on board and leave its cloak of moisture that
grows green mildew in a few hours over all. Noise you will not
be much troubled with: there is only that rain, a sound I have
known make men who are sick with fever well-nigh mad, and
now and again the depressing cry of the curlews which abound
here. This combination is such that after six or eight hours of it
you will be thankful to hear your shipmates start to work the
winch. I take it you are hard up when you relish a winch. And
you will say—let your previous experience of the world be what
it may—Good Heavens, what a place!

Five times have I been now in Bonny River and I like it. You
always do get to like it if you live long enough to allow the
strange fascination of the place to get a hold on you; but when
I first entered it, on a ship commanded by Captain Murray in
'93, in the wet season, *i.e.* in August, in spite of the confidence I
had by this time acquired in his skill and knowledge of the West
Coast, a sense of horror seized on me as I gazed upon the scene,
and I said to the old coaster who then had charge of my education, 'Good Heavens! what an awful accident. We've gone and
picked up the Styx'. He was evidently hurt and said, 'Bonny
was a nice place when you got used to it', and went on to discourse on the last epidemic here, when nine men out of the
resident eleven died in about ten days from yellow fever.

I went ashore that evening to have tea with Captain Boler,
and was told many more details about this particular epidemic,
to say nothing of other epidemics. In one which the captain
experienced, at the fourth funeral, two youngsters (junior clerks
of the deceased) from drink brought on by fright, fell into the
grave before the coffin, which got lowered on to them, and all
three had to be hauled out again. 'Barely necessary though, was
it?' said another member of the party, 'for those two had to have

a grave of their own before next sundown.' And the general consensus of opinion was that one of these periodic epidemics was 'just about due now'. Next to the scenery of 'a River', commend me for cheerfulness to the local conversation of its mangrove-swamp region; and every truly important West African river has its mangrove-swamp belt.

CHAPTER TWO

Libreville to Lambaréné

On first entering the great grim twilight regions of the forest you hardly see anything but the vast column-like grey tree stems in their countless thousands around you, and the sparsely vegetated ground beneath. But day by day, as you get trained to your surroundings, you see more and more, and a whole world grows up gradually out of the gloom before your eyes. Snakes, beetles, bats and beasts, people the region that at first seemed lifeless.

It is the same with the better lit regions, where vegetation is many-formed and luxuriant. As you get used to it, what seemed at first to be an inextricable tangle ceases to be so. The separate sorts of plants stand out before your eyes with ever increasing clearness, until you can pick out the one particular one you may want; and daily you find it easier to make your way through what looked at first an impenetrable wall, for you have learnt that it is in the end easier to worm your way in among networks of creepers, than to shirk these, and go for the softer walls of climbing grasses and curtains of lycopodium; and not only is it easier, but safer, for in the grass and lycopodium there are nearly certain to be snakes galore, and the chances are you may force yourself into the privacy of a gigantic python's sleeping place.

There is the same difference also between night and day in the forest. You may have got fairly used to it by day, and then some catastrophe keeps you out in it all night, and again you see another world. To my taste there is nothing so fascinating as spending a night out in an African forest, or plantation; but I beg you to note I do not advise anyone to follow the practice. Nor indeed do I recommend African forest life to any one. Unless you are interested in it and fall under its charm, it is the most awful life in death imaginable. It is like being shut up in a library whose books you cannot read, all the while tormented, terrified, and bored. And if you do fall under its spell, it takes all the colour out of other kinds of living. Still, it is good for a man to have an experience of it, whether he likes it or not, for it teaches you how very dependent you have been, during your

previous life, on the familiarity of those conditions you have been brought up among, and on your fellow citizens; moreover it takes the conceit out of you pretty thoroughly during the days you spend stupidly stumbling about among your new surroundings.

When this first period passes there comes a sense of growing power. The proudest day in my life was the day on which an old Fan hunter said to me—'Ah! you see'. Now he did not say this, I may remark, as a tribute to the hard work I had been doing in order to see, but regarded it as the consequence of a chief having given me a little ivory half-moon, whose special mission was 'to make man see Bush', and when you have attained to that power in full, a state I do not pretend to have yet attained to, you can say, 'Put me where you like in an African forest, and as far as the forest goes, starve me or kill me if you can'.

As it is with the forest, so it is with the minds of the natives. Unless you live alone among the natives, you never get to know them; if you do this you gradually get a light into the true state of their mind-forest. At first you see nothing but a confused stupidity and crime; but when you get to see—well! as in the other forest—you see things worth seeing. But it is beyond me to describe the process, so we will pass on to Congo Français.

My reasons for going to this wildest and most dangerous part of the West African regions were perfectly simple and reasonable. I had not found many fish in the Oil Rivers, and, as I have said, my one chance of getting a collection of fishes from a river north of the Congo lay in the attitude Mr C. G. Hudson might see fit to assume towards ichthyology. Mr Hudson I had met in 1893 at Kabinda, when he rescued me from dire dilemmas, and proved himself so reliable, that I had no hesitation in depending on his advice. Since those Kabinda days he had become a sort of commercial Bishop, *i.e.*, an Agent-General for Messrs Hatton and Cookson in Congo Français, and in this capacity had the power to let me get up the Ogowé river, the greatest river between the Niger and the Congo.

This river is mainly known in England from the works of Mr Du Chaillu, who, however, had the misfortune on both his expeditions to miss actually discovering it. Still, he knew it was there, and said so; and from his reports other explorers went out to look for it and duly found it. It has been in the possession of France nearly forty years now, and the French authorities keep quite as much order as one can expect along its navigable water way, considering that the density of the forest around it har-

bours and protects a set of notoriously savage tribes, chief among which are the Fans. These Fans are a great tribe that have, in the memory of living men, made their appearance in the regions known to white men, in a state of migration seawards, and are a bright, active, energetic sort of African, who by their pugnacious and predatory conduct do much to make one cease to regret and deplore the sloth and lethargy of the rest of the West Coast tribes; but of Fans I will speak by and by; and merely preface my diary by stating that Congo Français has a coast line of about 900 miles, extending from the Campo River to a point a few miles north of Landana, with the exception of the small Corisco region claimed by Spain.

The two main outlets of its trade are Gaboon and Fernan Vaz. Gaboon is the finest harbour on the western side of the continent, and was thought for many years to be what it looks like, namely, the mouth of a great river. Of late years, however, it has been found to be merely one of those great tidal estuaries like Bonny—that go thirty or forty miles inland and then end in a series of small rivers.

On 20th May 1895 Mary Kingsley landed at Gaboon from the Benguella 'amidst showers of good advice and wishes from Captain Eversfield and Mr Fothergill, to which an unknown but amiable French official, who came aboard at Batta, adds a lovely Goliath beetle'. At the Customs she abandoned her revolver rather than pay a licence fee of 15/-, but her collecting case and spirit were passed in free. After a few days spent in collecting specimens on the sea shore she was taken by M. Pichault and Mr Huyghens to Libreville 'to be registered'.

The road from Glass to Libreville is, at moments, very lovely, and a fine piece of work for the country and the climate. Round Glass the land is swampy, a thing that probably induced the English to settle here when they came to Gaboon, for the English love, above all things, settling in, or as near as possible to, a good reeking, stinking swamp. We pass first along a made piece of road with the swamp on the left hand, and on the other, a sandy bush-grown piece of land with native houses on it, beyond which lies the sea-shore, and whenever the swamp chooses to go down to the edge of the shore there is an iron viaduct thrown across it. The making of this road cost the lives of seventy out of one hundred of the Tonkinese convicts engaged in its construction. After this swampy piece the road runs through sandy land,

virtually the shore, with low hills on the one hand and the beach on the other.

A line of cocoanut palms has been planted along either side of the road for most of the way, looking beautiful but behaving badly, for there is a telephone wire running along it from Libreville to Glass, and these gossiping palms—the most inveterate chatterer in the vegetable kingdom is a cocoanut palm—talk to each other with their hard leaves on the wire, so that mere human beings can hardly get a word in edgeways. This irritates the human atom, and of course it uses bad words to the wire, and I fancy these are seventy-five per cent. of all the words that get through the palm leaves' patter.

Two and a half miles' walk brings us to the office of the Directeur de l'Administration de l'Intérieur, and we hang about a fine stone-built verandah. We wait so long that the feeling grows on us that elaborate preparations for incarcerating us for life must be going on, but just as Mr H. and I have made up our minds to make a dash for it and escape, we are ushered into a cool, whitewashed office, and find a French official, clean, tidy, dark-haired, and melancholy, seated before his writing-table. Courteously bidding us be seated, he asks our names, ages, and avocations, enters them in a book for future reference, and then writes out a permit for each of us to reside in the colony, as long as we behave ourselves, and conform to the laws thereof.

We feel happier and free, and then M. Pichault alarms us by saying, 'Now for the Police'; and off we trail, subdued, to the Palais de Justice, where we are promptly ushered into a room containing a vivacious, gesticulatory old gentleman, kindly civil beyond words, and a powerful, calm young man, with a reassuring 'He's-all-right; it's-only-his-way' manner regarding his chief. The chief is clad in a white shirt and white pantaloons cut *à la* Turque, but unfortunately these garments have a band that consists of a run-in string, and that string is out of repair. He writes furiously—blotting paper mislaid—frantic flurry round—pantaloons won't stand it—grab just saves them—something wanted the other side of the room—headlong flight towards it—'now's our chance,' think the pantaloons, and make off—recaptured.

Formalities being concluded regarding us, the chief makes a dash out from behind his writing-table, claps his heels together, and bows with a jerk that causes the pantaloons to faint in coils, like the White Knight in 'Alice in Wonderland', and my last view was of a combat with them, I hope a successful one, and

that their owner, who was leaving for home the next day, is now enjoying a well-earned, honourable repose after his long years of service to his country in Congo Français.

A few days later Mr Fildes, an agent under Mr Hudson for Hatton & Cookson, took Mary Kingsley in a gig up an inlet of the Ogowé.

As we go higher up, the river channel winds to and fro between walls and slopes of ink-black slime, more sparsely covered with mangrove bushes than near the entrance. This stinking, stoneless slime is honey-combed with crab holes, and the owners of these—green, blue, red, and black—are walking about on the tips of their toes sideways, with that comic pomp peculiar to the crab family. I expected only to have to sit in the boat and say 'Horrible' at intervals, but no such thing; my companion, selecting a peculiarly awful-looking spot, says he 'thinks that will do', steers the boat up to it, and jumps out with a squidge into the black slime. For one awful moment I thought it was suicide, and that before I could even get the address of his relations to break the news to them there would be nothing but a Panama hat lying on the slime before me. But he only sinks in a matter of a foot or so, and then starts off, to my horror, calling the boys after him, to hunt crabs for me. Now I have mentioned no desire for crabs, and was merely looking at them, as I always do when out with other white folk, noting where they were so as to come back alone next day and get them; for I don't want any one's blood, black or white, on my head. As soon as I recovered speech, I besought him to come back into the boat and leave them: but no, 'tears, prayers, entreaties, all in vain,' as Koko says; he would not, and dashed about in the stinking mud, regardless, with his four Kruboys far more cautiously paddling after him.

The affrighted crabs were in a great taking. It seems to be crab etiquette that, even when a powerfully built, lithe, six foot high young man is coming at you hard all with a paddle, you must not go rushing into anybody's house save your own, whereby it fell out many crabs were captured; but the thing did not end there. I had never suspected we should catch anything but our deaths of fever, and so had brought with me no collecting-box, and before I could remonstrate Mr. Fildes' handkerchief was full of crabs, and of course mine too. It was a fine sunny morning on the Equator, and therefore it was hot, and we had nothing to wipe our perspiring brows with.

All the crabs being caught or scared home on this mud bank, we proceed higher up river, and after some more crab hunts we got to a place where I noticed you did not sink very far in if you kept moving; so I got ashore, and we went towards a break in the mangroves, where some high trees were growing, where we fell in with some exceedingly lovely mayflies and had a great hunt. They have legs two to three inches long, white at the joints and black between; a very small body with purple wings belongs to the legs, but you do not suspect this until you have caught the legs, as they hover and swing to and fro over some mass of decaying wood stuff. At first I thought they were spiders hanging from some invisible thread, so strangely did they move in circumscribed spaces: but we swept our hands over them and found no thread, and then we went for the legs in sheer desperation, and found a tiny fly body belonging to them and not a tiny spider body.

We then made our way on to the slightly higher land fringing the swamp. There was at the river end of the swamp a belt of palms, and beyond this a belt of red-woods, acacias, and other trees, and passing through these, we were out on an open grass-covered country, with low, rolling hills, looking strangely English, with clumps of trees here and there, and running between the hills, in all directions, densely-wooded valleys—a pleasant, homely-looking country.

We wandered through a considerable lot of grass, wherein I silently observed there were millions of ticks, and we made for a group of hut-homesteads and chatted with the inhabitants, until Mr Fildes' conscience smote him with the fact that he had not given out cook's stores for the mid-day meal. Then we made a short cut to the boat, which involved us in a lot of mud-hopping, and so home to 12 o'clock breakfast.

After their meal the energetic Mr Fildes took his no less energetic guest, on foot, to Woermann's farm, an abandoned coffee plantation reverting to bush.

At 3 o'clock off we go, turning down the 'Boulevard' towards Libreville, and then up a road to the right opposite Woermann's beach, and follow it through miles of grass over low hills. Here and there are huts new to me, and quite unlike the mud ones of the West Coast, or the grass ones of the Congo and Angola districts. They are far inferior to the swish huts of the Effiks, or the Moorish-looking mud ones you see round Cape Coast Castle,

&c., and notably inferior to the exceedingly neat Dualla huts of Cameroons; but they are better than any other type of African house I have seen.

On either side of us show wooded valleys like those we saw this morning; and away to the east the line of mangrove swamp fringing the little river we rowed up. Away to the west are the groves of mango trees round Libreville; mango trees are only pretty when you are close to them, prettiest of all when you are walking through an avenue of them, and you can see their richness of colour; the deep myrtle-green leaves, with the young shoots a dull crimson, and the soft gray-brown stem, and the luscious-looking but turpentiny-tasting fruit, a glory of gold and crimson, like an immense nectarine.

We gradually get into a more beautiful type of country, and down into a forest. The high trees are the usual high forest series with a preponderance of acacias. It is a forest of varied forms, but flowerless now in the dry season. There are quantities of ferns; hart's-tongues and the sort that grows on the oil-palms, and elkshorn growing out of its great brown shields on the trees above, and bracken, and pretty trailing lycopodium climbing over things, but mostly over the cardamoms which abound in the under-bush, and here and there great banks of the most lovely ferns I have ever seen save the tree-fern, an ambitious climber, called, I believe, by the botanists *Nephrodium circutarium*, and walls of that strange climbing grass, and all sorts of other lovely things by thousands in all directions.

We pass through several villages which Mr Fildes tells me are Fan villages, and are highly interesting after all one has already heard of this tribe of evil repute. Their houses are built of sheets of bark, tied on to sticks.

Frequently in the street one sees the characteristic standing drum painted white in patterns with black or red-brown, and a piece of raw hide stretched across the top, and one or two talking-drums besides.

We cross several pretty streams in the forest carefully bridged with plank. This Woermann's road, I hear, is between six and seven miles long, and its breadth uniformly nine feet, and it must have cost a lot of money to make.

There is a considerable-sized Fan village just at the entrance to the farm in which is a big silk-cotton tree. It struck me as strange, after coming from Calabar where these trees are frequently smothered round the roots with fetish objects, to see

nothing on this one save a framed and glazed image of the Virgin and Child.

When we get so far it is too late to proceed further, and nothing but this consideration, backed by the memory of one night when he was compelled to walk to Glass from the farm, prevents Mr Fildes, I believe, from crossing to Corisco Bay.

So round we turn, and return in the same order we came in, Mr Fildes lashing along first, I behind him, going like a clock, which was my one chance. When at last we reached the 'Boulevard' he wanted to reverse this order, but remembering the awful state that the back of my blouse got in at Fernando Po from a black boot-lace I was reduced to employ as a stay-lace, I refuse to go in front, without explaining why.

The next few days are spent exploring the environs of Libreville, collecting shells and butterflies, and gathering general impressions of the French colony.

Before I know where I am I find myself in a network of little irrigating canals, running between neatly kept beds of tomatoes, salad, &c., whereon there are working busily a lot of Anamese convicts. The convicts are deported from the French Cochin China possessions and employed by the Public Works Department in various ways. Those who conduct themselves well, and survive, have grants of garden ground given them, which they cultivate in this tidy, carefully minute way, so entirely different from the slummacky African methods of doing things. The produce they sell to the residents in the town, and live very prosperously in this way: but the climate of Western Africa is almost, if not quite, as deadly to the Chinese races as to the white—a fact that has been amply demonstrated not only here; but in Congo Belge, where the railway company carried on a series of experiments with imported labour—a series of experiments that entailed an awful waste of human life—for none of the imported people stood the climate any better than the whites, and you know what that means.

This labour question out here, a question that increases daily with the development of plantation enterprise, I do not think will ever be solved by importing foreign labour. Nor is it advisable that it should be, for our European Government puts a stop to the action of those causes which used to keep the native population down, intertribal wars, sacrifices, &c., &c.; and to the deportation of surplus population in the form of slaves, and

so unless means of support are devised for 'the indigenous ones', as Mrs Gault calls them, Africa will have us to thank for some smart attacks of famine, for the natives, left to their own devices, will never cultivate the soil sufficiently to support a large population, and moreover a vast percentage of the West African soil is very poor, sour stuff, that will grow nothing but equally valueless vegetation. From this discourse you will argue I did get home at last.

On 27 May 1895 the vessel Mové *arrived with Mr Hudson on board, and on 5 June Mary Kingsley set off up-river with Mr Hudson, two traders, a missionary priest and a large crowd of deck passengers.*

She is a fine little vessel; far finer than I expected. The accommodation I am getting is excellent. A long, narrow cabin, with one bunk in it and pretty nearly everything one can wish for, and a copying press thrown in. Food is excellent, society charming, captain and engineer quite acquisitions. The saloon is square and roomy for the size of the vessel, and most things, from rowlocks to teapots, are kept under the seats in good nautical style.

We call at the guard-ship to pass our papers, and then steam ahead out of the Gaboon estuary to the south, round Pongara Point, keeping close into the land. About forty feet from shore there is a good free channel for vessels with a light draught which if you do not take, you have to make a big sweep seaward to avoid a reef. Between four and five miles below Pongara, we pass Point Gombi, which is fitted with a lighthouse, a lively and conspicuous structure by day as well as night.

As we pass round Gombi point, the weather becomes distinctly rough, particularly at lunch-time. The *Mové* minds it less than her passengers, and stamps steadily along past the wooded shore, behind which shows a distant range of blue hills. Silence falls upon the black passengers, who assume recumbent positions on the deck, and suffer. All the things from under the saloon seats come out and dance together, and play puss-in-the-corner, after the fashion of loose gear when there is any sea on.

As the night comes down, the scene becomes more and more picturesque. The moonlit sea, shimmering and breaking on the darkened shore, the black forest and the hills silhouetted against the star-powdered purple sky, and, at my feet, the engine-room stoke-hole, lit with the rose-coloured glow from its

furnace, showing by the great wood fire the two nearly naked Krumen stokers, shining like polished bronze in their perspiration, as they throw in on to the fire the billets of red wood that look like freshly-cut chunks of flesh. The white engineer hovers round the mouth of the pit, shouting down directions and ever and anon plunging down the little iron ladder to carry them out himself. At intervals he stands on the rail with his head craned round the edge of the sun deck to listen to the captain, who is up on the little deck above, for there is no telegraph to the engines, and our gallant commander's voice is not strong.

While the white engineer is roosting on the rail, the black engineer comes partially up the ladder and gazes hard at me; so I give him a wad of tobacco, and he plainly regards me as inspired, for of course that was what he wanted. Remember that whenever you see a man, black or white, filled with a nameless longing, it is tobacco he requires. Grim despair accompanied by a gusty temper indicates something wrong with his pipe, in which case offer him a straightened-out hairpin.

At last we anchor for the night just inside Nazareth Bay, for Nazareth Bay wants daylight to deal with, being rich in low islands and sand shoals. We crossed the Equator this afternoon.

Off at daybreak into Nazareth Bay. Anxiety displayed by navigators, sounding taken on both sides of the bows with long bamboo poles painted in stripes, and we go 'slow ahead' and 'hard astern' successfully, until we get round a good-sized island, and there we stick until four o'clock, high water, when we come off all right, and steam triumphantly but cautiously into the Ogowé. The shores of Nazareth Bay are fringed with mangroves, but once in the river the scenery soon changes, and the waters are walled on either side with a forest rich in bamboo, oil and wine palms. These forest cliffs seem to rise right up out of the mirror-like brown water. Many of the highest trees are covered with clusters of brown-pink young shoots that look like flowers, and others are decorated by my old enemy the climbing palm, now bearing clusters of bright crimson berries. Climbing plants of other kinds are wreathing everything, some blossoming with mauve, some with yellow, some with white flowers, and every now and then a soft sweet heavy breath of fragrance comes out to us as we pass by. There is a native village on the north bank, embowered along its plantations with some very tall cocoa-palms rising high above them.

The river winds so that it seems to close in behind us, opening out in front fresh vistas of superb forest beauty, with the great

brown river stretching away unbroken ahead like a broad road of burnished bronze. Astern, it has a streak of frosted silver let into it by the *Mové*'s screw. Just about six o'clock, we run up to the *Fallabar*, the *Mové*'s predecessor in working the Ogowé, now a hulk, used as a depot by Hatton and Cookson. She is anchored at the entrance of a creek that runs through to the Fernan Vaz; some say it is six hours' run, others that it is eight hours for a canoe; all agree that there are plenty of mosquitoes.

The *Fallabar* looks grimly picturesque, and about the last spot in which a person of a nervous disposition would care to spend the night. One half of her deck is dedicated to fuel logs, on the other half are plank stores for the goods, and a room for the black sub-trader in charge of them. I know that there must be scorpions which come out of those logs and stroll into the living room, and goodness only knows what one might not fancy would come up the creek or rise out of the floating grass, or the limitless-looking forest. I am told she was a fine steamer in her day, but those who had charge of her did not make allowances for the very rapid rotting action of the Ogowé water, so her hull rusted through before her engines were a quarter worn out; and there was nothing to be done with her then, but put a lot of concrete in, and make her a depot, in which state of life she is very useful, for during the height of the dry season, the *Mové* cannot get through the creek to supply the firm's Fernan Vaz factories.

All West African steamers have a mania for bush, and the delusion that they are required to climb trees. The *Fallabar* had the complaint severely, because of her defective steering powers, and the temptation the magnificent forest, and the rapid currents, and the sharp turns of the creek district, offered her; she failed, of course—they all fail—but it is not for want of practice. I have seen many West Coast vessels up trees, but never more than fifteen feet or so.

The trade of this lower part of the Ogowé, from the mouth to Lambaréné, a matter of 130 miles, is almost *nil*. Above Lambaréné, you are in touch with the rubber and ivory trade.

This *Fallabar* creek is noted for mosquitoes, and the black passengers made great and showy preparations in the evening time to receive their onslaught, by tying up their strong chintz mosquito bars to the stanchions and the cook-house. Conversation and atmosphere are full of mosquitoes. The decision of widely experienced sufferers amongst us is, that next to the

lower Ogowé, New Orleans is the worst place for them in this world.

The day closed with a magnificent dramatic beauty. Dead ahead of us, up through a bank of dun-coloured mist rose the moon, a great orb of crimson, spreading down the oil-like, still river, a streak of blood-red reflection. Right astern, the sun sank down into the mist, a vaster orb of crimson, and when he had gone out of view, sent up flushes of amethyst, gold, carmine and serpent-green, before he left the moon in undisputed possession of the black purple sky.

Next morning everyone was up at dawn, wood was loaded into the Mové and by 10.25 a.m. they were off at full speed up-river.

The day soon grew dull, and looked threatening, after the delusive manner of the dry season. The climbing plants are finer here than I have ever before seen them. They form great veils and curtains between and over the trees, often hanging so straight and flat, in stretches of twenty to forty feet or so wide, and thirty to sixty or seventy feet high, that it seems incredible that no human hand has trained or clipped them into their perfect forms. Sometimes these curtains are decorated with large bell-shaped, bright-coloured flowers, sometimes with delicate sprays of white blossoms.

This forest is beyond all my expectations of tropical luxuriance and beauty, and it is a thing of another world to the forest of the Upper Calabar, which, beautiful as it is, is a sad dowdy to this. There you certainly get a great sense of grimness and vastness; here you have an equal grimness and vastness with the addition of superb colour. This forest is a Cleopatra to which Calabar is but a Quaker. Not only does this forest depend on flowers for its illumination, for there are many kinds of trees having their young shoots, crimson, brown-pink, and creamy yellow: added to this there is also the relieving aspect of the prevailing fashion among West African trees, of wearing the trunk white with here and there upon it splashes of pale pink lichen, and vermilion-red fungus, which alone is sufficient to prevent the great mass of vegetation from being a monotony in green.

All day long we steam past ever-varying scenes of loveliness whose component parts are ever the same, yet the effect ever different. Doubtless it is wrong to call it a symphony, yet I know no other word to describe the scenery of the Ogowé. It is

as full of life and beauty and passion as any symphony Beethoven ever wrote: the parts changing, interweaving, and returning. There are *leit motifs* here in it, too. See the papyrus ahead; and you know when you get abreast of it you will find the great forest sweeping away in a bay-like curve behind it against the dull gray sky, the splendid columns of its cotton and red woods looking like a façade of some limitless inchoate temple. Then again there is that stretch of sword-grass, looking as if it grew firmly on to the bottom, so steady does it stand; but as the *Mové* goes by, her wash sets it undulating in waves across its broad acres of extent, showing it is only riding at anchor; and you know after a grass patch you will soon see a red dwarf clay cliff, with a village perched on its top, and the inhabitants thereof in their blue and red cloths standing by to shout and wave to the *Mové*, or legging it like lamp-lighters from the back streets and the plantation to the river frontage, to be in time to do so, and through all these changing phases there is always the strain of the vast wild forest, and the swift, deep, silent river.

At almost every village that we pass—and they are frequent after the *Fallabar*—there is an ostentatious display of firewood deposited either on the bank, or on piles driven into the mud in front of it, mutely saying in their uncivilised way, 'Try our noted chunks: best value for money'—(that is to say, tobacco, &c.), to the *Mové* or any other little steamer that may happen to come along hungry for fuel.

After leaving Ashchyouka, high land showed to the N.E., and at 5.15, without evident cause to the uninitiated, the *Mové* took to whistling like a liner. A few minutes later a factory shows up on the hilly north bank, which is Woermann's; then just beyond and behind it we see the Government Post; then Hatton and Cookson's factory, all in a line. Opposite Hatton and Cookson's there was a pretty little stern-wheel steamer [the *Éclaireur*] nestling against the steep clay bank of Lambaréné Island when we come in sight, but she instantly swept out from it in a perfect curve, which lay behind her marked in frosted silver on the water as she dropt down river. In a few minutes we have taken her berth close to the bank, and tied up to a tree. The white engineer yells to the black engineer 'Tom-Tom: Haul out some of them fire and open them drains one time', and the stokers, with hooks, pull out the glowing logs on to the iron deck in front of the furnace door, and throw water over them, and the *Mové* sends a cloud of oil-laden steam against the bank, coming perilously near scalding some of her black admirers assembled there. I am

escorted on to the broad verandah of Hatton and Cookson's factory, and I sit down under a lamp, prepared to contemplate, until dinner time, the wild beauty of the scene. This idea does not get carried out; in the twinkling of an eye I am stung all round the neck, and recognise there are lots too many mosquitoes and sandflies in the scenery to permit of contemplation of any kind. Never have I seen sandflies and mosquitoes in such appalling quantities. With a wild ping of joy the latter made for me, and I retired promptly into a dark corner of the verandah, swearing horribly, but internally, and fought them.

Mr Hudson, Agent-general, and Mr Cockshut, Agent for the Ogowé, walk up and down the beach in front, doubtless talking cargo, apparently unconscious of mosquitoes; but by and by, while we are having dinner, they get their share. I behave exquisitely, and am quite lost in admiration of my own conduct, and busily deciding in my own mind whether I shall wear one of those plain ring haloes, or a solid plate one, *à la* Cimabue, when Mr Hudson says in a voice full of reproach to Mr Cockshut, 'You have got mosquitoes here, Mr Cockshut'. Poor Mr Cockshut doesn't deny it; he has got four on his forehead and his hands are sprinkled with them, but he says: 'There are none at Njole,' which we all feel is an absurdly lame excuse, for Njole is some ninety miles above Lambaréné, where we now are. Mr Hudson says this to him, tersely, and feeling he has utterly crushed Mr Cockshut, turns on me, and utterly failing to recognise me as a suffering saint, says point blank and savagely, 'You don't seem to feel these things, Miss Kingsley'. Not feel them, indeed! Why, I could cry over them. Well! that's all the thanks one gets for trying not to be a nuisance in this world.

At Kangwe, on the river-bank the other side of Lambaréné island Mary Kingsley stayed with M. and Mme Jacot at their Mission station. Here she made her first contact with the Fans, who became her favourite tribe despite their cannibalistic habits.

I will not weary you with my diary during my first stay at Kangwe. It is a catalogue of the collection of fish, &c., that I made, and a record of the continuous, never-failing kindness and help that I received from M. and Mme Jacot. I daily saw there what it is possible to do, even in the wildest and most remote regions of West Africa, and recognised that there is still one heroic form of human being whose praise has never adequately been sung, namely, the missionary's wife. With all the draw-

backs and difficulties of the enervating climate, and the lack of
trained domestic help, and with the addition of two small
children of her own, and a tribe of school children of the Fan
and Igalwa tribes, Mme. Jacot had that mission house as clean
and tidy, and well ordered, as if it were in Paris.

One of the main comforts I had at Kangwe was the perfect
English spoken by both M. and Mme Jacot; what that amounted
to I alone know, for I cannot speak a word of French, neither
could I give you dates until I left Kangwe on the *Éclaireur*, for
it is one of my disastrous habits well known to my friends on the
Coast that whenever I am happy, comfortable and content, I
lose all knowledge of the date, the time of day, and my hairpins.
'It's the climate.' But I kept my fetish notes, except during two
days when my right elbow was out of repair in consequence of
my first visit to a Fan * fireside.

It happened this way. Down on the river bank, some one-and-
a-half miles below Kangwe, lies Fula, a large Fan village.
Through Fula that ill-starred day I passed with all the *éclat* of
Wombwell's menagerie. Having been escorted by half the population for a half mile or so beyond the town, and being then
nervous about Fans, from information received, I decided to
return to Kangwe by another road, if I could find it. I had not
gone far on my quest before I saw another village, and having
had enough village work for one day, I made my way quietly
up into the forest on the steep hillside overhanging the said
village. There was no sort of path up there, and going through
a clump of shenja, I slipped, slid, and finally fell plump through
the roof of an unprotected hut.

What the unfortunate inhabitants were doing, I don't know,
but I am pretty sure they were not expecting me to drop in,
and a scene of great confusion occurred. My knowledge of Fan
dialect then consisted of Kor-kor, so I said that in as fascinating
a tone as I could, and explained the rest with three pocket
handkerchiefs, a head of tobacco, and a knife which providentially I had stowed in what my nautical friends would call my
afterhold—my pockets. I also said I'd pay for the damage, and
although this important communication had to be made in trade
English, they seemed to understand, for when I pointed to the
roof and imitated writing out a book for it, the master of the

* The proper way to spell this tribe's name is Faung, but as they are
called by the first writer on them, Du Chaillu, Fans, I keep that name.
They are also referred to as the M'pangwe, the Pahouines, the Fam-Fam,
the Osheba, and the Ba-fann. The latter is a plural form. (MK)

house said 'Um', and then laid hold of an old lady and pointed to
her and then to the roof, meaning clearly I had equally damaged
both, and that she was equally valuable. I squared the family
all right, and I returned to Kangwe *via* Fula, without delay and
without the skin on my elbow. Wishing to get higher up the
Ogowé, I took the opportunity of the river boat of the Chargeurs
Réunis going up to the Njole on one of her trips, and joined
her.

The Éclaireur—*a 'charming little stern wheel steamer, exquisitely
kept'—steamed up the Ogowé, calling at villages and sub-factories
on the river banks. On the second day (23 June 1895) they reached
more mountainous country.*

The banks of the Ogowé just above Lambaréné Island are low;
with the forest only broken by village clearings and seeming to
press in on those, ready to absorb them should the inhabitants
cease their war against it. The blue mountains of Achango land
show away to the E.S.E. in a range. Behind us, gradually sinking
in the distance, is the high land on Lambaréné Island.

Soon we run up alongside a big street of a village with four
high houses rising a story above the rest, which are strictly
ground floor; it has also five or six little low open thatched huts
along the street in front. These may be fetish huts, or, as the
captain of the *Sparrow* would say, 'again they mayn't'. For I
have seen similar huts in the villages round Libreville, which
were store places for roof mats, of which the natives carefully
keep a store dry and ready for emergencies in the way of tornadoes, or to sell. We stop abreast of this village. Inhabitants in
scores rush out and form an excited row along the vertical
bank edge, several of the more excited individuals falling over it
into the water.

Yells from our passengers on the lower deck. Yells from inhabitants on shore. Yells of *vite, vite* from the Captain. Dogs
bark, horns bray, some exhilarated individual thumps the
village drum, canoes fly out from the bank towards us. Fearful
scrimmage heard going on all the time on the deck below. As
soon as the canoes are alongside, our passengers from the lower
deck, with their bundles and their dogs, pour over the side into
them. Canoes rock wildly and wobble off rapidly towards the
bank, frightening the passengers because they have got their
best clothes on, and fear that the *Éclaireur* will start and upset
them altogether with her wash.

We go on up stream; now and again stopping at little villages to land passengers or at little sub-factories to discharge cargo, until evening closes in, when we anchor and tie up at O'Soamo-kita.

Start off steaming up river early in the morning time. Land ahead showing mountainous. Rather suddenly the banks grow higher. Here and there in the forest are patches which look like regular hand-made plantations, which they are not, but only patches of engombie-gombie trees, showing that at this place was once a native town. Whenever land is clear along here, this tree springs up all over the ground. It grows very rapidly, and has great leaves something like a sycamore leaf, only much larger. These leaves growing in a cluster at the top of the straight stem give an umbrella-like appearance to the affair; so the natives call them and an umbrella by the same name, but whether they think the umbrella is like the tree or the tree is like the umbrella, I can't make out.

The uniformity of the height of the individual trees in one of these patches is striking, and it arises from their all starting fair. I cannot make out other things about them to my satisfaction, for you very rarely see one of them in the wild bush, and then it does not bear a fruit that the natives collect and use, and then chuck away the stones round their domicile. Anyhow, there they are, all one height, and all one colour, and apparently allowing no other vegetation to make any headway among them.

But I found when I carefully investigated engombie-gombie patches that there were a few of the great, slower-growing forest trees coming up amongst them, and in time when these attain a sufficient height, their shade kills off the engombie-gombie, and the patch goes back into the great forest from which it came. The frequency of these patches arises from the nomadic habits of the chief tribe in these regions, the Fans. They rarely occupy one site for a village for any considerable time on account—firstly, of their wasteful method of collecting rubber by cutting down the vine, which soon stamps it out of a district; and, secondly, from their quarrelsome ways. So when a village of Fans has cleared all the rubber out of its district, or has made the said district too hot to hold it by rows with other villages, or has got itself very properly shelled out and burnt for some attack on traders or the French flag in any form, its inhabitants clear off into another district, and build another village; for bark and palm thatch are cheap, and house removing just nothing; when

you are an unsophisticated cannibal Fan you don't require
a pantechnicon van to stow away your one or two mushroom-shaped stools, knives, and cooking-pots, and a calabash
or so.

If you are rich, maybe you will have a box with clothes in as
well, but as a general rule all your clothes are on your back. So
your wives just pick up the stools and the knives and the
cooking-pots, and the box, and the children toddle off with the
calabashes. You have, of course, the gun to carry, for sleeping or
waking a Fan never parts with his gun, and so there you are,
'finish', as M. Pichault would say, and before your new bark
house is up, there grows the engombie-gombie, where your house
once stood. Now and again, for lack of immediate neighbouring
villages to quarrel with, one end of a village will quarrel with the
other end. The weaker end then goes off and builds itself another
village, keeping an eye lifting for any member of the stronger
end who may come conveniently into its neighbourhood to be
killed and eaten. Meanwhile, the engombie-gombie grows over
the houses of the empty end, pretending it's a plantation belonging to the remaining half. I once heard a new-comer hold forth
eloquently as to how those Fans were maligned. 'They say',
said he, with a fine wave of his arm towards such a patch, 'that
these people do not till the soil—that they are not industrious
—that the few plantations they do make are ill-kept—that they
are only a set of wandering hunters and cannibals. Look there at
those magnificent plantations!' I did look, but I did not alter
my opinion of the Fans, for I know my old friend engombie-
gombie when I see him.

As we go on, the banks become hills and the broad river,
which has been showing sheets of sandbanks in all directions,
now narrows and shows only neat little beaches of white sand in
shallow places along the bank. The current is terrific. The
Éclaireur breathes hard, and has all she can do to fight her way
up against it. Masses of black weathered rock in great boulders
show along the exposed parts of both banks, left dry by the
falling waters. Each bank is steep, and quantities of great trees,
naked and bare, are hanging down from them, held by their
roots and bush-rope entanglement from being swept away with
the rushing current, and they make a great white fringe to the
banks. The hills become higher and higher, and more and more
abrupt, and the river runs between them in a gloomy ravine,
winding to and fro; we catch sight of a patch of white sand
ahead, which I mistake for a white painted house, but immedi-

ately after doubling round a bend we see the houses of the
Talagouga Mission Station. We run on up past Talagouga Island,
where the river broadens out again a little, but not much, and
reach Njole by nightfall, and tie up to a tree by Dumas factory
beach. Usual uproar, but as Mr Cockshut says, no mosquitoes.
The mosquito belt ends abruptly at O'Soamokita.

CHAPTER THREE

By Canoe up the Ogowé

At Njole the Éclaireur *turned round and proceeded a short way downstream to Talagouga, where Mary Kingsley disembarked (25 June 1895) to stay with M. and Mme Forget.*

Mme Forget received me most kindly and hospitably, she, with her husband and her infant daughter, and M. and Mme Gacon represent the Mission Évangélique and the white race at Talagouga. Mme Forget is a perfectly lovely French girl, with a pale transparent skin and the most perfect great dark eyes, with indescribable charm, grace of manner, and vivacity in conversation. It grieves me to think of her, wasted on this savage wilderness surrounded by its deadly fever air. Oranie Forget, otherwise the baby, although I am not a general admirer of babies of her age—a mere matter of months—is also charming; I am not saying this because she flattered me by taking to me— all babies and children do that—but she has great style, and I have no doubt she will grow up to be a beauty too, but she would have made a dead certainty of it, if she had taken after her mother.

The mission station at Talagouga is hitched on to the rocky hillside, which rises so abruptly from the river that there is hardly room for the narrow footpath which runs along the river frontage of it. And when you are on the Forgets' verandah it seems as if you could easily roll right off it into the dark, deep, hurrying Ogowé. I suggest this to Mme Forget as an awful future for Oranie, but she has thought of it and wired the verandah up. You go up a steep flight of steps into the house, which is raised on poles some fifteen feet above the ground in front, and you walk through it against the hillside, made up mostly of enormous boulders of quartz, for Talagouga mountains are the western termination of the side of the Sierra del Cristal range. When you get through the house you come to more stairs, cut out now in the hillside rock and leading to the kitchen to the right, and to the store buildings; to the left they continue up to the church, which is still higher up the hill-face. That church is the prettiest I have seen in Africa. I do not say I should like to

sit in it, because there seems to me no proper precautions taken to exclude snakes, lizards, or insects, and there would be great difficulty in concentrating one's mind on the higher life in the presence of these fearfully prevalent lower forms.

Across the other side of the ravine and high up, is perched the house which Dr Nassau built, when he first established mission work on the Upper Ogowé. The house is now in ruins; but in front of it, as an illustration of the transitory nature of European life in West Africa, is the grave of Mrs Nassau, among the great white blocks of quartz rock, its plain stone looking the one firm, permanent, human-made-thing about the place.

Talagouga is grand, but its scenery is undoubtedly grim, and its name, signifying the gateway of misery, seems applicable. It must be a melancholy place to live in, the very air lies heavy and silent. I never saw the trees stirred by a breeze the whole time I was there, even the broad plantain leaves seemed to stand sleeping day out and day in, motionless. The only sign of motion you get is in the Ogowé; if you look at it you see, in spite of its dark quiet face, that it is sweeping past at a terrific pace. One great gray rock sticks up through it just below the mission beach, and from that lies ever a silver streak from the hindrance it gives the current. Every now and again you will notice a canoe full of wild, naked, or nearly naked savages, silent because they are Fans, and don't sing like Igalwas or M'pongwe when in canoes. They are either paddling very hard and creeping very slowly upwards, against one of the banks, or just keeping her head straight and going rapidly down. Now and again you will hear the laboured beat of the engines of either the *Mové* or *Éclaireur*, before you see the vessel and hear the warning shriek of their whistles; and you can watch her as she comes up fighting her way to Njole, or see her as she comes down, slipping past like a dream in a few seconds, and that is all.

I spent the succeeding days in buying fish from the natives, who brought it in quantities, mostly of two sorts, and of course wanted enormous prices for it; but I confess I rather enjoy the give-and-take fun of bartering against their extortion, and my trading with them introduced us to each other so that when we met in the course of the long climbing walks I used to take beetle-hunting in the bush behind the mission station, we knew about each other, and did not get much shocked or frightened.

That forest round Talagouga was one of the most difficult bits of country to get about in I ever came across, for it was dense and there were no bush paths. No Fan village wants to walk to

another Fan village for social civilities, and all their trade goes up and down the river in canoes. No doubt some miles inland there are bush paths, but I never struck one, so they must be pretty far away. Neither did I come across any villages in the forest, they seem all to be on the river bank round here.

Now and again, on exposed parts of the hillside, one comes across great falls of timber which have been thrown down by tornadoes either flat on to the ground—in which case under and among them are snakes and scorpions, and getting over them is slippery work; or thrown sideways and hanging against their fellows, all covered with gorgeous drapery of climbing, flowering plants—in which case they present to the human atom a wall made up of strong tendrils and climbing grasses, through which the said atom has to cut its way with a matchette and push into the crack so made, getting, the while covered with red driver-ants, and such like, and having sensational meetings with blue-green snakes, dirty green snakes with triangular horned heads, black cobras, and boa constrictors. I never came back to the station without having been frightened half out of my wits, and with one or two of my small terrifiers in cleft sticks to bottle.

When you get into the way, catching a snake in a cleft stick is perfectly simple. Only mind you have the proper kind of stick, split far enough up, and keep your attention on the snake's head, that's his business end, and the tail which is whisking and winding round your wrist does not matter: there was one snake, by the way, of which it was impossible to tell, in the forest, which was his head. The natives swear he has one at each end; so you had better 'Lef 'em', even though you know the British Museum would love to have him, for he is very venomous, and one of the few cases of death from snake-bite I have seen, was from this species.

Several times, when further in the forest, I came across a trail of flattened undergrowth, for fifty or sixty yards, with a horrid musky smell that demonstrated it had been the path of a boa constrictor, and nothing more.

It gave me more trouble and terror to get to the top of those Talagouga hillsides than it gave me to go twenty miles in the forests of Old Calabar, and that is saying a good deal, but when you got to the summit there was the glorious view of the rest of the mountains, stretching away, interrupted only by Mount Talagouga to the S.E. by E. and the great, grim, dark forest, under the lowering gray sky common during the dry season on the Equator. No glimpse or hint did one have of the Ogowé up

here, so deep down in its ravine does it flow. A person coming to the hill tops close to Talagouga from the N. or N.N.W. and turning back in his track from here might be utterly unconscious that one of the great rivers of the world was flowing, full and strong, within some 800 feet of him. There is a strange sense of secretiveness about all these West African forests; but I never saw it so marked as in these that shroud the Sierra del Cristal. I very rarely met any natives in this part; those that I did were hunters, big, lithe men with all their toilet attention concentrated on their hair. On two occasions I ran some risk from having been stalked in mistake for game by these hunters. I escaped, however, because these men get as close as they can to their prey before firing; and when they found out their mistake they were not such cockney sportsmen as to kill me because I was something queer, and we stood and stared at each other, said a few words in our respective languages, and parted. One thing that struck me very much in these forests was the absence of signs of fetish worship which are so much in evidence in Calabar, where you constantly come across trees worshipped as the residences of spirits, and little huts put up over offerings to bush souls.

All the balance of the time I was at Talagouga I spent in trying to find means to get up into the rapids above Njole, for my heart got more and more set on them now that I saw the strange forms of the Talagouga fishes, and the differences between them and the fishes at Lambaréné. For some time no one whom I could get hold of regarded it as a feasible scheme, but, at last, M. Gacon thought it might be managed; I said I would give a reward of 100 francs to any one who would lend me a canoe and a crew, and I would pay the working expenses, food, wages, &c. M. Gacon had a good canoe and could spare me two English-speaking Igalwas, one of whom had been part of the way with MM. Allégret and Teisserès, when they made their journey up to Franceville and then across to Brazzaville and down the Congo two years ago. He also thought we could get six Fans to complete the crew.

I was delighted, packed my small portmanteau with a few things, got some trade goods, wound up my watch, ascertained the date of the day of the month, and borrowed three hairpins from Mme Forget, then down came disappointment. On my return from the bush that evening, Mme Forget said M. Gacon said 'it was impossible', the Fans round Talagouga wouldn't go at any price above Njole, because they were certain they would

be killed and eaten by the up-river Fans. Internally consigning the entire tribe to regions where they will get a rise in temperature, even in this climate, I went with Mme Forget to M. Gacon, and we talked it over; finally, M. Gacon thought he could let me have two more Igalwas from Hatton and Cookson's beach across the river. Sending across there we found this could be done, so I now felt I was in for it, and screwed my courage to the sticking point—no easy matter after all the information I had got into my mind regarding the rapids of the River Ogowé.

I establish myself on my portmanteau comfortably in the canoe, my back is against the trade box, and behind that is the usual mound of pillows, sleeping mats, and mosquito-bars of the Igalwa crew; the whole surmounted by the French flag flying from an indifferent stick.

M. and Mme Forget provide me with everything I can possibly require, and say, that the blood of half my crew is half alcohol; on the whole it is patent they don't expect to see me again, and I forgive them, because they don't seem cheerful over it; but still it is not reassuring—nothing is about this affair, and it's going to rain. It does, as we go up the river to Njole, where there is another risk of the affair collapsing, by the French authorities declining to allow me to proceed. On we paddled, M'bo the head man standing in the bows of the canoe in front of me, to steer, then I, then the baggage, then the able-bodied seamen, including the cook also standing and paddling; and at the other extremity of the canoe—it grieves me to speak of it in this unseamanlike way, but in these canoes both ends are alike, and chance alone ordains which is bow and which is stern— stands Pierre, the first officer, also steering; the paddles used are all of the long-handled, leaf-shaped Igalwa type.

In the canoe Mary Kingsley returns to Njole where she wrings a reluctant permission to proceed from the French officials, who 'part with me as one bent on self-destruction'.

Two hours after leaving Njole we are facing our first rapid. Great gray-black masses of smoothed rock rise up out of the whirling water in all directions. These rocks have a peculiar appearance which puzzle me at the time, but in subsequently getting used to it I accepted it quietly and admired. When the sun shines on them they have a soft light blue haze round them, like a halo. The effect produced by this, with the forested hillsides and the

little beaches of glistening white sand was one of the most perfect things I have ever seen.

We kept along close to the right-hand bank, dodging out of the way of the swiftest current as much as possible. Ever and again we were unable to force our way round projecting parts of the bank, so we then got up just as far as we could to the point in question, yelling and shouting at the tops of our voices. M'bo said 'Jump for bank, sar,' and I 'up and jumped', followed by half the crew. Such banks! sheets, and walls, and rubbish heaps of rock, mixed up with trees fallen and standing. One appalling corner I shall not forget, for I had to jump at a rock wall, and hang on to it in a manner more befitting an insect than an insect-hunter, and then scramble up it into a close-set forest, heavily burdened with boulders of all sizes.

I wonder whether the rocks or the trees were there first? There is evidence both ways, for in one place you will see a rock on the top of a tree, the tree creeping out from underneath it, and in another place you will see a tree on the top of a rock, clasping it with a network of roots and getting its nourishment, goodness knows how, for these are by no means tender, digestible sandstones, but uncommon hard gneiss and quartz which has no idea of breaking up into friable small stuff, and which only takes on a high polish when it is vigorously sanded and canvassed by the Ogowé. While I was engaged in climbing across these promontories, the crew would be busy shouting and hauling the canoe round the point by means of the strong chain provided for such emergencies fixed on to the bow. When this was done, in we got again and paddled away until we met our next affliction.

M'bo had advised that we should spend our first night at the same village that M. Allégret did: but when we reached it, a large village on the north bank, we seemed to have a lot of daylight still in hand, and thought it would be better to stay at one a little higher up, so as to make a shorter day's work for tomorrow, when we wanted to reach Kondo Kondo; so we went against the bank just to ask about the situation and character of the up-river villages. The row of low, bark huts was long, and extended its main frontage close to the edge of the river bank. The inhabitants had been watching us as we came, and when they saw we intended calling that afternoon, they charged down to the river-edge hopeful of excitement.

They had a great deal to say, and so had we. To M'bo's questions they gave a dramatic entertainment as answer, after the manner of these brisk, excitable Fans. One chief, however, soon

settled down to definite details, prefacing his remarks with the silence-commanding 'Azuna! Azuna!' and his companions grunted approbation of his observations. He took a piece of plantain leaf and tore it up into five different-sized bits. These he laid along the edge of our canoe at different intervals of space, while he told M'bo things, mainly scandalous, about the characters of the villages these bits of leaf represented, save of course about bit A, which represented his own. The interval between the bits was proportional to the interval between the villages, and the size of the bits was proportional to the size of the village. Village number four was the only one he should recommend our going to.

When all was said, I gave our kindly informants some heads of tobacco and many thanks. Then M'bo sang them a hymn, with the assistance of Pierre, half a line behind him in a different key, but every bit as flat. The Fans seemed impressed, but any crowd would be by the hymn-singing of my crew, unless they were inmates of deaf and dumb asylums. Then we took our farewell, and thanked the village elaborately for its kind invitation to spend the night there on our way home, shoved off and paddled away in great style just to show those Fans what Igalwas could do.

We hadn't gone 200 yards before we met a current coming round the end of a rock reef that was too strong for us to hold our own in, let alone progress. On to the bank I was ordered and went; it was a low slip of rugged confused boulders and fragments of rocks, carelessly arranged, and evidently under water in the wet season. I scrambled along, the men yelled and shouted and hauled the canoe, and the inhabitants of the village, seeing we were becoming amusing again, came, legging it like lamp-lighters, after us, young and old, male and female, to say nothing of the dogs. Some good souls helped the men haul, while I did my best to amuse the others by diving headlong from a large rock on to which I had elaborately climbed, into a thick clump of willow-leaved shrubs. They applauded my performance vociferously, and then assisted my efforts to extricate myself, and during the rest of my scramble they kept close to me, with keen competition for the front row, in hopes that I would do something like it again. But I refused the *encore*, because, bashful as I am, I could not but feel that my last performance was carried out with all the superb reckless *abandon* of a Sarah Bernhardt, and a display of art of this order should satisfy any African village for a year at least. At last I got across the rocks on to a

lovely little beach of white sand, and stood there talking, surrounded by my audience, until the canoe got over its difficulties
and arrived almost as scratched as I; and then we again said
farewell and paddled away, to the great grief of the natives, for
they don't get a circus up above Njole every week, poor dears.

*Darkness overtook the party before they could reach the village
recommended by the chief, and they found themselves caught in the
rapids, menaced by fallen tree-trunks and vicious rocks.*

About 8 P.M. we came to a corner, a bad one; but we were unable
to leap on to the bank and haul round, not being able to see
either the details or the exact position of the said bank, and we
felt, I think naturally, disinclined to spring in the direction of
such bits of country as we had had experience of during the
afternoon. We fought our way round that corner, yelling
defiance at the water, and dealt with succeeding corners on the
vi et armis plan, breaking, ever and anon, a pole.

About 9.30 we got into a savage rapid. We fought it inch by
inch. The canoe jammed herself on some barely sunken rocks in
it. We shoved her off over them. She tilted over and chucked us
out. The rocks round being just awash, we survived and got her
straight again, and got into her and drove her unmercifully; she
struck again and bucked like a broncho, and we fell in heaps
upon each other, but stayed inside that time—the men by the
aid of their intelligent feet, I by clinching my hands into the
bush rope lacing which ran round the rim of the canoe and the
meaning of which I did not understand when I left Talagouga.

We sorted ourselves out hastily and sent her at it again.
Smash went a sorely tried pole and a paddle. Round and round
we spun in an exultant whirlpool, which, in a light-hearted,
maliciously joking way, hurled us tail first out of it into the
current. Now the grand point in these canoes of having both
ends alike declared itself; for at this juncture all we had to do
was to revolve on our own axis and commence life anew with
what had been the bow for the stern. Of course we were defeated,
we could not go up any further without the aid of our lost poles
and paddles, so we had to go down for shelter somewhere,
anywhere, and down at a terrific pace in the white water we
went.

M'bo and Pierre, provided with our surviving poles, stood in
the bows to fend us off rocks, as we shot towards them; while we
midship paddles sat, helping to steer, and when occasion arose,

which occasion did with lightning rapidity, to whack the whirl-pools with the flat of our paddles, to break their force. Cook crouched in the stern concentrating his mind on steering only. We dashed full tilt towards high rocks, things twenty to fifty feet above water. Midship backed and flapped like fury; M'bo and Pierre received the shock on their poles; sometimes we glanced successfully aside and flew on; sometimes we didn't. The shock being too much for M'bo and Pierre they were driven back on me, who got flattened on to the cargo of bundles which, being now firmly tied in, couldn't spread the confusion further aft; but the shock of the canoe's nose against the rock did so in style, and the rest of the crew fell forward on to the bundles, me, and them-selves. So shaken up together were we several times that night, that it's a wonder to me, considering the hurry, that we sorted ourselves out correctly with our own particular legs and arms. And although we in the middle of the canoe did some very spirited flapping, our whirlpool-breaking was no more successful than M'bo and Pierre's fending off, and many a wild waltz we danced that night with the waters of the River Ogowé.

Unpleasant as going through the rapids was, when circum-stances took us into the black current we fared no better. For good all-round inconvenience, give me going full tilt in the dark into the branches of a fallen tree at the pace we were going then —and crash, swish, crackle and there you are, hung up, with a bough pressing against your chest, and your hair being torn out and your clothes ribboned by others, while the wicked river is trying to drag away the canoe from under you. After a good hour and more of these experiences, we went hard on to a large black reef of rocks. So firm was the canoe wedged that we in our rather worn-out state couldn't move her so we wisely decided to 'lef 'em' and see what could be done towards getting food and a fire for the remainder of the night. Our eyes, now trained to the darkness, observed pretty close to us a big lump of land, looming up out of the river. This we subsequently found out was Kembe Island. The rocks and foam on either side stretched away into the darkness, and high above us against the star-lit sky stood out clearly the summits of the mountains of the Sierra del Cristal.

The most interesting question to us now was whether this rock reef communicated sufficiently with the island for us to get to it. Abandoning conjecture; tying very firmly our canoe up to the rocks, a thing that seemed, considering she was jammed hard and immovable, a little unnecessary—but you can never be

sufficiently careful in this matter with any kind of boat—off we started among the rock boulders. I would climb up on to a rock table, fall off it on the other side on to rocks again, with more or less water on them—then get a patch of singing sand under my feet, then with varying suddenness get into more water, deep or shallow, broad or narrow pools among the rocks; out of that over more rocks, &c., &c., &c.: my companions, from their noises, evidently were going in for the same kind of thing, but we were quite cheerful, because the probability of reaching the land seemed increasing. Most of us arrived into deep channels of water which here and there cut in between this rock reef and the bank.

M'bo was the first to find the way into certainty; he was, and I hope still is, a perfect wonder at this sort of work. I kept close to M'bo, and when we got to the shore, the rest of the wanderers being collected, we said 'chances are there's a village round here'; and started to find it. After a gay time in a rock-encumbered forest, growing in a tangled, matted way on a rough hillside, at an angle of 45 degrees, M'bo sighted the gleam of fires through the tree stems away to the left, and we bore down on it, listening to its drum. Viewed through the bars of the tree stems the scene was very picturesque. The village was just a collection of palm mat-built huts, very low and squalid. In its tiny street, an affair of some sixty feet long and twenty wide, were a succession of small fires. The villagers themselves, however, were the striking features in the picture. They were painted vermilion all over their nearly naked bodies, and were dancing enthusiastically to the good old rump-a-tump-tump-tump tune, played energetically by an old gentleman on a long, high-standing, white-and-black painted drum. They said that as they had been dancing when we arrived they had failed to hear us.

M'bo secured a—well, I don't exactly know what to call it—for my use. It was, I fancy, the remains of the village club-house. It had a certain amount of palm-thatch roof and some of its left-hand side left, the rest of the structure was bare old poles with filaments of palm mat hanging from them here and there; and really if it hadn't been for the roof one wouldn't have known whether one was inside or outside it. The floor was trodden earth and in the middle of it a heap of white ash and the usual two bush lights, laid down with their burning ends propped up off the ground with stones, and emitting, as is their wont, a rather mawkish, but not altogether unpleasant smell, and volumes of smoke which finds its way out through the thatch, leaving on

the inside of it a rich oily varnish of a bright warm brown colour. They give a very good light, provided someone keeps an eye on them and knocks the ash off the end as it burns gray; the bush lights' idea of being snuffed. Against one of the open-work sides hung a drum covered with raw hide, and a long hollow bit of tree trunk, which served as a cupboard for a few small articles.

I gathered in all these details as I sat on one of the hard wood benches, waiting for my dinner, which Isaac was preparing outside in the street. The atmosphere of the hut, in spite of its remarkable advantages in the way of ventilation, was oppressive, for the smell of the bush lights, my wet clothes, and the natives who crowded into the hut to look at me, made anything but a pleasant combination. The people were evidently exceedingly poor; clothes they had very little of. The two head men had on old French military coats in rags; but they were quite satisfied with their appearance, and evidently felt through them in touch with European culture, for they lectured to the others on the habits and customs of the white man with great self-confidence and superiority.

The majority of the village had a slight acquaintance already with this interesting animal, being, I found, Adoomas. They had made a settlement on Kembe Island some two years or so ago. Then the Fans came and attacked them, and killed and ate several. The Adoomas left and fled to the French authority at Njole and remained under its guarding shadow until the French came up and chastised the Fans and burnt their village; and the Adoomas—when things had quieted down again and the Fans had gone off to build themselves a new village for their burnt one—came back to Kembe Island and their plantain patch. They had only done this a few months before my arrival and had not had time to rebuild, hence the dilapidated state of the village. As soon as my dinner arrived they politely cleared out, and I heard the devout M'bo holding a service for them, with hymns, in the street, and this being over they returned to their drum and dance, keeping things up distinctly late, for it was 11.10 P.M., when we first entered the village.

While the men were getting their food I mounted guard over our little possessions, and when they turned up to make things tidy in my hut, I walked off down to the shore by a path, which we had elaborately avoided when coming to the village, a very vertically inclined, slippery little path, but still the one whereby the natives went up and down to their canoes, which were kept tied up amongst the rocks. The moon was rising, illumining the

sky, but not yet sending down her light on the foaming, flying Ogowé in its deep ravine. The scene was divinely lovely; on every side out of the formless gloom rose the peaks of the Sierra del Cristal. Tomanjawki, on the further side of the river surrounded by his companion peaks, looked his grandest, silhouetted hard against the sky. In the higher valleys where the dim light shone faintly, one could see wreaths and clouds of silver-gray mist lying, basking lazily or rolling to and fro. Olangi seemed to stretch right across the river, blocking with his great blunt mass all passage; while away to the N.E. a cone-shaped peak showed conspicuous, which I afterwards knew as Kangwe.

In the darkness round me flitted thousands of fire-flies and out beyond this pool of utter night flew by unceasingly the white foam of the rapids; sound there was none save their thunder. The majesty and beauty of the scene fascinated me, and I stood leaning with my back against a rock pinnacle watching it. Do not imagine it gave rise, in what I am pleased to call my mind, to those complicated, poetical reflections natural beauty seems to bring out in other people's minds. It never works that way with me; I just lose all sense of human individuality, all memory of human life, with its grief and worry and doubt, and become part of the atmosphere. If I have a heaven, that will be mine, and I verily believe that if I were left alone long enough with such a scene as this, or on the deck of an African liner in the Bights, watching her funnel and masts swinging to and fro in the great long leisurely roll against the sky, I should be found soulless and dead; but I never have a chance of that.

This night my absent Kras, as my Fanti friends would call them, were sent hurrying home badly scared to their attributive body by a fearful shriek tearing through the voice of the Ogowé up into the silence of the hills. I woke with a shudder and found myself sore and stiff, but made hastily in the direction of the shriek, fancying some of our hosts had been spearing one of the crew—a vain and foolish fancy I apologise for. What had happened was that my men, thinking it wiser to keep an eye on our canoe, had come down and built a fire close to her and put up their mosquito-bars as tents. One of the men, tired out by his day's work, had sat down on one of the three logs, whose ends, pointed to a common centre where the fire is, constitute the universal stove of this region. He was taking a last pipe before turning in, but sleep had taken him, and the wretch of a fire had

sneaked along in the log under him and burnt him suddenly. The shriek was his way of mentioning the fact. Having got up these facts I left the victim seated in a remedial cool pool of water and climbed back to the village, whose inhabitants, tired at last, were going to sleep. M'bo, I found, had hung up my mosquito-bar over one of the hard wood benches, and going cautiously under it I lit a night-light and read myself asleep with my damp dilapidated old Horace.

Woke at 4 A M lying on the ground among the plantain stems, having by a reckless movement fallen out of the house. Thanks be there are no mosquitoes. I don't know how I escaped the rats which swarm here, running about among the huts and the inhabitants in the evening, with a tameness shocking to see. I turned in again until six o'clock, when we started getting things ready to go up river again, carefully providing ourselves with a new stock of poles, and subsidising a native to come with us and help us to fight the rapids.

We left the landing place rocks of Kembe Island about 8, and no sooner had we got afloat, than, in the twinkling of an eye, we were swept, broadside on, right across the river to the north bank, and then engaged in a heavy fight with a severe rapid. After passing this, the river is fairly uninterrupted by rock for a while, and is silent and swift. When you are ascending such a piece the effect is strange; you see the water flying by the side of your canoe, as you vigorously drive your paddle into it with short rapid strokes, and you forthwith fancy you are travelling at the rate of a North-Western express; but you just raise your eyes, my friend, and look at that bank, which is standing very nearly still, and you will realise that you and your canoe are standing very nearly still too; and that all your exertions are only enabling you to creep on at the pace of a crushed snail, and that it's the water that is going the pace. It's a most quaint and unpleasant disillusionment.

A bad rapid, called by our ally from Kembe Island 'Unfanga', being surmounted, we seem to be in a mountain-walled lake, and keeping along the left bank of this, we get on famously for twenty whole restful minutes, which lulls us all into a false sense of security, and my crew sing M'pongwe songs, descriptive of how they go to their homes to see their wives, and families, and friends, giving chaffing descriptions of their friends' character- istics and of their failings, which cause bursts of laughter from those among us who recognise the allusions, and how they go to their boxes, and take out their clothes, and put them on—a long

bragging inventory of these things is given by each man as a solo, and then the chorus, taken heartily up by his companions, signifies their admiration and astonishment at his wealth and importance—and then they sing how, being dissatisfied with that last dollar's worth of goods they got from 'Holty's', they have decided to take their next trade to Hatton and Cookson, or *vice versa*; and then comes the chorus, applauding the wisdom of such a decision, and extolling the excellence of Hatton and Cookson's goods or Holty's.

These M'pongwe and Igalwa boat songs are all very pretty, and have very elaborate tunes in a minor key. I do not believe there are any old words to them; I have tried hard to find out about them, but I believe the tunes, which are of a limited number and quite distinct from each other, are very old. The words are put in by the singer on the spur of the moment, and only restricted in this sense, that there would always be the domestic catalogue—whatever its component details might be —sung to the one fixed tune, the trade information sung to another, and so on. A good singer, in these parts, means the man who can make up the best song—the most impressive, or the most amusing; I have elsewhere mentioned pretty much the same state of things among the Ga's and Krumen and Bubi, and in all cases the tunes are only voice tunes, not for instrumental performance. The instrumental music consists of that marvellously developed series of drum tunes—the attempt to understand which has taken up much of my time, and led me into queer company—and the many tunes played on the 'mrimba and the orchid-root-stringed harp: they are, I believe, entirely distinct from the song tunes.

On we go singing elaborately, thinking no evil of nature, when a current, a quiet devil of a thing, comes round from behind a point of the bank and catches the nose of our canoe; wringing it well, it sends us scuttling right across the river in spite of our ferocious swoops at the water, upsetting us among a lot of rocks with the water boil'ng over them; this lot of rocks being however of the table-top kind, and not those precious, close-set pinnacles rising up sheer out of profound depths, between which you are so likely to get your canoe wedged in and split. We, up to our knees in water that nearly tears our legs off, push and shove the canoe free, and re-embarking return singing across the river, to have it out with that current. We do; and at its head find a rapid, and notice on the mountain-side a village clearing, the first sign of human habitation we have seen to-day.

Above this rapid we get a treat of still water, the main current of the Ogowé flying along by the south bank. On our side there are sandbanks with their graceful slop'ng backs and sudden ends, and there is a very strange and beautiful effect produced by the flakes and balls of foam thrown off the rushing main current into the quiet water. These whirl among the eddies and rush backwards and forwards as though they were still mad with wild haste, until, finding no current to take them down, they drift away into the land-locked bays, where they come to a standstill as if they were bewildered and lost and were trying to remember where they were going to and whence they had come; the foam of which they are composed is yellowish-white, with a spongy sort of solidity about it.

In a little bay we pass we see eight native women, Fans clearly, by their bright brown faces, and their loads of brass bracelets and armlets, intent on breaking up a stockaded fish-trap. We pause and chat, and watch them collecting the fish in baskets, and I acquire some specimens; and then, shouting farewells when we are well away, in the proper civil way, resume our course.

The middle of the Ogowé here is simply forested with high rocks, looking, as they stand with their grim forms above the foam, like a regiment of strange strong creatures breasting it, with their straight faces up river, and their more flowing curves down, as though they had on black mantles which were swept backwards. Our channel was free until we had to fight round the upper end of our bay into a long rush of strong current with bad whirlpools curving its face; then the river widens out and quiets down and then suddenly contracts—a rocky forested promon-tory running out from each bank. There is a little village on the north bank's promontory, and, at the end of each, huge monoliths rise from the water, making what looks like a gateway which had once been barred and through which the Ogowé had burst.

For the first time on this trip I felt discouraged; it seemed so impossible that we, with our small canoe and scanty crew, could force our way up through that gateway, when the whole Ogowé was rushing down through it. But we clung to the bank and rocks with hands, poles, and paddle, and did it; really the worst part was not in the gateway but just before it, for here there is a great whirlpool, its centre hollowed some two or three feet below its rim. It is caused, my Kembe islander says, by a great cave opening beneath the water. Above the gate the river

broadens out again and we see the arched opening to a large cave in the south bank; the mountain-side is one mass of rock covered with the unbroken forest; and the entrance to this cave is just on the upper wall of the south bank's promontory; so, being sheltered from the current here, we rest and examine it leisurely. The river runs into it, and you can easily pass in at this season, but in the height of the wet season, when the river level would be some twenty feet or more above its present one, I doubt if you could. They told me this place is called Boko Boko, and that the cave is a very long one, extending on a level some way into the hill, and then ascending and coming out near a mass of white rock that showed as a speck high up on the mountain.

If you paddle into it you go 'far far', and then 'no more water live', and you get out and go up the tunnel, which is sometimes broad, sometimes narrow, sometimes high, sometimes so low that you have to crawl, and so get out at the other end.

One French gentleman has gone through this performance, and I am told found 'plenty plenty' bats, and hedgehogs, and snakes. They could not tell me his name, which I much regretted. As we had no store of bush lights we went no further than the portals; indeed, strictly between ourselves, if I had had every bush light in Congo Français I personally should not have relished going further. I am terrified of caves; it sends a creaming down my back to think of them.

Paddling on beyond Boko Boko and 'soon again in the midst of a bristling forest of rocks', an elemental roar came to their ears which Mary Kingsley took to be a thunderstorm. 'No, sir, that's the Alemba,' M'bo replied.

We paddled on towards it, hugging the right-hand bank again to avoid the mid-river rocks. For a brief space the mountain wall ceased, and a lovely scene opened before us; we seemed to be looking into the heart of the chain of the Sierra del Cristal, the abruptly shaped mountains encircling a narrow plain or valley before us, each one of them steep in slope, every one of them forest-clad. The colour down this gap was superb, and very Japanese in the evening glow. The more distant peaks were soft gray-blues and purple, those nearer, indigo and black.

We soon passed this lovely scene and entered the walled-in channel, creeping up what seemed an interminable hill of black water, then through some whirlpools and a rocky channel to the

sand and rock shore of our desired island Kondo Kondo, along whose northern side tore in thunder the Alemba. We made our canoe fast in a little cove among the rocks, and landed, pretty stiff and tired and considerably damp. This island, when we were on it, must have been about half a mile or so long, but during the long wet season a good deal of it is covered, and only the higher parts—great heaps of stone, among which grows a long branched willow-like shrub—are above or nearly above water.

The Adooma from Kembe Island especially drew my attention to this shrub, telling me his people who worked the rapids always regarded it with an affectionate veneration; for he said it was the only thing that helped a man when his canoe got thrown over in the dreaded Alemba, for its long tough branches swimming in, or close to, the water are veritable life lines, and his best chance; a chance which must have failed some poor fellow, whose knife and leopard-skin belt we found wedged in among the rocks on Kondo Kondo. The main part of the island is sand, with slabs and tables of polished rock sticking up through it; and in between the rocks grew in thousands most beautiful lilies, their white flowers having a very strong scent of vanilla and their bright light-green leaves looking very lovely on the glistening pale sand among the black-gray rock. How they stand the long submersion they must undergo I do not know; the natives tell me they begin to spring up as soon as ever the water falls and leaves the island exposed; that they very soon grow up and flower, and keep on flowering until the Ogowé comes down again and rides roughshod over Kondo Kondo for months.

While the men were making their fire I went across the island to see the great Alemba rapid, of which I had heard so much, that lay between it and the north bank. Nobler pens than mine must sing its glory and its grandeur. Its face was like nothing I have seen before. Its voice was like nothing I have heard. Those other rapids are not to be compared to it; they are wild, headstrong, and malignant enough, but the Alemba is not as they. It does not struggle, and writhe, and brawl among the rocks, but comes in a majestic springing dance, a stretch of waltzing foam, triumphant.

The beauty of the night on Kondo Kondo was superb; the sun went down and the afterglow flashed across the sky in crimson, purple, and gold, leaving it a deep violet-purple, with the great stars hanging in it like moons, until the moon herself arose,

lighting the sky long before she sent her beams down on us in this valley. As she rose, the mountains hiding her face grew harder and harder in outline, and deeper and deeper black, while those opposite were just enough illumined to let one see the wefts and floating veils of blue-white mist upon them, and when at last, and for a short time only, she shone full down on the savage foam of the Alemba, she turned it into a soft silver mist. Around, on all sides flickered the fire-flies, who had come to see if our fire was not a big relation of their own, and they were the sole representatives, with ourselves, of animal life. When the moon had gone, the sky, still lit by the stars, seeming indeed to be in itself lambent, was very lovely, but it shared none of its light with us, and we sat round our fire surrounded by an utter darkness. Cold, clammy drifts of almost tangible mist encircled us; ever and again came cold faint puffs of wandering wind, weird and grim beyond description.

The individual names of the mountains round Kondo Kondo and above I cannot give you, though I was told them. For in my last shipwreck before reaching Kondo Kondo, I had lost my pencil; and my note-book, even if I had had a pencil, was unfit to get native names down on, being a pulpy mass, because I had kept it in my pocket after leaving the Okana river so as to be ready for submergencies. And I also had several fish and a good deal of water in my pocket too, so that I am thankful I have a note left.

Their return journey downstream from Kondo Kondo was accomplished without disaster, though not without mishap.

A comic incident happened to us one evening. The canoe jammed among a clump of rocks, and out we went anyhow into the water. Fortunately, there were lots of rocks about; unfortunately, we each chose different ones to perch on; mine was exceedingly inconvenient, being a smooth pillar affair, to which it was all I and the French flag, which always accompanied me in upsets, could do to hold on. There was considerable delay in making up our party again, for the murkiness of the night only allowed each of us to see the foam which flew round our own particular rock, and the noise of the rapids made it difficult for us to interchange information regarding our own individual position and plan of action.

However, owing to that weak-minded canoe swinging round broadside on to the rocks, she did not bolt down the river. When

Pierre got to her she was trying to climb sideways over them, 'like a crab,' he said. We seven of us got into her—number eight we could not find and were just beginning to think the Ogowé had claimed another victim when we heard the strains of that fine hymn 'Notre port est au Ciel'—which is a great favourite hereabouts owing to its noble tune—coming to us above the rapids' clamour in an agonised howl. We went joyfully and picked the singer off his rock, and then dashed downwards to further dilemmas and disasters.

Customs of the River Tribes

After reaching Talagouga, Mary Kingsley re-embarked on the
Éclaireur 'with all my bottles and belongings', and was once more
in the company of the ebullient Captain Verdier and his chief
engineer.

The captain is drowsily looking down the river. But repose is not
long allowed to that active spirit; he sees something in the
water—what? '*Hippopotame*,' he ejaculates. Now both he and
the engineer frequently do this thing, and then fly off to their
guns—bang, bang, finish; but this time he does not dash for his
gun, nor does the engineer, who flies out of his cabin at the sound
of the war shout '*Hippopotame*'. In vain I look across the broad
river with its stretches of yellow sandbanks, where the '*hippopotame*' should be, but I can see nothing but four black stumps
sticking up in the water away to the right. Meanwhile the
captain and the engineer are flying about getting off a crew of
blacks into the canoe we are towing alongside. This being done
the captain explains to me that on the voyage up 'the engineer
had fired at, and hit a hippopotamus, and without doubt this
was its body floating'.

We are now close enough even for me to recognise the four
stumps as the deceased's legs, and soon the canoe is alongside
them and makes fast to one, and then starts to paddle back,
hippo and all, to the *Éclaireur*. But no such thing; let them
paddle and shout as hard as they like, the hippo's weight
simply anchors them. The *Éclaireur* by now has dropped down
the river past them, and has to sweep round and run back.
Recognising promptly what the trouble is, the energetic captain
grabs up a broom, ties a light cord belonging to the leadline to it,
and holding the broom by the end of its handle, swings it round
his head and hurls it at the canoe. The arm of a merciful Pro-
vidence being interposed, the broom-tomahawk does not hit the
canoe, wherein, if it had, it must infallibly have killed some one,
but falls short, and goes tearing off with the current, well out
of reach of the canoe.

The captain seeing this gross dereliction of duty by a Chargeur

Réunis broom, hauls it in hand over hand and talks to it. Then he ties the other end of its line to the mooring rope, and by a better aimed shot sends the broom into the water, about ten yards above the canoe, and it drifts towards it. Breathless excitement! Surely they will get it now. Alas, no! Just when it is within reach of the canoe, a fearful shudder runs through the broom. It throws up its head and sinks beneath the tide. A sensation of stun comes over all of us. The crew of the canoe, ready and eager to grasp the approaching aid, gaze blankly at the circling ripples round where it sank.

The *Éclaireur* goes now close enough to the hippo-anchored canoe for a rope to be flung to the man in her bows; he catches it and freezes on gallantly. Saved! No! Oh horror! The lower deck hums with fear that after all it will not taste that toothsome hippo chop, for the man who has caught the rope is as nearly as possible jerked flying out of the canoe when the strain of the *Éclaireur* contending with the hippo's inertia flies along it, but his companion behind him grips him by the legs and is in his turn grabbed, and the crew holding on to each other with their hands, and on to their craft with their feet, save the man holding on to the rope and the whole situation; and slowly bobbing towards us comes the hippopotamus, who is shortly hauled on board by the winners in triumph.

My esteemed friends, the captain and the engineer, who of course have been below during this hauling, now rush on to the upper deck, each coatless, and carrying an enormous butcher's knife. They dash into the saloon, where a terrific sharpening of these instruments takes place on the steel belonging to the saloon carving-knife, and down stairs again. By looking down the ladder, I can see the pink, pig-like hippo, whose colour has been soaked out by the water, lying on the lower deck and the captain and engineer slitting down the skin intent on gralloching operations. Providentially, my prophetic soul induces me to leave the top of the ladder and go forward—'run to win'ard', as Captain Murray would say—for within two minutes the captain and engineer are up the ladder as if they had been blown up by the boilers bursting, and go as one man for the brandy bottle; and they wanted it if ever man did; for remember that hippo had been dead and in the warm river-water for more than a week.

The captain had had enough of it, he said, but the engineer stuck to the job with a courage I profoundly admire, and he saw it through and then retired to his cabin; sand-and-can-

vassed himself first, and then soaked and saturated himself in
Florida water. The flesh gladdened the hearts of the crew and
lower-deck passengers and also of the inhabitants of Lambaréné, who got dashes of it on our arrival there. Hippo flesh is
not to be despised by black man or white; I have enjoyed it far
more than the stringy beef or vapid goat's flesh one gets down
here.

Back at Kangwe, Mary Kingsley again left the Éclaireur *and was
welcomed once more by the Jacots, looking 'all the better for my
having been away'. Under their tuition she 'saw and learnt many
things', and under her own learnt how to manage a native canoe.*

My first attempt was made at Talagouga one very hot afternoon.
I was too frightened to go into the forest that afternoon, because on the previous afternoon I had been stalked as a wild
beast by a cannibal savage, and I am nervous. Besides, and
above all, it is quite impossible to see other people gliding about
in canoes, without wishing to go and glide about yourself. So I
went down to where the canoes were tied by their noses to the
steep bank, and finding a paddle, a broken one, I unloosed the
smallest canoe. Unfortunately this was fifteen feet or so long,
but I did not know the disadvantage of having, as it were, a
long-tailed canoe then—I did shortly afterwards.

The promontories running out into the river on each side of
the mission beach give a little stretch of slack water between the
bank and the mill-race-like current of the Ogowé, and I wisely
decided to keep in the slack water, until I had found out how to
steer—most important thing, steering. I got into the bow of the
canoe, and shoved off from the bank all right; then I knelt
down—learn how to paddle standing up by and by—good so
far. I rapidly learnt how to steer from the bow, but I could not
get up any pace. Intent on acquiring pace, I got to the edge of
the slack water; and then displaying more wisdom, I turned
round to avoid it, proud as a peacock, you understand, at
having found out how to turn round. At this moment, the
current of the greatest equatorial river in the world grabbed my
canoe by its tail. We spun round and round for a few seconds,
like a teetotum, I steering the whole time for all I was worth,
and then the current dragged the canoe ignominiously down
river, tail foremost.

Fortunately a big tree was at that time temporarily hanging
against the rock in the river, just below the sawmill beach. Into

that tree the canoe shot with a crash, and I hung on, and shipping my paddle, pulled the canoe into the slack water again, by the aid of the branches of the tree, which I was in mortal terror would come off the rock, and insist on accompanying me and the canoe, *via* Kama country, to the Atlantic Ocean; but it held, and when I had got safe against the side of the pinnacle-rock I wiped a perspiring brow, and searched in my mind for a piece of information regarding navigation that would be applicable to the management of long-tailed Adooma canoes.

I could not think of one for some minutes. Captain Murray has imparted to me at one time and another an enormous mass of hints as to the management of vessels, but those vessels were all presupposed to have steam power. But he having been the first man to take an ocean-going steamer up to Matadi on the Congo, through the terrific currents that whirl and fly in Hell's Cauldron, knew about currents, and I remembered he had said regarding taking vessels through them, 'Keep all the headway you can on her.' Good! that hint nverted will fit this situation like a glove, and I'll keep all the tailway I can off her.

Feeling now as safe as only a human being can feel who is backed up by a sound principle, I was cautiously crawling to the tail-end of the canoe, intent on kneeling in it to look after it, when I heard a dreadful outcry on the bank. Looking there I saw Mme Forget, Mme Gacon, M. Gacon, and their attributive crowd of mission children all in a state of frenzy. They said lots of things in chorus. 'What?' said I. They said some more and added gesticulations. Seeing I was wasting their time as I could not hear, I drove the canoe from the rock and made my way, mostly by steering, to the bank close by; and then tying the canoe firmly up I walked over the mill stream and divers other things towards my anxious friends. 'You'll be drowned,' they said. 'Gracious goodness!' said I, 'I thought that half an hour ago, but it's all right now; I can steer.' After much conversation I lulled their fears regarding me, and having received strict orders to keep in the stern of the canoe, because that is the proper place when you are managing a canoe single-handed, I returned to my studies. I had not however lulled my friends' interest regarding me, and they stayed on the bank watching.

I found first, that my education in steering from the bow was of no avail; second, that it was all right if you reversed it. For instance, when you are in the bow, and make an inward stroke with the paddle on the right-hand-side, the bow goes to the right; whereas, if you make an inward stroke on the right-hand

side, when you are sitting in the stern, the bow then goes to the left. Understand? Having grasped this law, I crept along up river; and, by Allah! before I had gone twenty yards, if that wretch, the current of the greatest, &c., did not grab hold of the nose of my canoe, and we teetotummed round again as merrily as ever.

However, I got into the slack water again, by some very showy, high-class steering. Still steering, fine as it is, is not all you require and hanker after. You want pace as well, and pace, except when in the clutches of the current, I had not so far attained. Perchance, thought I, the pace region in a canoe may be in its centre; so I got along on my knees into the centre to experiment. Bitter failure; the canoe took to sidling down river broadside on, like Mr Winkle's horse. Shouts of laughter from the bank. Both bow and stern education utterly inapplicable to centre; and so, seeing I was utterly thrown away there, I crept into the bows, and in a few more minutes I steered my canoe, perfectly, in among its fellows by the bank and secured it there. Mme Forget ran down to meet me and assured me she had not laughed so much since she had been in Africa, although she was frightened at the time lest I should get capsized and drowned.

Well, when I got down to Lambaréné I naturally went on with my canoeing studies, in pursuit of the attainment of pace. Success crowned my efforts, and I can honestly and truly say that there are only two things I am proud of—one is that Doctor Günther has approved of my fishes, and the other is that I can paddle an Ogowé canoe. Pace, style, steering and all, 'All same for one' as if I were an Ogowé African. A strange, incongruous pair of things: but I often wonder what are the things other people are really most proud of; it would be a quaint and repaying subject for investigation.

The sandbanks were showing their yellow heads in all directions when I came down from Talagouga, and just opposite Andande there was sticking up out of the water a great, graceful, palm frond. It had been stuck into the head of the pet sandbank, and every day was visited by the boys and girls in canoes to see how much longer they would have to wait for the sandbank's appearance. A few days after my return it showed, and in two days more there it was, acres and acres of it, looking like a great, golden carpet spread on the surface of the centre of the clear water.

There was great rejoicing. Canoe-load after canoe-load of boys

and girls went to the sandbank, some doing a little fishing round its rim, others bringing the washing there, all skylarking and singing. Few prettier sights have I ever seen than those on that sandbank—the merry brown forms dancing or lying stretched on it: the gaudy-coloured patchwork quilts and chintz mosquito-bars that have been washed, spread out drying, looking from Kangwe on the hill above, like beds of bright flowers. By night when it was moonlight there would be bands of dancers on it with bush-light torches, gyrating, intermingling and separating till you could think you were looking at a dance of stars. Ah me! if the aim of life were happiness and pleasure, Africa should send us missionaries instead of our sending them to her—but, fortunately for the work of the world, happiness is not.

One thing I remember which struck me very much regarding the sandbank, and this was that Mme Jacot found such pleasure in taking her work on to the verandah, where she could see it. I knew she did not care for the songs and the dancing. One day she said to me, 'It is such a relief.' 'A relief?' I said. 'Yes, do you not see that until it shows, there is nothing but forest, forest, forest, and that still stretch of river. That bank is the only piece of clear ground I see in the year, and that only lasts a few weeks until the wet season comes, and then it goes, and there is nothing but forest, forest, forest, for another year. It is two years now since I came to this place; it may be I know not how many more before we go home again.'

I grieve to say, for my poor friend's sake, that her life at Kangwe was nearly at its end. Soon after my return to England I heard of the death of her husband from malignant fever. M. Jacot was a fine, powerful, energetic man, in the prime of life. He was a teetotaler and a vegetarian; and although constantly travelling to and fro in his district on his evangelising work, he had no foolish recklessness in him. No one would have thought that he would have been the first to go of us who used to sit round his hospitable table. His delicate wife, his two young children or I would have seemed far more likely. His loss will be a lasting one to the people he risked his life to (what he regarded) save. The natives held him in the greatest affection and respect, and his influence over them was considerable, far more profound than that of any other missionary I have ever seen. His loss is also great to those students of Africa who are working on the culture or on the languages; his knowledge of both was extensive, particularly of the little known languages of the Ogowé

district. He was, when I left, busily employed in compiling a dictionary of the Fan tongue, and had many other works on language in contemplation. His work in this sphere would have had a high value, for he was a man with a university education and well grounded in Latin and Greek, and thoroughly acquainted with both English and French literature, for although born a Frenchman, he had been brought up in America. He was also a cultivated musician, and he and Mme Jacot in the evenings would sing old French songs, Swiss songs, English songs, in their rich full voices; and then if you stole softly out on to the verandah, you would often find it crowded with a silent, black audience, listening intently.

Mary Kingsley explains the trading system of the area, on which she became an expert in order to reinforce her own slender means.

Payments on the Ogowé are made in goods; the natives do not use any coinage-equivalent, save in the strange case of the Fans. They have not even the brass bars and cheetems that are in use in Calabar, or cowries as in Lagos. In order to expedite and simplify this goods traffic, a written or printed piece of paper is employed—practically a cheque, which is called a 'bon' or 'book', and these 'bons' are cashed—*i.e.* gooded, at the store. They are for three amounts. Five fura = a dollar. One fura = a franc. Desu = fifty centimes = half a fura. The value given for these 'bons' is the same from government, trade, and mission. All the native evangelists, black teachers, Bible-readers and labourers on the stations are paid off in these bons; and when any representative of the mission is away on a journey, food bought for themselves and their canoe crews is paid for in bons, which are brought in by the natives at their convenience, and changed for goods at the store. Therefore for several hours every weekday the missionary has to devote himself to store work, and store work out here is by no means playing at shop. It is very hard, tiring, exasperating work when you have to deal with it in full, as a trader. But it is quite enough to try the patience of any saint when you are only keeping store to pay on bons, *à la* missionary; for each class of article used in trade—and there are some hundreds of them—has a definite and acknowledged value, but where the trouble comes in is that different articles have the same value; for example, six fishhooks and one pocket-handkerchief have the same value, or you can make up that value in lucifer matches,

pomatum, a mirror, a hair comb, tobacco, or scent in bottles. Picture to yourself the perplexities of a Christian minister, engaged in such an occupation as storekeeping under these circumstances, with, likely enough, a touch of fever on him and jiggers in his feet; and when the store is closed the goods in it requiring constant vigilance to keep them free from mildew and white ants.

There follows an account of the educational system in the Congo Français, where French was decreed to be the language of instruction; on methods of cookery and diet, and on their connection with polygamy.

The Negroes cook uniformly very well, and at moments are inspired in the direction of palm-oil chop and fish cooking. Not so the Bantu, whose methods cry aloud for improvement, they having just the very easiest and laziest way possible of dealing with food. The food supply consists of plantain, yam, koko, sweet potatoes, maize, pumpkin, pineapple and ochres, fish both wet and smoked, and flesh of many kinds—including human in certain districts—snails, snakes and cray-fish, and big maggot-like pupae of the rhinoceros beetle and the *Rhyncophorus palmatorum*. For sweetmeats the sugar-cane abounds, but it is only chewed *au naturel*. For seasoning there is that bark that tastes like an onion, an onion distinctly *passé*, but powerful and permanent, particularly if it has been used in one of the native-made, rough earthen pots. These pots have a very cave-man look about them; they are unglazed, unlidded bowls. They stand the fire wonderfully well, and you have got to stand, as well as you can, the taste of the aforesaid bark that clings to them, and that of the smoke which gets into them during cooking operations over an open wood fire, as well as the soot-like colour they impart to even your own white rice.

Out of all this varied material the natives of the Congo Français forests produce, dirtily, carelessly and wastefully, a dull, indigestible diet. Yam, sweet potatoes, ochres and maize are not so much cultivated or used as among the Negroes, and the daily food is practically plantain—picked while green and the rind pulled off, and the tasteless woolly interior baked or boiled, and the widely distributed manioc treated in the usual way. The sweet or non-poisonous manioc I have rarely seen cultivated, because it gives a much smaller yield, and is much longer coming to perfection. The poisonous kind is that in general use; its

great dahlia-like roots are soaked in water to remove the poisonous principle, and then dried and grated up, or more commonly
beaten up into a kind of dough in a wooden trough that looks
like a model canoe, with wooden clubs, which I have seen the
curiosity hunter happily taking home as war clubs to alarm his
family with.

The thump, thump, thump of this manioc beating is one of
the most familiar sounds in a bush village. The meal, when
beaten up, is used for thickening broths, and rolled up into
bolsters about a foot long and two inches in diameter, and then
wrapped in plantain leaves, and tied round with tie-tie and
boiled, or more properly speaking steamed, for a lot of the rolls
are arranged in a brass skillet. A small quantity of water is
poured over the rolls of plantain, a plantain leaf is tucked over
the top tightly, so as to prevent the steam from escaping, and
the whole affair is poised on the three cooking-stones over a
wood fire, and left there until the contents are done, or more
properly speaking, until the lady in charge of it has delusions on
the point, and the bottom rolls are a trifle burnt or the whole
insufficiently cooked.

This manioc meal is the staple food, the bread equivalent, all
along the coast. As you pass along you are perpetually meeting
with a new named food, fou-fou on the Leeward, kank on the
Windward, m'vada in Corisco, agooma in the Ogowé; but
acquaintance with it demonstrates that it is all the same—
manioc. If I ever meet a tribe that refers to buttered muffins I
shall know what to expect and so not get excited.

It is a good food when it is properly prepared; but when a
village has soaked its soil-laden manioc tubers in one and the
same pool of water for years, the water in that pool becomes a
trifle strong, and both it and the manioc get a smell which
once smelt is never to be forgotten; it is something like that
resulting from bad paste with a dash of vinegar, but fit to pass
all these things, and has qualities of its own that have no civilised equivalent.

I believe that this way of preparing the staple article of diet
is largely responsible for that dire and frequent disease 'cut him
belly', and several other quaint disorders, possibly even for the
sleep disease. The natives themselves say that a diet too
exclusively maniocan produces dimness of vision, ending in
blindness if the food is not varied; the poisonous principle
cannot be anything like soaked out in the surcharged water,
and the meal when it is made up and cooked has just the

same sour, acrid taste you would expect it to have from the smell.

The smoked meat is badly prepared, just hung up in the smoke of the fires, which hardens it, blackening the outside quickly; but when the lumps are taken out of the smoke, in a short time cracks occur in them, and the interior part proceeds to go bad, and needless to say maggoty. If it is kept in the smoke, as it often is to keep it out of the way of dogs and driver ants, it acquires the toothsome taste and texture of a piece of old tarpaulin. I have gone into this bush cooking here in detail, so that you may understand why on the Coast, when a man comes in and says he has been down on native chop, we say 'Good gracious!' and give out the best tins on the spot.

I now ask the surviving reader who has waded through this dissertation on cookery if something should not be done to improve the degraded condition of the Bantu cooking culture? Not for his physical delectation only, but because his present methods are bad for his morals, and drive the man to drink, let alone assisting in riveting him in the practice of polygamy, which the missionary party say is an exceedingly bad practice for him to follow.

The inter-relationship of these two subjects may not seem on the face of it very clear, but inter-relationships of customs very rarely are; I well remember M. Jacot coming home one day at Kangwe from an evangelising visit to some adjacent Fan towns, and saying he had had given to him that afternoon a new reason for polygamy, which was that it enabled a man to get enough to eat. This sounds sinister from a notoriously cannibal tribe; but the explanation is that the Fans are an exceedingly hungry tribe, and require a great deal of providing for. It is their custom to eat about ten times a day when in village, and the men spend most of their time in the palaver-houses at each end of the street, the women bringing them bowls of food of one kind or another all day long. When the men are away in the forest rubber or elephant-hunting, and have to cook their own food, they cannot get quite so much; but when I have come across them on these expeditions, they halted pretty regularly every two hours and had a substantial snack, and the gorge they all go in for after a successful elephant hunt is a thing to see—once.

There are other reasons which lead to the prevalence of this custom, beside the cooking. One is that it is totally impossible for one woman to do the whole work of a house—look after the

children, prepare and cook the food, prepare the rubber, carry the same to the markets, fetch the daily supply of water from the stream, cultivate the plantation, &c., &c. The more wives the less work, says the African lady; and I have known men who would rather have had one wife and spent the rest of the money on themselves, in a civilised way, driven into polygamy by the women; and of course this state of affairs is most common in non-slave-holding tribes like the Fan. But then there is that custom which, as far as I know, is common to all African tribes, and I suspect to Asiatic, which is well known to ethnologists, and which once caused a missionary to say to me: 'A blow must be struck at polygamy, and that blow must be dealt with a feeding-bottle'.* He was a practical man, so there are a gross or two of Alexandra feeding-bottles at a place on the Coast; but they don't go off, and the missionary has returned to America.

Polygamy is the institution which above all others governs the daily life of the native; and it is therefore the one which the missionaries who enter into this daily life, and not merely into the mercantile and legal, as do the trader and the government official, are constantly confronted with and hindered by. All the missionaries have set their faces against it and deny Church membership to those men who practise it; whereby it falls out that many men are excluded from the fold who would make quite as good Christians as those within it. They hesitate about turning off from their homes women who have lived and worked for them for years, and not only for them, but often for their fathers before them.

One case in the Rivers I know of is almost tragic if you put yourself in his place. An old chief, who had three wives, profoundly and vividly believed that exclusion from the Holy Communion meant an eternal damnation. The missionary had instructed him in the details of this damnation thoroughly, and the chief did not like the prospect at all; but on the other hand he did not like to turn off the three wives he had lived with for years. He found the matter was not even to be compromised, by turning off two and going to church to be married with accompanying hymns and orange-blossoms with number three, for the ladies held together; not one of them would marry him and let the other two go, so the poor old chief worried himself

* A reference to the custom whereby a man forgoes sexual relations with his wife so long as she is suckling, and infants are kept at the breast for up to three years. (EH)

to a shammock and anybody else he could get to listen to him.

His white trader friends told him not to be such an infernal ass. Some of his black fellow chiefs said the missionary was quite right, and the best thing for him to do would be to hand over to them the three old wives, and go and marry a young girl from the mission school. Personally they were not yet afflicted with scruples on the subject of polygamy, and of course (being 'missionary man' now) he would not think of taking anything for his wives, so they would do their best, as friends, to help him out of the difficulty. Others of his black fellow chiefs, less advanced in culture, just said: 'What sort of fool palaver you make'; and spat profusely. The poor old man smelt hell fire, and cried 'Yo, yo, yo', and beat his hands upon the ground. It was a moral mess of the first water all round. Still do not imagine the mission-field is full of yo yo-ing old chiefs; for although the African is undecided, he is also very ingenious, particularly in dodging inconvenient moral principles.

I am unsympathetic, for reasons of my own, with Christian missions, so my admiration for [the Mission Évangélique] does not arise from the usual ground of admiration for missions, namely, that however they may be carried on, they are engaged in a great and holy work; but I regard this one, judging from the results I have seen, as the perfection of what one may call a purely spiritual mission.

Lambaréné Island is the largest of the islands on the Ogowé. It is some fifteen miles long, east and west, and a mile to a mile and a half wide. It is hilly and rocky, uniformly clad with forest, and several little permanent streams run from it on both sides into the Ogowé. It is situated 130 miles from the sea, at the point, just below the entrance of the N'guni, where the Ogowé commences to divide up into that network of channels by which, like all great West African rivers save the Congo, it chooses to enter the ocean. The island, as we mainlanders at Kangwe used to call it, was a great haunt of mine, particularly after I came down from Talagouga and saw fit to regard myself as competent to control a canoe.

Now my pet canoe at Andande was about six feet long, pointed at both ends, flat bottomed, so that it floated on the top of the water; its freeboard was, when nothing was in it, some three inches, and the poor thing had seen trouble in its time, for it had a hole you could put your hand in at one end; so in order

to navigate it successfully, you had to squat in the other, which immersed that to the water level but safely elevated the damaged end in the air. Of course you had to stop in your end firmly, because if you went forward the hole went down into the water, and the water went into the hole, and forthwith you foundered with all hands—*i.e.*, you and the paddle and the calabash baler. This craft also had a strong weather helm, owing to a warp in the tree of which it had been made.

The next voyage I made, I decided to go by myself to the factory, which is on the other side of the island, and did so. I got some goods to buy fish with, and heard from Mr Cockshut that the poor boy-agent at O'Soamokita, had committed suicide. It was a grievous thing. He was a bright, intelligent young Frenchman; but living in the isolation, surrounded by savage, tiresome tribes, the strain of his responsibility had been too much for him. He had had a good deal of fever, and the very kindly head agent for Woermann's had sent Dr Pélessier to see if he had not better be invalided home; but he told the Doctor he was much better, and as he had no one at home to go to he begged him not to send him, and the Doctor, to his subsequent regret, gave in.

No one knows, who has not been to visit Africa, how terrible is the life of a white man in one of these out-of-the-way factories, with no white society, and with nothing to look at, day out and day in, but the one set of objects—the forest, the river, and the beach, which in a place like O'Soamokita you cannot leave for months at a time, and of which you soon know every plank and stone. I felt utterly wretched as I started home again to come up to the end of the island, and go round it and down to Andande; and paddled on for some little time, before I noticed that I was making absolutely no progress. I redoubled my exertions, and crept slowly up to some rocks projecting above the water; but pass them I could not, as the main current of the Ogowé flew in hollow swirls round them against my canoe.

Several passing canoefuls of natives gave me good advice in Igalwa; but facts were facts, and the Ogowé was too strong for me. After about twenty minutes an old Fan gentleman came down river in a canoe and gave me good advice in Fan, and I got him to take me in tow—that is to say, he got into my canoe and I held on to his and we went back down river. I then saw his intention was to take me across to that disreputable village, half Fan, half Bakele, which is situated on the main bank of the river opposite the island; this I disapproved of, because I had heard

that some Senegal soldiers who had gone over there, had been stripped of every rag they had on, and maltreated; besides, it was growing very late, and I wanted to get home to dinner. I communicated my feelings to my pilot, who did not seem to understand at first, so I feared I should have to knock them into him with the paddle; but at last he understood I wanted to be landed on the island and duly landed me, when he seemed much surprised at the reward I gave him in pocket-handker-chiefs. Then I got a powerful young Igalwa dandy to paddle me home.

The Igalwas are a tribe very nearly akin, if not ethnically identical with, the M'pongwe, and the culture of these two tribes is on a level with the highest native African culture. African culture, I may remark, varies just the same as European in this, that there is as much difference in the manners of life between, say, an Igalwa and a Bubi of Fernando Po, as there is between a Londoner and a Laplander.

The Igalwa builds his house like that of the M'pongwe, of bamboo, and he surrounds himself with European-made articles. The neat houses, fitted with windows, with wooden shutters to close at night, and with a deal door—a carpenter-made door—are in sharp contrast with the ragged ant-hill looking perform-ances of the Akkas, or the bark huts of the Fan, with no windows, and just an extra broad bit of bark to slip across the hole that serves as a door. On going into an Igalwa house you will see a four-legged table, often covered with a bright-coloured tablecloth, on which stands a water bottle, with two clean glasses, and round about you will see chairs—Windsor chairs.

These houses have usually three, sometimes more rooms, and a separate closed-in little kitchen, built apart, wherein you may observe European-made saucepans, in addition to the ubiquit-ous skillet. Outside, all along the clean sandy streets, the inhabitants are seated. The Igalwa is truly great at sitting, the men pursuing a policy of masterly inactivity, broken occasion-ally by leisurely netting a fishing net, the end of the netting hitched up on to the roof thatch, and not held by a stirrup. The ladies are employed in the manufacture of articles pertaining to a higher culture—I allude, as Mr Micawber would say, to bed-quilts and pillow cases—the most gorgeous bed-quilts and pillow-cases—made of patchwork, and now and again you will see a mosquito-bar in course of construction, of course not made of net or muslin because of the awesome strength and ferocity of the Lambaréné strain of mosquitoes, but of stout, fair-

flowered and besprigged chintzes; and you will observe these
things are often being sewn with a sewing machine.

Here and there you will see a misguided woman making a
Hubbard. Forgive me, but I must break out on the subject of
Hubbards; I will promise to keep clear of bad language let the
effort cost me what it may. A Hubbard is a female garment
patronised by the whole set of missions from Sierra Leone to
Congo Belge, so please understand I am not criticising the
Mission Evangélique in this affair. I think these things are one of
the factors producing the well-known torpidity of the mission-
trained girl; and they should be suppressed in her interest, apart
from their appearance, which is enough to constitute a hanging
matter. Their formation is this—a yoke round the neck and
shoulders fastens at the back with three buttons—two usually
lost; from this yoke protrude dwarf sleeves, and round its lower
rim, on a level with the armpits, is sewn on a flounce, set in with
full gathers, which falls to the heels of the wearer.

The constant habit of the garment is to fall forward and reap
the dirt whenever the wearer stoops forward to do anything,
going into the fire, and the cooking, and things in general, and
impeding all rapid movement. These garments are usually made
at working parties in Europe; and what idea the pious ladies in
England, Germany, Scotland and France can have of the
African figure I cannot think, but evidently part of their opinion
is that it is very like a tub. I was once helping to unpack a
mission box. 'What have they sent out these frills for palm-oil
puncheons for?' I inquired of my esteemed friend, the lady
missionary. 'Don't be more foolish than you can help,' she
answered. 'Don't you see the sleeves? They are Hubbards.' I
was crushed; but even she acknowledged that it was trying of
the home folk to make them like that, all the more so because
their delusion on the African figure was not confined to the
making of Hubbards, but extended to the making of shirts and
chemises. There is nothing like measurements in ethnology, so I
measured and found one that with a depth of thirty inches had
a breadth of beam of forty-two inches; one with a depth of
thirty-six inches had a breadth of sixty inches. It is not in
nature for people to be made to fit these things.

Those among them who may not be busy sewing, are busy
doing each other's hair. Hair-dressing is quite an art among the
Igalwa and M'pongwe women, and their hair is very beautiful;
very crinkly, but fine. It is plaited up, close to the head, partings
between the plaits making elaborate parterres. Into the beds

of plaited hair are stuck long pins of river ivory (hippo),
decorated with black tracery and openwork, and made by their
good men. A lady will stick as many of these into her hair as she
can get, but the prevailing mode is to have one stuck in behind
each ear, showing their broad, long heads above like two horns;
they are exceedingly becoming to these black but comely ladies,
verily I think, the comeliest ladies I have ever seen on the
Coast. Very black they are, blacker than any of their neighbours, always blacker than the Fans, and although their skin
lacks that velvety pile of the true negro, it is not too shiny, but
it is fine and usually unblemished, and their figures are charm-
ingly rounded, their hands and feet small, almost as small as a
high-class Calabar woman's, and their eyes large, lustrous, soft
and brown, and their teeth as white as the sea surf and undis-
figured by filing.

The native dress for men and women alike is the cloth or
paun. The men wear it by rolling the upper line round the waist,
and in addition they frequently wear a singlet or a flannel shirt
worn *more Africano*, flowing free. Rich men will mount a
European coat and hat, and men connected with the mission or
trading stations occasionally wear trousers. The personal
appearance of the men does not amount to much when all's
done, so we will return to the ladies. They wrap the upper hem
of these cloths round under the armpits, a graceful form of
drapery, but one which requires continual readjustment. The
cloth is about four yards long and two deep, and there is always
round the hem a border, or false hem, of turkey red twill, or
some other coloured cotton cloth to the main body of the paun.
In addition to the cloth there is worn, when possible, a European
shawl, either one of those thick cotton cloth ones printed with
Chinese-looking patterns in dull red on a dark ground, this
sort is wrapped round the upper part of the body: or what is
more highly esteemed is a bright, light-coloured, fancy wool
shawl, pink or pale blue preferred, which being carefully folded
into a roll is placed over one shoulder, and is entirely for dandy.

Add to this costume a sober-coloured silk parasol, not one of
your green or red young tent-like, brutally masculine, knobby-
sticked umbrellas, but a fair, lady-like parasol, which, being
carefully rolled up, is carried handle foremost right in the
middle of the head, also for dandy. Then a few strings of
turquoise-blue beads, or imitation gold ones, worn round the
shapely throat; and I will back my Igalwa or M'pongwe belle
against any of those South Sea Island young ladies we nowadays

hear so much about, thanks to Mr Stevenson, yea, even though
these may be wreathed with fragrant flowers, and the African
lady very rarely goes in for flowers. The only time I have seen
the African ladies wearing them for ornament has been among
these Igalwas, who now and again stud their night-black hair
with pretty little round vividly red blossoms in a most fetching
way. I wonder the Africans do not wear flowers more frequently,
for they are devoted to scent, both men and women.

The Igalwas are a proud race, one of the noble tribes, like
the M'pongwe and the Ajumba. The women do not intermarry
with lower-class tribes, and in their own tribe they are much
restricted, owing to all relations on the mother's side being
forbidden to intermarry. This well-known form of accounting
relationships only through the mother (*Mutterrecht*) is in a more
perfected and elaborated form among the Igalwa than among
any other tribe I am personally acquainted with; brothers and
cousins on the mother's side being in one class of relationship,
and called by one name, Ndako.

The father's responsibility, as regards authority over his own
children, is very slight. The really responsible male relative
is the mother's elder brother. From him must leave to marry
be obtained for either girl, or boy; to him and the mother must
the present be taken which is exacted on the marriage of a girl;
and should the mother die, on him and not on the father, lies
the responsibility of rearing the children; they go to his house,
and he treats and regards them as nearer and dearer to himself
than his own children, and at his death, after his own brothers
by the same mother, they become his heirs.

Marriage among the Igalwa and M'pongwe is not direct
marriage by purchase, but a certain fixed price present is made
to the mother and uncle of the girl. Other propitiatory presents
are made, but do not count legally, and have not necessarily to
be returned in case of post-nuptial differences arising leading to
a divorce—a very frequent catastrophe in the social circle; for
the Igalwa ladies are spirited, and devoted to personal adornment, and they are naggers at their husbands. Many times when
walking on Lambaréné Island, have I seen a lady stand in the
street and let her husband, who had taken shelter inside the
house, know what she thought of him, in a way that reminded
me of some London slum scenes. When the husband loses his
temper, as he surely does sooner or later, being a man, he whacks
his wife—or wives, if they have been at him in a body. This crisis
usually takes place at night; and when staying on board the

Mové, or the *Éclaireur*, moored alongside the landing place at Lambaréné Island, I have heard yells and squalls of a most dismal character. He may whack with impunity so long as he does not draw blood; if he does, be it never so little, his wife is off to her relations, the present he has given for her is returned, the marriage is annulled, and she can re-marry as soon as she is able.

Her relations are only too glad to get her, because, although the present has to be returned, yet the propitiatory offerings remain theirs, and they know more propitiatory offerings as well as another present will accrue with the next set of suitors. This of course is only the case with the younger women; the older women for one thing do not nag so much, and moreover they have usually children willing and able to support them. If they have not, their state is, like that of all old childless women in Africa, a very desolate one.

Infant marriage is now in vogue among the Igalwa, and to my surprise I find it is of quite recent introduction and adoption. Their own account of this retrograde movement in culture is that in the last generation—some of the old people indeed claim to have known him—there was an exceedingly ugly and deformed man who could not get a wife, the women being then, as the men are now, great admirers of physical beauty. So this man, being very cunning, hit on the idea of becoming betrothed to one before she could exercise her own choice in the matter; and knowing a family in which an interesting event was likely to occur, he made heavy presents in the proper quarters and bespoke the coming infant if it should be a girl. A girl it was, and thus, say the Igalwa, arose the custom; and nowadays, although they do not engage their wives so early as did the founder of the custom, they adopt infant marriage as an institution.

I inquired carefully as to what methods of courting were in vogue previously. They said people married each other because they loved each other. I think other ethnologists will follow this inquiry up, for we may here find a real golden age, which in other races of humanity lies away in the mists of the ages behind the kitchen middens and the Cambrian rocks. My own opinion in this matter is that the earlier courting method of the Igalwa involved a certain amount of effort on the man's part, a thing abhorrent to an Igalwa. It necessitated his dressing himself up, and likely enough fighting that impudent scoundrel who was engaged in courting her too; and above all serenading her at night on the native harp, with its strings made from the tendrils

of a certain orchid, or on the marimba, amongst crowds of mosquitoes. Any institution that involved being out at night amongst crowds of those Lambaréné mosquitoes would have to disappear, let that institution be what it might.

The Igalwa are one of the dying-out coast tribes. As well as on Lambaréné Island, their villages are scattered along the banks of the Lower Ogowé, and on the shores and islands of Elivā Z'onlange. On the island they are, so far, undisturbed by the Fan invasion, and laze their lives away like lotus-eaters. Their slaves work their large plantations, and bring up to them magnificent yams, ready prepared agooma, sweet-potatoes, papaw, &c., not forgetting that delicacy Odeaka cheese; this is not an exclusive inspiration of theirs, for the M'pongwe and the Benga use it as well.

It is made from the kernel of the wild mango, a singularly beautiful tree of great size and stately spread of foliage. In due season (August) it is covered—not ostentatiously like the real mango, with great spikes of bloom, looking each like a gigantic head of mignonette—but with small yellow-green flowers tucked away under the leaves, filling the air with a soft sweet perfume, and then falling on to the bare shaded ground beneath to make a deep-piled carpet. I do not know whether it is a mango tree at all, for I am no botanist: but anyhow the fruit is rather like that of the mango in external appearance, and in internal still more so, for it has a disproportionately large stone.

These stones are cracked, and the kernel taken out. The kernels are spread a short time in the shade to dry; then they are beaten up into a pulp with a wooden pestle, and the pulp put into a basket lined carefully with plantain leaves and placed in the sun, which melts it up into a stiff mass. The basket is then removed from the sun and stood aside to cool. When cool, the cheese can be turned out in shape, and can be kept a long time if it is wrapped round with leaves and a cloth, and hung up inside the house. Its appearance is that of almond rock, and it is cut easily with a knife; but at any period of its existence, if it is left in the sun it melts again rapidly into an oily mass.

The natives use it as a seasoning in their cookery, stuffing fish and plantains with it and so on, using it also in the preparation of a sort of sea-pie they make with meat and fish. To make this, a thing well worth doing, particularly with hippo or other coarse meat, reduce the wood fire to embers, and make plantain leaves into a sort of bag, or cup; small pieces of the meat should then be packed in layers with red pepper and odeaka in

between. The tops of the leaves are then tied together with fine
tie-tie, and the bundle, without any saucepan of any kind, stood
on the glowing embers, the cook taking care there is no flame.
The meat is done, and a superb gravy formed, before the containing plantain leaves are burnt through—plantain leaves will
stand an amazing lot in the way of fire. This dish is really
excellent, even when made with boa constrictor, hippo or
crocodile. It makes the former most palatable; but of course it
does not remove the musky taste from crocodile; nothing I
know of will.

The great and important difference between the M'pongwe,
Igalwa, and Ajumba fetish, and the fetish of those tribes round
them, consists in their conception of a certain spirit called
Mbuiri. They have, as is constant among the Bantu races of
South-West Africa, a great god—the creator, a god who has
made all things, and who now no longer takes any interest in
the things he has created. This god, unlike other forms of the
creating god in fetish, has a viceroy or minister who is a god he
has created, and to whom he leaves the government of affairs.
This god is Mbuiri or Ombwiri, and this Ombwiri is of very high
interest to the student of comparative fetish. He has never
been, nor can he ever become, a man, *i.e.* be born as a man, but
he can transfuse with his own personality that of human beings,
and also the souls of all those things we white men regard as
inanimate, such as rocks, trees, &c., in a similar manner.

The M'pongwe know that his residence is in the sea, and some
of them have seen him as an old white man, not flesh-colour
white, but chalk white. Mbuiri's appearance in a corporeal form
denotes ill luck, not death to the seer, but misfortune of a
severe and diffused character. The ruin of a trading enterprise,
the destruction of a village or a family, are put down to Mbuiri's
action. Yet he is not regarded as a malevolent god, a devil, but
as an avenger, or punisher of sin; and the M'pongwe look on
him as the Being to whom they primarily owe the good things
and fortunes of this life, and as the Being who alone has power
to govern the host of truly malevolent spirits that exist in
nature.

The great difference between Mbuiri and the lesser spirits is
this:—the lesser spirits cannot incarnate themselves except
through extraneous things; Mbuiri can, he can become visible
without anything beyond his own will to do so. The other spirits
must be *in* something to become visible. This is an extremely

delicate piece of fetish which it took me weeks to work out. Among the M'pongwe and the tribe who are the parent tribe of the M'pongwe—the now rapidly dying out Ajumba, and their allied tribe the Igalwa—Mbuiri is a distinct entity, while among the neighbouring tribes he is a class, *i.e.* there are hundreds of Mbuiri or Ombwiri, one for every remarkable place or thing, such as rock, tree, or forest thicket, and for every dangerous place in a river. Had I not observed a similar state of affairs regarding Sasabonsum, a totally different kind of spirit on the Windward coast, I should have had even greater trouble than I had, in finding a key to what seemed at first a mass of conflicting details regarding this important spirit Mbuiri.

There is one other very important point in M'pongwe fetish; and that is that the souls of men exist before birth as well as after death. This is indeed, as far as I have been able to find out, a doctrine universally held by the West African tribes, but among the M'pongwe there is this modification in it, which agrees strangely well with the idea I found regarding reincarnated diseases, existent among the Okÿon tribes (pure Negroes). The malevolent minor spirits are capable of being born with, what we will call, a man's soul, as well as going in with the man's soul during sleep. For example, an Olâgâ may be born with a man and that man will thereby be born mad; he may at any period of his life, given certain conditions, become possessed by an evil spirit, Onlogho Abambo, Iniembe, Nkandada, and become mad, or ill; but if he is born mad, or sickly, one of the evil spirits such as an Olâgâ or an Ibambo, the soul of a man that has not been buried properly, has been born with him.

CHAPTER FIVE

In the Country of the Fans

On 22 July 1895 Mary Kingsley sets out to explore the lower reaches of the Ogowé river with a crew of four Ajumba men, spending her first night at the village of Arevooma.

I own I did not much care for these Ajumbas on starting, but they are evidently going to be kind and pleasant companions. One of them is a gentlemanly-looking man, who wears a gray shirt; another looks like a genial Irishman who has accidentally got black, very black; he is distinguished by wearing a singlet; another is a thin, elderly man, notably silent; and the remaining one is a strapping, big fellow, as black as a wolf's mouth, of gigantic muscular development, and wearing quantities of fetish charms hung about him. The two first mentioned are Christians; the other two pagans, and I will refer to them by their characteristic points, for their honourable names are awfully alike when you do hear them, and, as is usual with Africans, rarely used in conversation.

Gray Shirt places his house at my disposal, and both he and his exceedingly pretty wife do their utmost to make me comfortable. The house lies at the west end of the town. It is one room inside, but has, I believe, a separate cooking shed. In the verandah in front is placed a table, an ivory bundle chair and a gourd of water, and I am also treated to a calico tablecloth, and most thoughtfully screened off from the public gaze with more calico so that I can have my tea in privacy. After this meal, to my surprise Ndaka turns up. Certainly he is one of the very ugliest men—black or white—I have ever seen, and I fancy one of the best. He is now on a holiday from Kangwe, seeing to the settlement of his dead brother's affairs. The dead brother was a great man in Arevooma and a pagan, but Ndaka, the Christian Bible-reader, seems to get on perfectly with the family and is holding to-night a meeting outside his brother's house and comes with a lantern to fetch me to attend it. Of course I have to go, headache or no headache.

Most of the town was there, mainly as spectators. Ndaka and my two Christian boatmen manage the service between them,

and what with the hymns and the mosquitoes the experience is slightly awful. We sit in a line in front of the house, which is brilliantly lit up—our own lantern on the ground before us acting as a rival entertainment to the house lamps inside for some of the best insect society in Africa, who after the manner of the insect world, insist on regarding us as responsible for their own idiocy in getting singed, and sting us in revenge, while we slap hard, as we howl hymns in the fearful Igalwa and M'ponge way. Next to an English picnic, the most uncomfortable thing I know is an open-air service in this part of Africa.

Service being over, Ndaka takes me over the house to show its splendours. The most remarkable point about the house is the floor which is made of split, plaited bamboo, the like of which I have never before seen. It gives under your feet in an alarming way, being raised some three or four feet above the ground, and I am haunted by the fear that I shall go through it and give pain to myself, and great trouble to others before I could be got out. It is a beautiful piece of workmanship, and Arevooma has every reason to be proud of it. Having admired these things, I go, dead tired and still headachy, down the road with my host who carries the lantern, through an atmosphere that has 45 per cent. of solid matter in the shape of mosquitoes; then wishing him good-night, I shut myself in, and illuminate, humbly, with a candle. The furniture of the house consists mainly of boxes, containing the wealth of Gray Shirt, in clothes, mirrors, &c. One corner of the room is taken up by great calabashes full of some sort of liquor, and there is an ivory bundle chair, a hanging mirror, several rusty guns, and a considerable collection of china basins and jugs. Evidently Gray Shirt is rich. The most interesting article to me, however, just now is the bed hung over with a clean, substantial, chintz mosquito bar, and spread with clean calico and adorned with patchwork-covered pillows. So I take off my boots and put on my slippers; for it never does in this country to leave off boots altogether at any time, and risk getting bitten by mosquitoes on the feet, when you are on the march; because the rub of your boot on the bite always produces a sore, and a sore when it comes in the Gorilla country, comes to stay.

After a disturbed night, Mary Kingsley sets out again next morning.

We paddle still westwards down the broad quiet waters of the O'Rembo Vongo. I notice great quantities of birds about

here—great hornbills, vividly coloured kingfishers, and for the
first time the great vulture I have often heard of, and the skin
of which I will take home before I mention even its approximate
spread of wing. There are also noble white cranes, and flocks
of small black and white birds, new to me, with heavy razor-
shaped bills, reminding one of the Devonian puffin.

The hornbill is perhaps the most striking in appearance. It is
the size of a small, or say a good-sized, hen-turkey. Gray Shirt
says the flocks, which are of eight or ten, always have the same
quantity of cocks and hens, and that they live together 'white
man fashion', *i.e.*, each couple keeping together. They certainly
do a great deal of courting, the cock filling out his wattles on
his neck like a turkey, and spreading out his tail with great
pomp and ceremony, but very awkwardly. To see hornbills on
a bare sandbank is a solemn sight, but when they are dodging
about in the hippo grass they sink ceremony, and roll and
waddle, looking—my man said—for snakes and the little sand-
fish, which are close in under the bank; and their killing way of
dropping their jaws—I should say opening their bills—when
they are alarmed is comic. I think this has something to do with
their hearing, for I often saw two or three of them in a line on a
long branch, standing, stretched up to their full height, their
great eyes opened wide, and all with their great beaks open,
evidently listening for something. Their cry is most peculiar and
can only be mistaken for a native horn; and although there
seems little variety in it to my ear, there must be more to theirs,
for they will carry on long confabulations with each other across
a river, and, I believe, sit up half the night and talk scandal.

There were plenty of plantain-eaters here, but, although their
screech was as appalling as I have heard in Angola, they were
not regarded, by the Ajumba at any rate, as being birds of evil
omen, as they are in Angola. Still, by no means all the birds here
only screech and squark. Several of them have very lovely
notes. There is one who always gives a series of infinitely beautiful, soft, rich-toned whistles just before the first light of the
dawn shows in the sky, and one at least who has a prolonged
and very lovely song. This bird, I was told in Gaboon, is called
Telephonus erythropterus. I expect an ornithologist would enjoy
himself here, but I cannot—and will not—collect birds. I hate
to have them killed anyhow, and particularly in the barbarous
way in which these natives kill them.

We have an addition to our crew this morning—a man who
wants to go and get work at John Holt's sub-factory away on

the Rembwé. He has been waiting a long while at Arevooma, unable to get across, I am told, 'because the road is now stopped between Ayzingo and the Rembwé by "those fearful Fans"'. 'How are we going to get through that way?' says I, with natural feminine alarm. 'We are not, sir,' says Gray Shirt. This is what Lady MacDonald would term a chatty little incident; and my hair begins to rise as I remember what I have been told about those Fans and the indications I have already seen of its being true when on the Upper Ogowé. Now here we are going to try to get through the heart of their country, far from a French station, and without the French flag. Why did I not obey Mr Hudson's orders not to go wandering about in a reckless way! Anyhow I am in for it, and Fortune favours the brave. The only question is: Do I individually come under this class? I go into details. It seems Pagan thinks he can depend on the friendship of two Fans he once met and did business with, and who now live on an island in Lake Ncovi—Ncovi is not down on my map and I have never heard of it before—anyhow thither we are bound now.

Each man has brought with him his best gun, loaded to the muzzle, and tied on to the baggage against which I am leaning —the muzzles sticking out each side of my head: the flint locks covered with cases, or sheaths, made of the black-haired skins of gorillas, leopard skin, and a beautiful bright bay skin, which I do not know, which they say is bush cow—but they call half a dozen things bush cow. These guns are not the 'gas-pipes' I have seen up north; but decent rifles which have had the rifling filed out and the locks replaced by flint locks and converted into muzzle loaders, and many of them have beautiful barrels.

The forest on either bank is very lovely. Some enormously high columns of green are formed by a sort of climbing plant having taken possession of lightning-struck trees, and in one place it really looks exactly as if someone had spread a great green coverlet over the forest, so as to keep it dry. No high land showing in any direction. Beautiful effect of a gleam of sunshine lighting up a red sandbank till it glows like the Nibelungen gold. Indeed the effects are Turneresque today owing to the mist, and the sun playing in and out among it.

Most luxurious, charming, and pleasant trip this. The men are standing up swinging in rhythmic motion their long, rich red wood paddles in perfect time to their elaborate melancholy, minor key boat song. Nearly lost with all hands. Sandbank palaver—only when we were going over the end of it, slipped

sideways over its edge. River deep, bottom sand and mud.
Lovely stream falls into this river over cascades. The water is
now rough in a small way and the width of the river great, but
it soon is crowded again with wooded islands. There are patches
and wreaths of a lovely, vermilion-flowering bush rope decorat-
ing the forest, and now and again clumps of a plant that shows a
yellow and crimson spike of bloom, very strikingly beautiful. We
pass a long tunnel in the bush, quite dark as you look down it—
evidently the path to some native town. The south bank is
covered, where the falling waters have exposed it, with hippo
grass. Terrible lot of mangrove flies about, although we are more
than one hundred miles above the mangrove belt.

We turn at this point into a river on the north bank that runs
north and south—the current is running very swift to the north.
We run into it, and then, it being more than time enough for
chop, we push the canoe on to a sandbank in our new river,
which I am told is the Karkola. I, after having had my tea,
wander off. I find behind our high sandbank, which like all the
other sandbanks above water now, is getting grown over with
hippo grass—a fine light green grass, the beloved food of both
hippo and manatee—a forest, and entering this I notice a succession of strange mounds or heaps, made up of branches,
twigs, and leaves, and dead flowers. Many of these heaps are
recent, while others have fallen into decay. Investigation shows
they are burial places. Among the *débris* of an old one there are
human bones, and out from one of the new ones comes a stench
and a hurrying, exceedingly busy line of ants, demonstrating
what is going on. I own I thought these mounds were some kind
of bird's or animal's nest. They look entirely unhuman in this
desolate reach of forest.

Leaving these, I go down to the water edge of the sand, and
find in it a quantity of pools of varying breadth and expanse,
but each surrounded by a rim of dark red-brown deposit, which
you can lift off the sand in a skin. On the top of the water is a
film of exquisite iridescent colours like those on a soap bubble,
only darker and brighter. In the river alongside the sand, there
are thousands of those beautiful little fish with a black line each
side of their tails. They are perfectly tame, and I feed them with
crumbs in my hand. After making every effort to terrify the
unknown object containing the food—gallant bulls, quite two
inches long, sidling up and snapping at my fingers—they come
and feed right in the palm, so that I could have caught them by
the handful had I wished.

There are also a lot of those weird, semi-transparent, yellow, spotted little sand-fish with cup-shaped pectoral fins, which I see they use to enable them to make their astoundingly long leaps. These fish are of a more nervous and distrustful disposition, and hover round my hand but will not come into it. Indeed I do not believe the other cheeky little fellows would allow them to. They have grand butting matches among themselves, which wind up with a most comic tail fight, each combatant spinning round and going in for a spanking match with his adversary with his pretty little red-edged tail—the red rim round it and round his gill covers going claret-coloured with fury.

The men, having had their rest and their pipes, shout for me, and off we go again. The Karkola soon widens to about 100 feet; it is evidently very deep here; the right bank (the east) is forested, the left, low and shrubbed, one patch looking as if it were being cleared for a plantation, but no village showing. On the opposite bank, on a high dwarf cliff, is a Fan town. 'All Fan now', says Singlet in anything but a gratified tone of voice.

It is a strange, wild, lonely bit of the world we are now in, apparently a lake or broad—full of sandbanks, some bare and some in the course of developing into permanent islands by the growth on them of that floating coarse grass, any joint of which being torn off either by the current, a passing canoe, or hippos, floats down and grows wherever it settles. The grass is stubbled down into paths by hippos, and just as I have realised who are the road-makers, they appear in person. One immense fellow, hearing us, stands up and shows himself about six feet from us in the grass, gazes calmly, and then yawns a yawn a yard wide and grunts his news to his companions, some of whom—there is evidently a large herd—get up and stroll towards us with all the flowing grace of Pantechnicon vans in motion. We put our helm paddles hard a starboard and leave that bank.

Our hasty trip across to the bank of the island on the other side being accomplished, we, in search of seclusion and in the hope that out of sight would mean out of mind to hippos, shot down a narrow channel between semi-island sandbanks, and those sandbanks, if you please, are covered with specimens—as fine a set of specimens as you could wish for—of the West African crocodile. These interesting animals are also having their siestas, lying sprawling in all directions on the sand, with their mouths wide open. One immense old lady has a family of lively young crocodiles running over her, evidently playing like

a lot of kittens. The heavy musky smell they give off is most repulsive, but we do not rise up and make a row about this, because we feel hopelessly in the wrong in intruding into these family scenes uninvited, and so apologetically pole ourselves along rapidly, not even singing. The pace the canoe goes down that channel would be a wonder to Henley Regatta.

Continuing along the river 'dotted with sandbanks and islands in all directions', they come to a 'lovely, strangely melancholy, lone-looking lake' called by her companions Lake Ncovi.

It is exceedingly beautiful. The rich golden sunlight of the late afternoon soon followed by the short-lived, glorious flushes of colour of the sunset and the after-glow, play over the scene as we paddle across the lake to the N.N.E.—our canoe leaving a long trail of frosted silver behind her as she glides over the mirror-like water, and each stroke of the paddle sending down air with it to come up again in luminous silver bubbles—not as before in swirls of sand and mud. The lake shore is, in all directions, wreathed with nobly forested hills, indigo and purple in the dying daylight.

Sign of human habitation at first there was none; and in spite of its beauty, there was something which I was almost going to say was repulsive. The men evidently felt the same as I did. Had anyone told me that the air that lay on the lake was poison, or that in among its forests lay some path to regions of utter death, I should have said—'It looks like that'; but no one said anything, and we only looked round uneasily, until the comfortable-souled Singlet made the unfortunate observation that he 'smelt blood', a common African sensation among natives when alarmed, somewhat akin to our feeling someone walk over our graves. We all called him an utter fool to relieve our minds, and made our way towards the second island.

When we got near enough to it to see details, a large village showed among the trees on its summit, and a steep dwarf cliff, overgrown with trees and creeping plants, came down to a small beach covered with large water-washed gray stones. There was evidently some kind of a row going on in that village, that took a lot of shouting too. We made straight for the beach, and drove our canoe among its outlying rocks, and then each of my men stowed his paddle quickly, slung on his ammunition bag, and picked up his ready loaded gun, sliding the skin sheath off the lock. Pagan got out on to the stones alongside the canoe just as

the inhabitants became aware of our arrival, and came—a brown mass of naked humanity—down the steep cliff path to attend to us.

Things did not look restful, nor these Fans personally pleasant. Every man among them—no women showed—was armed with a gun, and they loosened their shovel-shaped knives in their sheaths as they came, evidently regarding a fight quite as imminent as we did. They drew up about twenty paces from us in silence. Pagan and Gray Shirt, who had joined him, held out their unembarrassed hands, and shouted out the name of the Fan man they had said they were friendly with: 'Kiva-Kiva'. The Fans stood still and talked angrily among themselves for some minutes, and then, Silence said to me, 'It would be bad palaver if Kiva no live for this place,' in a tone that conveyed to me the idea he thought this unpleasant contingency almost a certainty. The Passenger exhibited unmistakable symptoms of wishing he had come by another boat.

I got up from my seat in the bottom of the canoe and leisurely strolled ashore, saying to the line of angry faces 'M'boloani' in an unconcerned way, although I well knew it was etiquette for them to salute first. They grunted, but did not commit themselves further. A minute after, they parted to allow a fine-looking, middle-aged man, naked save for a twist of dirty cloth round his loins and a bunch of leopard and wild cat tails hung from his shoulder by a strip of leopard skin, to come forward. Pagan went for him with a rush, as if he were going to clasp him to his ample bosom, but holding his hands just off from touching the Fan's shoulder in the usual way, while he said in Fan, 'Don't you know me, my beloved Kiva? Surely you have not forgotten your old friend?' Kiva grunted feelingly, and raised up his hands and held them just off touching Pagan, and we breathed again.

Then Gray Shirt made a rush at the crowd and went through great demonstrations of affection with another gentleman whom he recognised as being a Fan friend of his own, and whom he had not expected to meet here. I looked round to see if there was not any Fan from the Upper Ogowé whom I knew to go for, but could not see one that I could on the strength of a previous acquaintance, and on their individual merits I did not feel inclined to do even this fashionable imitation embrace. Indeed I must say that never—even in a picture book—have I seen such a set of wild wicked-looking savages as those we faced this night, and with whom it was touch-and-go for twenty of the longest

minutes I have ever lived, whether we fought—for our lives, I was going to say, but it would not have been even for that, but merely for the price of them.

Peace having been proclaimed, conversation became general. Gray Shirt brought his friend up and introduced him to me, and we shook hands and smiled at each other in the conventional way. Pagan's friend, who was next introduced, was more alarming, for he held his hands for half a minute just above my elbows without quite touching me, but he meant well; and then we all disappeared into a brown mass of humanity and a fog of noise. You would have thought, from the violence and vehemence of the shouting and gesticulation, that we were going to be forthwith torn to shreds; but not a single hand really touched me, and as I, Pagan and Gray Shirt went up to the town in the midst of the throng, the crowd opened in front and closed in behind, evidently half frightened at my appearance.

The row when we reached the town redoubled in volume from the fact that the ladies, the children and the dogs joined in. Every child in the place as soon as it saw my white face let out a howl as if it had seen his Satanic Majesty, horns, hoofs, tail and all, and fled into the nearest hut, headlong, and I fear, from the continuance of the screams, had fits. The town was exceedingly filthy—the remains of the crocodile they had been eating the week before last, and piles of fish offal, and remains of an elephant, hippo or manatee—I really can't say which, decomposition was too far advanced—united to form a most impressive stench. The bark huts are, as usual in a Fan town, in unbroken rows; but there are three or four streets here, not one only, as in most cases. The palaver house is in the innermost street, and there we went, and noticed that the village view was not in the direction in which we had come, but across towards the other side of the lake. I told the Ajumba to explain we wanted hospitality for the night, and wished to hire three carriers for tomorrow to go with us to the Rembwé.

For an hour and three-quarters by my watch I stood in the suffocating, smoky, hot atmosphere listening to, but only faintly understanding, the war of words and gesture that raged round us. At last the fact that we were to be received being settled, Gray Shirt's friend led us out of the guard house—the crowd flinching back as I came through it—to his own house on the right-hand side of the street of huts. It was a very different dwelling to Gray Shirt's residence at Arevooma. I was as high as its roof ridge and had to stoop low to get through the door-hole.

Inside, the hut was fourteen or fifteen feet square, unlit by any window. The door-hole could be closed by pushing a broad piece of bark across it under two horizontally fixed bits of stick. The floor was sand like the street outside, but dirtier. On it in one place was a fire, whose smoke found its way out through the roof. In one corner of the room was a rough bench of wood, which from the few filthy cloths on it and a wood pillow I saw was the bed. There was no other furniture in the hut save some boxes, which I presume held my host's earthly possessions.

From the bamboo roof hung a long stick with hooks on it, the hooks made by cutting off branching twigs. This was evidently the hanging wardrobe, and on it hung some few fetish charms, and a beautiful ornament of wild cat and leopard tails, tied on to a square piece of leopard skin, in the centre of which was a little mirror, and round the mirror were sewn dozens of common shirt buttons. In among the tails hung three little brass bells and a brass rattle; these bells and rattles are not only 'for dandy', but serve to scare away snakes when the ornament is worn in the forest. A fine strip of silky-haired, young gorilla skin made the band to sling the ornament from the shoulder when worn. Gorillas seem well enough known round here. One old lady in the crowd outside, I saw, had a necklace made of sixteen gorilla canine teeth slung on a pine-apple fibre string. Gray Shirt explained to me that this is the best house in the village, and my host the most renowned elephant hunter in the village.

We then returned to the canoe, whose occupants had been getting uneasy about the way affairs were going 'on top', on account of the uproar they heard and the time we had been away. We got into the canoe and took her round the little promontory at the end of the island, to the other beach, which is the main beach. By arriving at the beach when we did, we took our Fan friends in the rear, and they did not see us coming in the gloaming. This was all for the best it seems, as they said they should have fired on us before they had had time to see we were rank outsiders, on the apprehension that we were coming from one of the Fan towns we had passed, and with whom they were on bad terms regarding a lady who bolted there from her lawful lord, taking with her—cautious soul!—a quantity of rubber.

All the goods were brought up to my hut, and while Ngouta gets my tea we started talking the carrier palaver again. The Fans received my offer, starting at two dollars ahead of what M. Jacot said would be enough, with utter scorn, and every

dramatic gesture of dissent; one man, pretending to catch Gray Shirt's words in his hands, flings them to the ground and stamps them under his feet. I affected an easy take-it-or-leave-it-manner, and looked on. A woman came out of the crowd to me, and held out a mass of slimy gray abomination on a bit of plantain leaf—smashed snail. I accepted it and gave her fish hooks. She was delighted and her companions excited, so she put them into her mouth for safe keeping. I hurriedly explained in my best Fan that I do not require any more snail; so another lady tried the effect of a pine-apple. There might be no end to this, so I retired into trade and asked what she would sell it for. She did not want to sell it—she wanted to give it me; so I gave her fish hooks. Silence and Singlet interposed, saying the price for pine-apples is one leaf of tobacco, but I explained I was not buying.

Ngouta turned up with my tea, so I went inside, and had it on the bed. The door-hole was entirely filled with a mosaic of faces, but no one attempted to come in. All the time the carrier palaver went on without cessation, and I went out and offered to take Gray Shirt's and Pagan's place, knowing they must want their chop, but they refused relief, and also said I must not raise the price; I was offering too big a price now, and if I once rise the Fan will only think I will keep on rising, and so make the palaver longer to talk. 'How long does a palaver usually take to talk round here?' I ask. 'The last one I talked,' says Pagan, 'took three weeks, and that was only a small price palaver.' 'Well,' say I, 'my price is for a start tomorrow—after then I have no price—after that I go away.'

Another hour however sees the jam made, and to my surprise I find the three richest men in this town of M'fetta have personally taken up the contract—Kiva my host, Fika a fine young fellow, and Wiki, another noted elephant hunter. These three Fans, the four Ajumba and the Igalwa, Ngouta, I think will be enough. Moreover I fancy it safer not to have an overpowering percentage of Fans in the party, as I know we shall have considerable stretches of uninhabited forest to traverse; and the Ajumba say that the Fans will kill people, *i.e.*, the black traders who venture into their country, and cut them up into neat pieces, eat what they want at the time, and smoke the rest of the bodies for future use.

No one, either Ajumba or Fan, knew the exact course we were to take. The Ajumba had never been this way before and the Fans said they only knew the way to a big Fan town called

Efoua, where no white man or black trader had yet been. There is a path from there to the Rembwé they knew, because the Efoua people take their trade all to the Rembwé. They would, they said, come with me all the way if I would guarantee them safety if they 'found war' on the road. This I agreed to do, and arranged to pay off at Hatton and Cookson's sub-factory on the Rembwé, and they have 'Look my mouth and it be sweet, so palaver done set.' Every load then, by the light of the bush lights held by the women, we arranged. I had to unpack my bottles of fishes so as to equalise the weight of the loads. Every load is then made into a sort of cocoon with bush rope.

I was left in peace at about 11.30 P.M., and clearing off the clothes from the bench threw myself down and tried to get some sleep, for we were to start, the Fans said, before dawn. Sleep impossible—mosquitoes! lice!!—so at 12.40 I got up and slid aside my bark door. I found Pagan asleep under his mosquito bar outside, across the doorway, but managed to get past him without rousing him from his dreams of palaver which he was still talking aloud, and reconnoitred the town. The inhabitants seemed to have talked themselves quite out and were sleeping heavily. I went down then to our canoe and found it safe, high up among the Fan canoes on the stones, and then I slid a small Fan canoe off, and taking a paddle from a cluster stuck in the sand, paddled out on to the dark lake.

It was a wonderfully lovely quiet night with no light save that from the stars. One immense planet shone pre-eminent in the purple sky, throwing a golden path down on to the still waters. Quantities of big fish sprung out of the water, their glistening silver-white scales flashing so that they look like slashing swords. Some bird was making a long, low boom-booming sound away on the forest shore. I paddled leisurely across the lake to the shore on the right, and seeing crawling on the ground some large glow-worms, drove the canoe on to the bank among some hippo grass, and got out to get them.

While engaged on this hunt I felt the earth quiver under my feet, and heard a soft big soughing sound, and looking round saw I had dropped in on a hippo banquet. I made out five of the immense brutes round me, so I softly returned to the canoe and shoved off, stealing along the bank, paddling under water, until I deemed it safe to run out across the lake for my island. I reached the other end of it to that on which the village is situated; and finding a miniature rocky bay with a soft patch of sand and no hippo grass, the incidents of the Fan hut suggested

the advisability of a bath. Moreover, there was no china collection in that hut, and it would be a long time before I got another chance, so I go ashore again, and, carefully investigating the neighbourhood to make certain there was no human habitation near, I then indulged in a wash in peace. Drying one's self on one's cummerbund is not pure joy, but it can be done when you put your mind to it.

While I was finishing my toilet I saw a strange thing happen. Down through the forest on the lake bank opposite came a violet ball the size of a small orange. When it reached the sand beach it hovered along it to and fro close to the ground. In a few minutes another ball of similarly coloured light came towards it from behind one of the islets, and the two waver to and fro over the beach, sometimes circling round each other. I made off towards them in the canoe, thinking—as I still do—they were some brand new kind of luminous insect. When I got on to their beach one of them went off into the bushes and the other away over the water. I followed in the canoe, for the water here is very deep, and, when I almost thought I had got it, it went down into the water and I could see it glowing as it sunk until it vanished in the depths.

I made my way back hastily, fearing my absence with the canoe might give rise, if discovered, to trouble, and by 3.30 I was back in the hut safe, but not so comfortable as I had been on the lake. A little before five my men are stirring and I get my tea. I do not state my escapade to them, but ask what those lights were. 'Akom,' said the Fan, and pointing to the shore of the lake where I had been during the night they said, 'they came there, it was an "Aku" '—or devil bush. More than ever did I regret not having secured one of those sort of two phenomena. What a joy a real devil, appropriately put up in raw alcohol, would have been to my scientific friends!

CHAPTER SIX

On Foot through the Great Forest

*Next day (25 July) the party, with the three Fans in a separate
canoe, reached the north-east end of Lake Ncovi and entered a
smaller lake 'studded with islands of fantastic shapes'. They
disembarked for their overland journey 'up to our knees in black
slime'.*

Our first day's march was a very long one. Path in the ordinary
acceptance of the term there was none. Hour after hour, mile
after mile, we passed on, in the under-gloom of the great forest.
The pace made by the Fans, who are infinitely the most rapid
Africans I have ever come across, severely tired the Ajumba,
who are canoe men, and who had been as fresh as paint, after
their exceedingly long day's paddling from Arevooma to
M'fetta. Ngouta, the Igalwa interpreter, felt pumped, and said
as much, very early in the day. I regretted very much having
brought him; for, from a mixture of nervous exhaustion arising
from our M'fetta experiences, and a touch of chill, he had almost
entirely lost his voice, and I feared would fall sick. The Fans
were evidently quite at home in the forest, and strode on over
fallen trees and rocks with an easy, graceful stride.

What saved us weaklings was the Fans' appetites; every two
hours they sat down, and had a snack of a pound or so of meat
and aguma apiece, followed by a pipe of tobacco. We used to
come up with them at these halts. Ngouta and the Ajumba used
to sit down and rest with them, and I also, for a few minutes, for
a rest and chat, and then I would go on alone, thus getting a
good start. I got a good start, in the other meaning of the word,
on the afternoon of the first day when descending into a ravine.
I saw in the bottom, wading and rolling in the mud, a herd of
five elephants. I am certain that owing to some misapprehen-
sion among the Fates I was given a series of magnificent sporting
chances, intended as a special treat for some favourite Nimrod
of those three ladies, and I know exactly how I ought to have
behaved. I should have felt my favourite rifle fly to my
shoulder, and then, carefully sighting for the finest specimen,
have fired. The noble beast should have stumbled forward,

recovered itself, and shedding its life blood behind it have crashed away into the forest. I should then have tracked it, and either with one well-directed shot have given it its quietus, or have got charged by it, the elephant passing completely over my prostrate body; either termination is good form, but I never have these things happen, and never will.

It was evident from the utter unconcern of these monsters that I was down wind now, so I had only to attend to dodging, and I promptly dodged round a tree, and lay down. Seeing they still displayed no emotion on my account, and fascinated by the novelty of the scene, I crept forward from one tree to another, until I was close enough to have hit the nearest one with a stone, and spats of mud, which they sent flying with their stamping and wallowing came flap, flap among the bushes covering me.

Presently when they had had enough of it they all strolled off up wind, in Indian file, now and then breaking off a branch, but leaving singularly little dead water for their tonnage and breadth of beam. One laid his trunk affectionately on the back of the one in front of him, which I believe to be the elephant equivalent to walking arm-in-arm. When they had gone I rose up, turned round to find the men, and trod on Kiva's back then and there, full and fair, and fell sideways down the steep hillside until I fetched up among some roots.

It seems Kiva had come on, after his meal, before the others, and seeing the elephants, and being a born hunter, had crawled like me down to look at them. He had not expected to find me there, he said. I do not believe he gave a thought of any sort to me in the presence of these fascinating creatures, and so he got himself trodden on. I suggested to him we should pile the baggage, and go and have an elephant hunt. He shook his head reluctantly, saying 'Kor, kor,' like a depressed rook, and explained we were not strong enough; there were only three Fans—the Ajumba and Ngouta did not count—and moreover that we had not brought sufficient ammunition owing to the baggage having to be carried.

We had by now joined the rest of the party, and were all soon squattering about on our own account in the elephant bath. It was shocking bad going—like a ploughed field exaggerated by a terrific nightmare. It pretty nearly pulled all the legs off me, and to this hour I cannot tell you if it is best to put your foot into a footmark—a young pond, I mean—about the size of the bottom of a Madeira work arm-chair, or whether you should poise yourself on the rim of the same, and stride forward to its

bank boldly and hopefully. The footmarks and the places where
the elephants had been rolling were by now filled with water,
and the mud underneath was in places hard and slippery.

I followed the Ajumba, and before I joined them felt a fearful
pricking irritation. Investigation of the affected part showed a
tick of terrific size with its head embedded in the flesh; pursuing
this interesting subject, I found three more, and had awfully
hard work to get them off, and painful too, for they give one not
only a feeling of irritation at their holding-on place, but a streak
of rheumatic-feeling pain up from it. On completing operations I
went on and came upon the Ajumba in a state more approved of
by Praxiteles than by the general public nowadays. They had
found out about elephant ticks, so I went on and got an excellent start for the next stage.

By this time, shortly after noon on the first day, we had
struck into a mountainous and rocky country, and also struck
a track—a track you had to keep your eye on or you lost it in a
minute, but still a guide as to direction.

The forest trees here were mainly ebony and great hard wood
trees, (*Diospyros* and *Copaifua mopane*), with no palms save my
old enemy the climbing palm, *Calamus*, as usual going on its
long excursions, up one tree and down another, bursting into a
plume of fronds, and in the middle of each plume one long spike
sticking straight up, which was an unopened frond, whenever it
got a gleam of sunshine; running along the ground over anything
it meets, rock or fallen timber, all alike, its long, dark-coloured,
rope-like stem simply furred with thorns. Immense must be the
length of some of these climbing palms.

Sometimes for hours we passed among thousands upon
thousands of gray-white columns of uniform height (about 100–
150 feet); at the top of these the boughs branched out and inter-
laced among each other, forming a canopy or ceiling, which
dimmed the light even of the equatorial sun to such an extent
that no undergrowth could thrive in the gloom. The statement
of the struggle for existence was published here in plain figures,
but it was not, as in our climate, a struggle against climate
mainly, but an internecine war from over-population. Now and
again we passed among vast stems of buttressed trees, sometimes enormous in girth; and from their far-away summits hung
great bush-ropes, some as straight as plumb lines, other coiled
round, and intertwined among each other, until one could fancy
one was looking on some mighty battle between armies of
gigantic serpents, that had been arrested at its height by some

magic spell. All these bush-ropes were as bare of foliage as a ship's wire rigging, but a good many had thorns. I was very curious as to how they got up straight, and investigation showed me that many of them were carried up with a growing tree. The only true climbers were the *Calamus* and the rubber vine (*Landolphia*), both of which employ hook tackle.

Some stretches of this forest were made up of thin, spindly stemmed trees of great height, and among these stretches I always noticed the ruins of some forest giant, whose death by lightning, or by his superior height having given the demoniac tornado wind an extra grip on him, had allowed sunlight to penetrate the lower regions of the forest; and then evidently the seedlings and saplings, who had for years been living a half-starved life for light, shot up. They seemed to know that their one chance lay in getting with the greatest rapidity to the level of the top of the forest. No time to grow fat in the stem. No time to send out side branches, or any of those vanities. Up, up to the light level, and he among them who reached it first won in this game of life or death; for when he gets there he spreads out his crown of upper branches, and shuts off the life-giving sunshine from his competitors, who pale off and die, or remain dragging on an attenuated existence waiting for another chance, and waiting sometimes for centuries. There must be tens of thousands of seeds which perish before they get their chance; but the way the seeds of the hard wood African trees are packed, as it were, in cases specially made durable, is very wonderful.

We saw this influence of light on a large scale as soon as we reached the open hills and mountains of the Sierra del Cristal, and had to pass over those fearful avalanche-like timber falls on their steep sides. The worst of these lay between Efoua and Egaja, where we struck a part of the range that was exposed to the south-east. These falls had evidently arisen from the tornados, which from time to time have hurled down the gigantic trees whose hold on the superficial soil over the sheets of hard bed rock was insufficient, in spite of all the anchors they had out in the shape of roots and buttresses, and all the rigging in the shape of bush ropes. Down they had come, crushing and dragging down with them those near them or bound to them by the great tough climbers.

Getting over these falls was perilous, not to say scratchy work. One or another member of our party always went through; and precious uncomfortable going it was I found, when I tried it in one above Egaja; ten or twelve feet of crashing

creaking timber, and then flump on to a lot of rotten, wet *débris*, with more snakes and centipedes among it than you had any immediate use for, even though you were a collector; but there you had to stay, while Wiki, who was a most critical connoisseur, selected from the surrounding forest a bush-rope that he regarded as the correct remedy for the case, and then up you were hauled, through the sticks you had turned the wrong way on your down journey.

The Duke had a bad fall, going twenty feet or so before he found the rubbish heap; while Fika, who went through with a heavy load on his back, took us, on one occasion, half an hour to recover; and when we had just got him to the top, and able to cling on to the upper sticks, Wiki, who had been superintending operations, slipped backwards, and went through on his own account. The bush-rope we had been hauling on was too worn with the load to use again, and we just hauled Wiki out with the first one we could drag down and cut; and Wiki, when he came up, said we were reckless, and knew nothing of bush ropes, which shows how ungrateful an African can be. It makes the perspiration run down my nose whenever I think of it. The sun was out that day; we were neatly situated on the Equator, and the air was semi-solid, with the stinking exhalations from the swamps with which the mountain chain is fringed and intersected; and we were hot enough without these things, because of the violent exertion of getting these twelve to thirteen-stone gentlemen up among us again, and the fine varied exercise of getting over the fall on our own account.

When we got into the cool forest beyond it was delightful; particularly if it happened to be one of those lovely stretches of forest, gloomy down below, but giving hints that far away above us was a world of bloom and scent and beauty which we saw as much of as earth-worms in a flower-bed. Here and there the ground was strewn with great cast blossoms, thick, wax-like, glorious cups of orange and crimson and pure white, each one of which was in itself a handful, and which told us that some of the trees around us were showing a glory of colour to heaven alone. Sprinkled among them were bunches of pure stephanotis-like flowers, which said that the gaunt bush-ropes were rubber vines that had burst into flower when they had seen the sun. These flowers we came across in nearly every type of forest all the way, for rubber abounds here.

A certain sort of friendship soon arose between the Fans and me. We each recognised that we belonged to that same section of

the human race with whom it is better to drink than to fight.
We knew we would each have killed the other, if sufficient
inducement were offered, and so we took a certain amount of
care that the inducement should not arise. Gray Shirt and
Pagan also, their trade friends, the Fans treated with an inde-
pendent sort of courtesy; but Silence, Singlet, the Passenger,
and above all Ngouta, they openly did not care a row of pins for,
and I have small doubt that had it not been for us other three
they would have killed and eaten these very amiable gentlemen
with as much compunction as an English sportsman would kill
as many rabbits.

They on their part hated the Fan, and never lost an opportunity of telling me 'these Fan be bad man too much'. I must
not forget to mention the other member of our party, a Fan
gentleman with the manners of a duke and the habits of a dust-
bin. He came with us, quite uninvited by me, and never asked
for any pay; I think he only wanted to see the fun, and drop in
for a fight if there was one going on, and to pick up the pieces
generally. He was evidently a man of some importance, from the
way the others treated him; and moreover he had a splendid
gun, with a gorilla skin sheath for its lock, and ornamented all
over its stock with brass nails. His costume consisted of a small
piece of dirty rag round his loins; and whenever we were going
through dense undergrowth, or wading a swamp, he wore that
filament tucked up scandalously short. Whenever we were sitting down in the forest having one of our nondescript meals, he
always sat next to me and appropriated the tin. Then he would
fill his pipe, and turning to me with the easy grace of aristocracy,
would say what may be translated as 'My dear Princess, could
you favour me with a lucifer?'

I used to say, 'My dear Duke, charmed, I'm sure,' and give
him one ready lit.

I dared not trust him with the box whole, having a personal
conviction that he would have kept it. I asked him what he
would do suppose I was not there with a box of lucifers; and he
produced a bush-cow's horn with a neat wood lid tied on with tie
tie, and from out of it he produced a flint and steel and demonstrated. Unfortunately all his grace's minor possessions, owing
to the scantiness of his attire, were in one and the same pine-
apple-fibre bag which he wore slung across his shoulder; and
these possessions, though not great, were as dangerous to the
body as a million sterling is said to be to the soul, for they consisted largely of gunpowder and snuff, and their separate

receptacles leaked and their contents commingled, so that demonstration on fire-making methods among the Fan ended in an awful bang and blow-up in a small way, and the Professor and his pupil sneezed like fury for ten minutes, and a cruel world laughed till it nearly died, for twenty. Still that bag with all its failings was a wonder for its containing power.

The first day in the forest we came across a snake (*Vipera nasicornis;* M'pongwe, *Ompenle*)—a beauty with a new red-brown and yellow-patterned velvety skin, about three feet six inches long and as thick as a man's thigh. Ngouta met it, hanging from a bough, and shot backwards like a lobster, Ngouta having among his many weaknesses a rooted horror of snakes. This snake the Ogowé natives all hold in great aversion. For the bite of other sorts of snakes they profess to have remedies, but for this they have none. If, however, a native is stung by one he usually conceals the fact that it was this particular kind, and tries to get any chance the native doctor's medicine may give. The Duke stepped forward and with one blow flattened its head against the tree with his gun butt, and then folded the snake up and got as much of it as possible into the bag, while the rest hung dangling out. We had the snake for supper, that is to say the Fan and I; the others would not touch it, although a good snake, properly cooked, is one of the best meats one gets out here, far and away better than the African fowl.

During the first day's march they encountered a band of gorillas.

On one occasion, between Egaja and Esoon, when we got to the edge of some cleared ground, we lay down, and wormed our way, with elaborate caution, among a patch of Koko; Wiki first, I following in his trail. After about fifty yards of this, Wiki sank flat, and I saw before me, some thirty yards off, busily employed in pulling down plantains, and other depredations, five gorillas: one old male, one young male, and three females. One of these had clinging to her a young fellow, with beautiful wavy black hair with just a kink in it. The big male was crouching on his haunches, with his long arms hanging down on either side, with the backs of his hands on the ground, the palms upwards. The elder lady was tearing to pieces and eating a pine-apple, while the others were at the plantains destroying more than they ate.

They kept up a sort of a whinnying, chattering noise, quite different from the sound I have heard gorillas give when enraged, or from the one you can hear them giving when they are

what the natives call 'dancing' at night. I noticed that their reach of arm was immense, and that when they went from one tree to another, they squattered across the open ground in a most inelegant style, dragging their long arms with the knuckles downwards. I should think the big male and female were over six feet each. The others would be from four to five. I put out my hand and laid it on Wiki's gun to prevent him from firing, and he, thinking I was going to fire, gripped my wrist.

I watched the gorillas with great interest for a few seconds, until I heard Wiki make a peculiar small sound, and looking at him saw his face was working in an awful way as he clutched his throat with his hand violently.

Heavens! think I, this gentleman's going to have a fit; it's lost we are entirely this time. He rolled his head to and fro, and then buried his face into a heap of dried rubbish at the foot of a plantain stem, clasped his hands over it, and gave an explosive sneeze. The gorillas let go all, raised themselves up for a second, gave a quaint sound between a bark and a howl, and then the ladies and the young gentleman started home. The old male rose to his full height and looked straight towards us, or rather towards where that sound came from. Wiki went off into a paroxysm of falsetto sneezes the like of which I have never heard; nor evidently had the gorilla, who went off after his family with a celerity that was amazing the moment he touched the forest, and disappeared as they had, swinging himself along through it from bough to bough, in a way that convinced me that, given the necessity of getting about in tropical forests, man has made a mistake in getting his arms shortened. I have seen many wild animals in their native wilds, but never have I seen anything to equal gorillas going through bush; it is a graceful, powerful, superbly perfect hand-trapeze performance.

I have no hesitation in saying that the gorilla is the most horrible wild animal I have seen. I have seen at close quarters specimens of the most important big game of Central Africa, and, with the exception of snakes, I have run away from all of them; but although elephants, leopards and pythons give you a feeling of alarm, they do not give that feeling of horrible disgust that an old gorilla gives on account of its hideousness of appearance.

After this sporting adventure, we returned, as I usually return from a sporting adventure, without measurements or the body.

Our first day's march, though the longest, was the easiest, though, providentially I did not know this at the time. From my

Woermann road walks I judge it was well twenty-five miles. It was easiest however, from its lying for the greater part of the way through the gloomy type of forest. All day long we never saw the sky once.

We had to hurry because Kiva, who was the only one among us who had been to Efoua, said that unless we did we should not reach Efoua that night. I said, 'Why not stay for bush?' not having contracted any love for a night in a Fan town by the experience of M'fetta; moreover the Fans were not sure that after all the whole party of us might not spend the evening at Efoua, when we did get there, simmering in its cooking-pots. I kept going, as it was my only chance, because I found I stiffened if I sat down, and they always carefully told me the direction to go in when they sat down; with their superior pace they soon caught me up, and then passed me, leaving me and Ngouta and sometimes Singlet and Pagan behind, we, in our turn, overtaking them, with this difference that they were sitting down when we did so.

About five o'clock I was off ahead and noticed a path which I had been told I should meet with, and, when met with, I must follow. The path was slightly indistinct, but by keeping my eye on it I could see it. Presently I came to a place where it went out, but appeared again on the other side of a clump of underbush fairly distinctly. I made a short cut for it and the next news was I was in a heap, on a lot of spikes, some fifteen feet or so below ground level, at the bottom of a bag-shaped game pit.

It is at these times you realise the blessing of a good thick skirt. Had I paid heed to the advice of many people in England, who ought to have known better, and did not do it themselves, and adopted masculine garments, I should have been spiked to the bone, and done for. Whereas, save for a good many bruises, here I was with the fulness of my skirt tucked under me, sitting on nine ebony spikes some twelve inches long, in comparative comfort, howling lustily to be hauled out. The Duke came along first, and looked down at me. I said, 'Get a bush-rope, and haul me out.' He grunted and sat down on a log. The Passenger came next, and he looked down. 'You kill?' says he. 'Not much,' say I; 'get a bush-rope and haul me out.' 'No fit', says he, and sat down on the log. Presently, however, Kiva and Wiki came up, and Wiki went and selected the one and only bush-rope suitable to haul an English lady, of my exact complexion, age, and size, out of that one particular pit.

They seemed rare round there from the time he took; and I

was just casting about in my mind as to what method would be best to employ in getting up the smooth, yellow, sandy-clay, incurved walls, when he arrived with it, and I was out in a twinkling, and very much ashamed of myself, until Silence, who was then leading, disappeared through the path before us with a despairing yell. Each man then pulled the skin cover off his gun lock, carefully looked to see if things there were all right and ready loosened his knife in its snake-skin sheath; and then we set about hauling poor Silence out, binding him up where necessary with cool green leaves; for he, not having a skirt, had got a good deal frayed at the edges on those spikes. Then we closed up, for the Fans said these pits were symptomatic of the immediate neighbourhood of Efoua.

We sounded our ground, as we went into a thick plantain patch, through which we could see a great clearing in the forest, and the low huts of a big town. We charged into it, going right through the guard-house gateway, at one end, in single file, as its narrowness obliged us, and into the street-shaped town, and formed ourselves into as imposing a looking party as possible in the centre of the street. The Efouerians regarded us with much amazement, and the women and children cleared off into the huts, and took stock of us through the door-holes. There were but few men in the town, the majority, we subsequently learnt, being away after elephants. But there were quite sufficient left to make a crowd in a ring round us. Fortunately Wiki and Kiva's friends were present, and we were soon in another word-fog, but not so bad a one as that at M'fetta; indeed Efoua struck me, from the first, favourably; it was, for one thing, much cleaner than most Fan towns I have been in.

As a result of the confabulation, one of the chiefs had his house cleared out for me. It consisted of two apartments almost bare of everything save a pile of boxes, and a small fire on the floor, some little bags hanging from the roof poles, and a general supply of insects. The inner room contained nothing save a hard plank, raised on four short pegs from the earth floor.

After much more palaver Mary Kingsley, exhausted by the day's adventures, at last retires to bed in the chief's hut.

Every hole in the side walls had a human eye in it, and I heard new holes being bored in all directions; so I deeply fear the chief, my host, must have found his palace sadly draughty. I felt

perfectly safe and content, however, although Ngouta suggested the charming idea that 'P'r'aps them M'fetta Fan done sell we.' The only grave question I had to face was whether I should take off my boots or not; they were wet through, from wading swamps, &c., and my feet were very sore; but on the other hand, if I took those boots off, I felt confident that I should not be able to get them on again next morning, so I decided to lef 'em.

As soon as all my men had come in, and established themselves in the inner room for the night, I curled up among the boxes, with my head on the tobacco sack, and dozed. Waking up I noticed the smell in the hut was violent, from being shut up I suppose, and it had an unmistakably organic origin. Knocking the ash end off the smouldering bush-light that lay burning on the floor, I investigated, and tracked it to those bags, so I took down the biggest one, and carefully noted exactly how the tie-tie had been put round its mouth; for these things are important and often mean a lot. I then shook its contents out in my hat, for fear of losing anything of value. They were a human hand, three big toes, four eyes, two ears, and other portions of the human frame. The hand was fresh, the others only so so, and shrivelled.

Replacing them I tied the bag up, and hung it up again. I subsequently learnt that although the Fans will eat their fellow friendly tribesfolk, yet they like to keep a little something belonging to them as a memento. This touching trait in their character I learnt from Wiki; and, though it's to their credit, under the circumstances, still it's an unpleasant practice when they hang the remains in the bedroom you occupy, particularly if the bereavement in your host's family has been recent. I did not venture to prowl round Efoua; but slid the bark door aside and looked out to get a breath of fresh air.

It was a perfect night, and no mosquitoes. The town, walled in on every side by the great cliff of high black forest, looked very wild as it showed in the starlight, its low, savage-built bark huts, in two hard rows, closed at either end by a guard-house. In both guard-houses there was a fire burning, and in their flickering glow showed the forms of sleeping men. Nothing was moving save the goats, which are always brought into the special house for them in the middle of the town, to keep them from the leopards, which roam from dusk to dawn.

Dawn found us stirring, me getting my tea, and the rest of the party their chop, and binding up anew the loads with Wiki's fresh supple bush-ropes. Kiva amused me much; during our march his costume was exceeding scant, but when we reached

the towns he took from his bag garments, and attired himself so resplendently that I feared the charm of his appearance would lead me into one of those dreadful wife palavers which experience had taught me of old to dread: and in the morning time he always devoted some time to repacking. I gave a big dash to both chiefs, and they came out with us, most civilly, to the end of their first plantations; and then we took farewell of each other, with many expressions of hope on both sides that we should meet again, and many warnings from them about the dissolute and depraved character of the other towns we should pass through before we reached the Rembwé.

Our second day's march was infinitely worse than the first, for it lay along a series of abruptly shaped hills with deep ravines between them; each ravine had its swamp and each swamp its river. This bit of country must be absolutely impassable for any human being, black or white, except during the dry season. There were representatives of the three chief forms of the West African bog. The large deep swamps were best to deal with, because they make a break in the forest, and the sun can come down on their surface and bake a crust, over which you can go, if you go quickly. From experience in Devonian bogs, I knew pace was our best chance, and I fancy I earned one of my nicknames among the Fans on these.

The Fans went across all right with a rapid striding glide, but the other men erred from excess of caution, and while hesitating as to where was the next safe place to plant their feet, the place that they were standing on went in with a glug. Moreover, they would keep together, which was more than the crust would stand. The portly Pagan and the Passenger gave us a fine job in one bog, by sinking in close together. Some of us slashed off boughs of trees and tore off handfuls of hard canna leaves, while others threw them round the sinking victims to form a sort of raft, and then with the aid of bush-rope, of course, they were hauled out.

The worst sort of swamp, and the most frequent hereabouts, is the deep narrow one that has no crust on, because it is too much shaded by the forest. The slopes of the ravines too are usually covered with an undergrowth of shenja, beautiful beyond description, but right bad to go through. I soon learnt to dread seeing the man in front going down hill, or to find myself doing so, for it meant that within the next half hour we should be battling through a patch of shenja. I believe there are few effects that can compare with the beauty of them, with the

golden sunlight coming down through the upper forest's branches on to their exquisitely shaped, hard, dark green leaves, making them look as if they were sprinkled with golden sequins. Their long green stalks, which support the leaves and bear little bunches of crimson berries, take every graceful curve imaginable, and the whole affair is free from insects; and when you have said this, you have said all there is to say in favour of shenja, for those long green stalks of theirs are as tough as twisted wire, and the graceful curves go to the making of a net, which rises round you shoulder high, and the hard green leaves when lying on the ground are fearfully slippery. It is not nice going down through them, particularly when nature is so arranged that the edge of the bank you are descending is a rock-wall ten or twelve feet high with a swamp of unknown depth at its foot. It is still less pleasant going up the other side of the ravine when you have got through your swamp. You have to fight your way upwards among rough rocks, through this hard tough network of stems; and it took it out of all of us except the Fans.

These narrow shaded swamps gave us a world of trouble and took up a good deal of time. Sometimes the leader of the party would make three or four attempts before he found a ford, going on until the black, batter-like ooze came up round his neck, and then turning back and trying in another place; while the rest of the party sat upon the bank until the ford was found, feeling it was unnecessary to throw away human life, and that the more men there were paddling about in that swamp, the more chance there was that a hole in the bottom of it would be found; and when a hole is found, the discoverer is liable to leave his bones in it.

If I happened to be in front, the duty of finding the ford fell on me; for none of us after leaving Efoua knew the swamps personally. I was too frightened of the Fan, and too nervous and uncertain of the stuff my other men were made of, to dare show the white feather at anything that turned up. The Fan took my conduct as a matter of course, never having travelled with white men before, or learnt the way some of them require carrying over swamps and rivers and so on. I should have fared very differently had I entered a region occupied by a powerful and ferocious tribe like the Fan, from some districts on the West Coast, where the inhabitants are used to find the white man incapable of personal exertion, requiring to be carried in a hammock, or wheeled in a go-cart or a Bath-chair about the

streets of their coast towns, depending for the defence of their settlement on a body of black soldiers.

This is not so in Congo Français and I had behind me the prestige of a set of white men to whom for the native to say, 'You shall not do such and such a thing;' 'You shall not go to such and such a place,' would mean that those things would be done. I soon found the name of Hatton and Cookson's agent-general for this district, Mr Hudson, was one to conjure with among the trading tribes; and the Ajumba, moreover, although their knowledge of white men had been small, yet those they had been accustomed to see were fine specimens. Mr Fildes, Mr Cockshut, M. Jacot, Dr Pélessier, Pere Lejeune, M. Gacon, Mr Whittaker, and that vivacious French official, were not men any man, black or white, would willingly ruffle; and in addition there was the memory among the black traders of 'that white man MacTaggart', whom an enterprising trading tribe near Setta Khama had had the hardihood to tackle, shooting him, and then towing him behind a canoe and slashing him all over with their knives the while; yet he survived, and tackled them again in a way that must almost pathetically have astonished those simple savages, after the real good work they had put in to the killing of him. Of course it was hard to live up to these ideals, and I do not pretend to have succeeded, or rather that I should have succeeded had the real strain been put on me.

All the rivers we crossed on the first, second and third day I was told went into one or other of the branches of the Ogowé, showing that the long slope of land between the Ogowé and the Rembwé is towards the Ogowé. The stone of which the mountains were composed was that same hard black rock that I had found on the Sierra del Cristal, by the Ogowé rapids; only hereabouts there was not amongst it those great masses of white quartz, which are so prominent a feature from Talagouga upwards in the Ogowé valley; neither were the mountains anything like so high, but they had the same abruptness of shape. They look like very old parts of the same range worn down to stumps by the disintegrating forces of the torrential rain and sun, and the dense forest growing on them. Frost of course they had not been subject to, but rocks, I noticed, were often being somewhat similarly split by rootlets having got into some tiny crevice, and by gradual growth enlarged it to a crack.

In the evening they approach Egaja, 'a town of extra evil repute', and come to the edge of a ravine.

'Oh, bless those swamps!' thought I, 'here's another,' but no—not this time. Across the bottom of the steep ravine, from one side to another, lay an enormous tree as a bridge, about fifteen feet above a river, which rushed beneath it over a boulder-encumbered bed. I took in the situation at a glance, and then and there I would have changed that bridge for any swamp I have ever seen, yea, even for a certain bush-rope bridge in which I once wound myself up like a buzzing fly in a spider's web. I was fearfully tired, and my legs shivered under me after the falls and emotions of the previous part of the day, and my boots were slippery with water soaking.

The Fans went into the river, and half swam, half waded across. All the Ajumba, save Pagan, followed, and Ngouta got across with their assistance. Pagan thought he would try the bridge, and I thought I would watch how the thing worked. He got about three yards along it and then slipped, but caught the tree with his hands as he fell, and hauled himself back to my side again; then he went down the bank and through the water. This was not calculated to improve one's nerve; I knew by now I had got to go by the bridge, for I saw I was not strong enough in my tired state to fight the water. If only the wretched thing had had its bark on it would have been better, but it was bare, bald, and round, and a slip meant death on the rocks below. I rushed it, and reached the other side in safety, whereby poor Pagan got chaffed about his failure by the others, who said they had gone through the water just to wash their feet.

The other side, when we got there, did not seem much worth reaching, being a swampy fringe at the bottom of a steep hillside, and after a few yards the path turned into a stream or backwater of the river. It was hedged with thickly pleached bushes, and covered with liquid water on the top of semi-liquid mud. Now and again for a change you had a foot of water on top of fearfully slippery harder mud, and then we light-heartedly took headers into the bush, sideways, or sat down.

At last we came to a sandy bank, and on that bank stood Egaja, the town with an evil name even among the Fan, but where we had got to stay, fair or foul. We went into it through its palaver house, and soon had the usual row.

After a noisy and unsatisfactory palaver, the senior chief arrives.

I saw at once he was a very superior man to any of the chiefs I had yet met with. It was not his attire, remarkable though that

was for the district, for it consisted of a gentleman's black frock-coat such as is given in the ivory bundle, a bright blue felt sombrero hat, an ample cloth of Boma check; but his face and general bearing was distinctive, and very powerful and intelligent; and I knew that Egaja, for good or bad, owed its name to this man. He was exceedingly courteous, ordering his people to bring me a stool and one for himself, and then a fly-whisk to battle with the evening cloud of sandflies. I got Pagan to come and act as interpreter while the rest were stowing the baggage, &c. After compliments, 'Tell the chief,' I said, 'that I hear this town of his is thief town.'

'Better not, sir,' says Pagan.

'Go on,' said I, 'or I'll tell him myself.'

So Pagan did. It was a sad blow to the chief.

'Thief town, this highly respectable town of Egaja! a town whose moral conduct in all matters was an example to all towns, called a thief town! Oh, what a wicked world!'

I said it was; but I would reserve my opinion as to whether Egaja was a part of the wicked world or a star-like exception, until I had experienced it myself. We then discoursed on many matters, and I got a great deal of interesting fetish information out of the chief, which was valuable to me, because the whole of this district had not been in contact with white culture; and altogether I and the chief became great friends.

Just when I was going in to have my much-desired tea, he brought me his mother—an old lady, evidently very bright and able, but, poor woman, with the most disgusting hand and arm I have ever seen. I am ashamed to say I came very near being sympathetically sick in the African manner on the spot. I felt I could not attend to it, and have my tea afterwards, so I directed one of the canoe-shaped little tubs, used for beating up the manioc in, to be brought and filled with hot water, and then putting into it a heavy dose of Condy's fluid, I made her sit down and lay the whole arm in it, and went and had my tea.

As soon as I had done I went outside, and getting some of the many surrounding ladies to hold bushlights, I examined the case. The whole hand was a mass of yellow pus, streaked with sanies, large ulcers were burrowing into the fore-arm, while in the arm-pit was a big abscess. I opened the abscess at once, and then the old lady frightened me nearly out of my wits by gently subsiding, I thought dying, but I soon found out merely going to sleep. I then washed the abscess well out, and having got a lot of baked plantains, I made a big poultice of them,

mixed with boiling water and more Condy in the tub, and laid her arm right in this; and propping her up all round and covering her over with cloths I requisitioned from her son, I left her to have her nap while I went into the history of the case, which was that some forty-eight hours ago she had been wading along the bank, catching crawfish, and had been stung by 'a fish like a snake'; so I presume the ulcers were an old-standing palaver. The hand had been a good deal torn by the creature, and the pain and swelling had been so great she had not had a minute's sleep since.

As soon as the poultice got chilled I took her arm out and cleaned it again, and wound it round with dressing, and had her ladyship carried bodily, still asleep, into her hut, and after rousing her up, giving her a dose of that fine preparation, *pil. crotonis cum hydrargi*, saw her tucked up on her own plank bedstead for the night, sound asleep again. The chief was very anxious to have some pills too; so I gave him some, with firm injunctions only to take one at the first time. I knew that that one would teach him not to take more than one for ever after, better than I could do if I talked from June to January.

Then all the afflicted of Egaja turned up, and wanted medical advice. There was evidently a good stiff epidemic of the yaws about; lots of cases of dūm with the various symptoms; ulcers of course galore; a man with a bit of a broken spear head in an abscess in the thigh; one which I believe a professional enthusiast would call a 'lovely case' of filaria, the entire white of one eye being full of the active little worms and a ridge of surplus population migrating across the bridge of the nose into the other eye, under the skin, looking like the bridge of a pair of spectacles.

It was past eleven before I had anything like done, and my men had long been sound asleep, but the chief had conscientiously sat up and seen the thing through. He then went and fetched some rolls of bark cloth to put on my plank, and I gave him a handsome cloth I happened to have with me, a couple of knives, and some heads of tobacco and wished him good-night; blockading my bark door, and picking my way over my sleeping Ajumba into an inner apartment which I also blockaded, hoping I had done with Egaja for some hours. No such thing. At 1.45 the whole town was roused by the frantic yells of a woman. I judged there was one of my beauties of Fans mixed up in it, and there was, and after paying damages, got back again by 2.30 AM, and off to sleep again instantly. At four sharp, whole

town of Egaja plunged into emotion, and worse shindy. I suggested to the Ajumba they should go out; but no, they didn't care a row of pins if one of our Fans did get killed, so I went, recognising Kiva's voice in high expostulation. Kiva, it seems, a long time ago had a transaction *in re* a tooth of ivory with a man who, unfortunately, happened to be in this town tonight, and Kiva owed the said man a coat.

Mary Kingsley finds Kiva tied up and about to be killed and eaten, and it takes what was left of the night for her to settle the dispute.

So at last I paid the equivalent value of the coat out of my own trade-stuff; and the affair was regarded by all parties as satisfactorily closed by the time the gray dawn was coming up over the forest wall. I went in again and slept in snatches until I got my tea about seven, and then turned out to hurry my band out of Egaja. This I did not succeed in doing until past ten. One row succeeded another with my men; but I was determined to get them out of that town as quickly as possible, for I had heard so much from perfectly reliable and experienced people regarding the treacherousness of the Fan. I feared too that more cases still would be brought up against Kiva, from the *résumé* of his criminal career I had had last night, and I knew it was very doubtful whether my other three Fans were any better than he.

The chief was very anxious for me to stay and rest, but as his mother was doing wonderfully well, and the other women seemed quite to understand my directions regarding her, I did not feel inclined to risk it.

The two chiefs saw us courteously out of the town as far as where the river crosses the out-going path again, and the blue-hatted one gave me some charms 'to keep my foot in path', and the mourning chief lent us his son to see us through the lines of fortification of the plantation. I gave them an equal dash, and in answer to their question as to whether I had found Egaja a thief town, I said that to call Egaja a thief town was rank perjury, for I had not lost a thing while in it; and we parted with mutual expression of esteem and hopes for another meeting at an early date.

We went on into the gloom of the Great Forest again; that forest that seemed to me without end, wherein, in a lazy, hazy-minded sort of way, I expected to wander through by day and drop in at night to a noisy savage town for the rest of my days.

We climbed up one hill, skirted its summit, went through our

athletic sports over sundry timber falls, and struck down into the ravine as usual. But at the bottom of that ravine, which was exceeding steep, ran a little river free from swamp. As I was wading it I noticed it had a peculiarity that distinguished it from all the other rivers we had come through; and then and there I sat down on a boulder in its midst and hauled out my compass. Yes, by Allah! it's going north-west and bound as we are for Rembwé River. I went out the other side of that river with a lighter heart than I went in, and shouted the news to the boys, and they yelled and sang as we went on our way.

All along this bit of country we had seen quantities of rubber vines, and between Egaja and Esoon we came across quantities of rubber being collected. Evidently there was a big camp of rubber hunters out in the district very busy. Wiki and Kiva did their best to teach me the trade. Along each side of the path we frequently saw a ring of stout bush rope, raised from the earth on pegs about a foot to eighteen inches. On the ground in the middle stood a calabash, into which the ends of the pieces of rubber vine were placed, the other ends being supported by the bush rope ring. Round the outside of some of these rings was a slow fire, which just singes the tops of the bits of rubber vine as they project over the collar or ring, and causes the milky juice to run out of the lower end into the calabash, giving out as it does so a strong ammoniacal smell. When the fire was alight there would be a group of rubber collectors sitting round it watching the cooking operations, removing those pieces that had run dry and placing others, from a pile at their side, in position.

The method of collection employed by the Fan is exceedingly wasteful, because this fool of a vegetable *Landolphia florida* (*Ovariensis*) does not know how to send up suckers from its root, but insists on starting elaborately from seeds only. I do not, however, see any reasonable hope of getting them to adopt more economical methods. When a Fan town has exhausted the rubber in its vicinity, it migrates, bag and baggage, to a new part of the forest. The young unmarried men are the usual rubber hunters. Parties of them go out into the forest, wandering about in it and camping under shelters of boughs by night, for a month and more at a time, during the dry seasons, until they have got a sufficient quantity together; then they return to their town, and it is manipulated by the women, and finally sold, either to the white trader, in districts where he is within reach, or to the M'pongwe trader who travels round buying it and the

collected ivory and ebony, like a Norfolk higgler. In districts like these I was in, remote from the M'pongwe trader, the Fans carry the rubber to the town nearest to them that is in contact with the black trader, and sell it to the inhabitants, who in their turn resell it to their next town, until it reaches him.

This passing down of the rubber and ivory gives rise between the various towns to a series of commercial complications which rank with women palaver for the production of rows; it being the sweet habit of these Fans to require a life for a life and to regard one life as good as another. Also rubber trade and wife palavers sweetly intertwine, for a man on the kill *in re* a wife palaver knows his best chance of getting the life from the village he has a grudge against lies in catching one of that village's men when he may be out alone rubber hunting. So he does this thing, and then the men from the victim's village, go and lay for a rubber hunter, from the killer's village; and then of course the men from the killer's village go and lay for rubber hunters from victim number one's village, and thus the blood feud rolls down the vaulted chambers of the ages, so that you, dropping in on affairs, cannot see one end or the other of it, and frequently the people concerned have quite forgotten what the killing was started for. Not that this discourages them in the least.

Wiki, being great on bush rope, gave me much information regarding rubber, showing me the various other vines besides the true rubber vine, whose juice, mingled with the true sap by the collector when in the forest, adds to the weight; a matter of importance, because rubber is bought by weight. The other adulteration gets done by the ladies in the villages when the collected sap is handed over to them to prepare for the markets.

It is during the moulding process that most of the adulteration gets in. Down by the side of many of the streams there is a white chalky-looking clay which is brought up into the villages, powdered up, and then hung up over the fire in a basket to attain a uniform smuttiness; it is then worked into the rubber when it is being made up into balls. Then a good chunk of Koko, *Arum esculentum* (Koko is better than yam, I may remark, because it is heavier), also smoked approximately the right colour, is often placed in the centre of the rubber ball. In fact, anything is put there, that is hopefully regarded as likely to deceive the white trader.

I once overheard a long discussion between two ladies: 'I always clay my rubber up well,' says number one. 'I think,' says number two, 'a bit of yam is better, with just a coat of rubber

outside, then he hop good too much when Mr—— frows him for floor.' They did not convince each other as to the superiority of their individual methods, but became very friendly over the foolishness of a mutual friend, who both clayed and yammed her rubber to such an extent that when Mr—— 'frowed him for floor he done squat'. Mr—— then cut him open and 'frowed' both the pieces at her head—a performance that raised Mr—— in their esteem, as it demonstrated commercial intelligence, a thing universally admired down here.

So great is the adulteration, that most of the traders have to cut each ball open. Even the Kinsembo rubber, which is put up in clusters of bits shaped like little thimbles formed by rolling pinches of rubber between the thumb and finger, and which one would think difficult to put anything inside of, has to be cut, because 'the simple children of nature' who collect it and bring it to that 'swindling white trader' struck upon the ingenious notion that little pieces of wood shaped like the thimbles and coated by a dip in rubber were excellent additions to a cluster.

'Pursuits, Sports and Pastimes of my Friends the Fans'

At Esoon, their next halting-place, Mary Kingsley takes off her boots for the first time and guards her men 'with the vigilance of a dragon' to keep them out of trouble with their hosts' wives. Next day they march westwards over difficult hilly country until they approach the Rembwé river.

All our paths took us during the early part of the day up and down hills, through swamps and little rivers, all flowing Rembwéwards. About the middle of the afternoon, when we had got up to the top of a high hill, after having had a terrible time on a timber fall of the first magnitude, into which four of us had fallen, I of course for one, I saw a sight that made my heart stand still. Stretching away to the west and north, winding in and out among the feet of the now isolated mound-like mountains, was that never to be mistaken black-green forest swamp of mangrove; doubtless the fringe of the River Rembwé, which evidently comes much further inland than the mangrove belt on the Ogowé.

Cheered by this pleasing prospect, we marched on forgetful of our scratches, down the side of the hill, and down the foot slope of it, until we struck the edge of the swamp. We skirted this for some mile or so, going N.E. Then we struck into the swamp, to reach what we had regarded as the Rembwé river. 'Nature was at its ghastliest', as *Chambers's Magazine* said, and hurt the feelings of the locality by saying, of the Oil Rivers scenery. We found ourselves at the edge of that open line we had seen from the mountain. Not standing, because you don't so much as try to stand on mangrove roots unless you are a born fool, and then you don't stand long, but clinging, like so many monkeys, to the net of aërial roots which surrounded us, looking blankly at a lake of ink-black slime.

It was half a mile across, and some miles long. We could not see either the west or east termination of it, for it lay like a rotten serpent twisted between the mangroves. It never entered

into our heads to try to cross it, for when a swamp is too deep for mangroves to grow in it, 'No bottom lib for them dam ting,' as a Kruboy once said to me, anent a small specimen of this sort of ornament to a landscape. But we just looked round to see which direction we had better take. Then I observed that the roots, aërial and otherwise, were coated in mud, and had no leaves on them, for a foot above our heads. Next I noticed that the surface of the mud before us had a sort of quiver running through it, and here and there it exhibited swellings on its surface, which rose in one place and fell in another. No need for an old coaster like me to look at that sort of thing twice to know what it meant, and feeling it was a situation more suited to Mr Stanley than myself, I attempted to emulate his methods and addressed my men.

'Boys,' said I, 'this beastly hole is tidal, and the tide is coming in. As it took us two hours to get to this sainted swamp, it's time we started out, one time, and the nearest way. It's to be hoped the practice we have acquired in mangrove roots in coming, will enable us to get up sufficient pace to get out on to dry land before we are all drowned.' The boys took the hint. Fortunately one of the Ajumbas had been down in Ogowé, it was Gray Shirt, who 'sabed them tide palaver'. The rest of them, and the Fans, did not know what tide meant, but Gray Shirt hustled them along and I followed, deeply regretting that my ancestors had parted prematurely with prehensile tails for four limbs, particularly when two of them are done up in boots and are not sufficient to enable one to get through a mangrove swamp network of slimy roots rising out of the water, and swinging lines of aërial ones coming down to the water *à la* mangrove, with anything approaching safety. Added to these joys were any quantity of mangrove flies, a broiling hot sun, and an atmosphere three quarters solid stench from the putrifying ooze all round us. For an hour and a half, thought I, Why did I come to Africa, or why, having come, did I not know when I was well off and stay in Glass? Before these problems were settled in my mind we were close to the true land again, with the water under us licking lazily among the roots and over our feet.

We did not make any fuss about it, but we meant to stick to dry land for some time, and so now took to the side of a hill that seemed like a great bubble coming out of the swamp, and bore steadily E. until we found a path. This path, according to the nature of paths in this country, promptly took us into another swamp, but of a different kind to our last—a knee-deep affair,

full of beautiful palms and strange water plants, the names whereof I know not. There was just one part where that abomination, *pandanus*, had to be got through, but, as swamps go, it was not at all bad. I ought to mention that there were leeches in it, lest I may be thought too enthusiastic over its charms. But the great point was that the mountains we got to on the other side of it, were a good solid ridge, running, it is true, E. and W., while we wanted to go N.; still on we went waiting for developments, and watching the great line of mangrove-swamp spreading along below us to the left hand, seeing many of the lines in its dark face, which betokened more of those awesome slime lagoons that we had seen enough of at close quarters.

About four o'clock we struck some more plantations, and passing through these, came to a path running north-east, down which we went. I must say the forest scenery here was superbly lovely. Along this mountain-side cliff to the mangrove-swamp the sun could reach the soil, owing to the steepness and abruptness and the changes of curves of the ground; while the soft steamy air which came up off the swamp swathed everything, and although unpleasantly strong in smell to us, was yet evidently highly agreeable to the vegetation. Lovely wine palms and rafia palms, looking as if they had been grown under glass, so deliciously green and profuse was their feather-like foliage, intermingled with giant red woods, and lovely dark glossy green lianes, blooming in wreaths and festoons of white and mauve flowers, which gave a glorious wealth of beauty and colour to the scene. Even the monotony of the mangrove-belt alongside gave an additional charm to it, like the frame round a picture.

As we passed on, the ridge turned N. and the mangrove line narrowed between the hills. Our path now ran east and more in the middle of the forest, and the cool shade was charming after the heat we had had earlier in the day. We crossed a lovely little stream coming down the hillside in a cascade; and then our path plunged into a beautiful valley. We had glimpses through the trees of an amphitheatre of blue mist-veiled mountains coming down in a crescent before us, and on all sides, save due west where the mangrove-swamp came in.

Never shall I forget the exceeding beauty of that valley, the foliage of the trees round us, the delicate wreaths and festoons of climbing plants, the graceful delicate plumes of the palm trees, interlacing among each other, and showing through all a background of soft, pale, purple-blue mountains and forest, not

really far away, as the practised eye knew, but only made to look so by the mist, which has this trick of giving suggestion of immense space without destroying the beauty of detail. Those African misty forests have the same marvellous distinctive quality that Turner gives one in his greatest pictures. I am no artist, so I do not know exactly what it is, but I see it is there.

I luxuriated in the exquisite beauty of that valley, little thinking or knowing what there was in it besides beauty, as Allah 'in mercy hid the book of fate'. On we went among the ferns and flowers until we met a swamp, a different kind of swamp to those we had heretofore met, save the little one last mentioned. This one was much larger, and a gem of beauty; but we had to cross it. It was completely furnished with characteristic flora. Fortunately when we got to its edge we saw a woman crossing before us, but unfortunately she did not take a fancy to our appearance, and instead of staying and having a chat about the state of the roads, and the shortest way to N'dorko, she bolted away across the swamp. I noticed she carefully took a course, not the shortest, although that course immersed her to her arm-pits.

In we went after her, and when things were getting unpleasantly deep, and feeling highly uncertain under foot, we found there was a great log of a tree under the water which, as we had seen the lady's care at this point, we deemed it advisable to walk on. All of us save one, need I say that one was myself, effected this with safety. I took a header, and am thereby able to inform the world, that there is between fifteen and twenty feet of water each side of that log. I conscientiously went in on one side, and came up on the other.

Having survived this and reached the opposite bank, we shortly fell in with a party of men and women, who were taking, they said, a parcel of rubber to Holty's. They told us N'dorko was quite close, and that the plantations we saw before us were its outermost ones, but spoke of a swamp, a bad swamp. We knew it, we said, in the foolishness of our hearts thinking they meant the one we had just forded, and leaving them resting, passed on our way; half-a-mile further on we were wiser and sadder, for then we stood on the rim of one of the biggest swamps I have ever seen south of the Rivers. It stretched away in all directions, a great sheet of filthy water, out of which sprang gorgeous marsh plants, in islands, great banks of screw pine, and coppices of wine palm, with their lovely fronds reflected back by the still, mirror-like water.

Our path went straight into this swamp over the black rocks forming its rim, in an imperative, no alternative, 'Come-along-this-way' style. Singlet, who was leading, carrying a good load of bottled fish and a gorilla specimen, went at it like a man, and disappeared before the eyes of us close following him, then and there down through the water. He came up, thanks be, but his load is down there now, worse luck. Then I said we must get the rubber carriers who were coming this way to show us the ford; and so we sat down on the bank a tired, disconsolate, dilapidated-looking row, until they arrived. When they came up they did not plunge in forthwith; but leisurely set about making a most nerve-shaking set of preparations, taking off their clothes, and forming them into bundles, which, to my horror, they put on the tops of their heads. The women carried the rubber on their backs still, but rubber is none the worse for being under water. The men went in first, each holding his gun high above his head. They skirted the bank before they struck out into the swamp, and were followed by the women and by our party, and soon we were all up to our chins.

We were two hours and a quarter passing that swamp. I was one hour and three-quarters; but I made good weather of it, closely following the rubber-carriers, and only going in right over head and all twice. Other members of my band were less fortunate. One finding himself getting out of his depth, got hold of a palm frond and pulled himself into deeper water still, and had to roost among the palms until a special expedition of the tallest men went and gathered him like a flower. Another got himself much mixed up and scratched because he thought to make a short cut through screw pines. He did not know the screw pine's little ways, and he had to have a special relief expedition. One and all, we got horribly infested with leeches, having a frill of them round our necks like astrakhan collars, and our hands covered with them, when we came out. It was for the best that we had some trade salt with us. It was most comic to see us salting each other; but in spite of the salt's efficacious action I was quite faint from loss of blood, and we all presented a ghastly sight as we made our way on into N'dorko. Of course the bleeding did not stop at once, and it attracted flies and—but I am going into details, so I forbear.

We had to pass across the first bit of open country I had seen for a long time—a real patch of grass on the top of a low ridge, which is fringed with swamp on all sides save the one we made our way to, the eastern. Shortly after passing through another

plantation, we saw brown huts, and in a few minutes were standing in the middle of a ramshackle village, at the end of which, through a high stockade, with its gateway smeared with blood which hung in gouts, we saw our much longed for Rembwé River.

I made for it, taking small notice of the hubbub our arrival occasioned, and passed through the gateway to its bank; then, setting its guarding bell ringing violently, I stood on the steep, black, mud slime bank, surrounded by a noisy crowd. It is a big river, but nothing to the Ogowé, either in breadth or beauty; what beauty it has is of the Niger delta type—black mud-laden water, with a mangrove swamp fringe to it in all directions. I soon turned back into the village and asked for Ugumu's factory. 'This is it,' said an exceedingly dirty, good-looking, civil-spoken man in perfect English, though as pure blooded an African as ever walked. 'This is it, sir,' and he pointed to one of the huts on the right-hand side, indistinguishable in squalor from the rest. 'Where's the Agent?' said I. 'I'm the Agent,' he answered.

You could have knocked me down with a feather. 'Where's John Holt's factory?' said I. 'You have passed it; it is up on the hill.' This showed Messrs Holt's local factory to be no bigger than Ugumu's. At this point a big, scraggy, very black man with an irregularly formed face the size of a tea-tray and looking generally as if he had come out of a pantomime on the *Arabian Nights*, dashed through the crowd, shouting, 'I'm for Holty, I'm for Holty.' 'This is my trade, you go 'way,' says Agent number one. Fearing my two Agents would fight and damage each other, so that neither would be any good for me, I firmly said, 'Have you got any rum?' Agent number one looked crestfallen, Holty's triumphant. 'Rum, fur sure,' says he; so I gave him a five-franc piece, which he regarded with great pleasure, and putting it in his mouth, he legged it like a lamplighter away to his store on the hill. 'Have you any tobacco?' said I to Agent number one. He brightened, 'Plenty tobacco, plenty cloth,' said he; so I told him to give me out twenty heads. I gave my men two heads apiece. I told them rum was coming, and ordered them to take the loads on to Hatton and Cookson's Agent's hut and then to go and buy chop and make themselves comfortable.

They highly approved of this plan, and grunted assent ecstatically; and just as the loads were stowed Holty's anatomy hove in sight with a bottle of rum under each arm, and one in each hand; while behind him came an acolyte, a fat, small boy,

panting and puffing and doing his level best to keep up with his long-legged flying master. I gave my men some and put the rest in with my goods, and explained that I belonged to Hatton and Cookson's (it's the proper thing to belong to somebody), and that therefore I must take up my quarters at their Store.

After more palaver it transpires that Hatton and Cookson's factory is at Agonjo, an hour's paddle upstream, and a message brings Mr Glass, the senior Agent, to N'dorko.

Mr Glass I found an exceedingly neat, well-educated M'pongwe gentleman in irreproachable English garments, and with irreproachable, but slightly *floreate*, English language. We started talking trade, with my band in the middle of the street, making a patch of uproar in the moonlit surrounding silence. As soon as we thought we had got one gentleman's mind settled as to what goods he would take his pay in, and were proceeding to investigate another gentleman's little fancies; gentleman number one's mind came all to pieces again, and he wanted 'to room his bundle', *i.e.* change articles in it for other articles of an equivalent value, if it must be, but of a higher, if possible. Oh ye shopkeepers in England who grumble at your lady customers, just you come out here and try to serve, and satisfy a set of Fans! Mr Glass was evidently an expert at the affair, but it was past 11 p.m. before we got the orders written out, and getting my baggage into some canoes that Mr Glass had brought down from Agonjo, for N'dorko only had a few very wretched ones, I started off up river with him and all the Ajumba, and Kiva, the Fan, who had been promised a safe conduct. He came to see the bundles for his fellow Fans were made up satisfactorily.

The canoes being small there was quite a procession of them. Mr Glass and I shared one, which was paddled by two small boys; how we ever got up the Rembwé that night I do not know, for although neither of us were fat, the canoe was a one man canoe, and the water lapped over the edge in an alarming way. Had any of us sneezed, or had it been daylight when two or three mangrove flies would have joined the party, we must have foundered; but all went well; and on arriving at Agonjo Mr Glass most kindly opened his store, and by the light of lamps and lanterns, we picked out the goods from his varied and ample supply, and handed them over to the Ajumba and Kiva, and all, save three of the Ajumba, were satisfied.

The three, Gray Shirt, Silence and Pagan quietly explained to

me that they found the Rembwé price so little better than the Lambaréné price that they would rather get their pay off Mr Cockshut, than risk taking it back through the Fan country, so I gave them books on him. I gave all my remaining trade goods, and the rest of the rum to the Fans as a dash, and they were more than satisfied. I must say they never clamoured for dash for top. The Passenger we had brought through with us, who had really made himself very helpful, was quite surprised at getting a bundle of goods from me.

I had a touching farewell with the Fans: and so in peace, good feeling, and prosperity I parted company for the second time with 'the terrible M'pongwe', whom I hope to meet with again, for with all their many faults and failings, they are real men. I am faint-hearted enough to hope that our next journey together, may not be over a country that seems to me to have been laid down as an obstacle race track for Mr G. F. Watts's Titans, and to have fallen into shocking bad repair.

Several 'lazy, pleasant days' are passed as the guest of Mr Glass and his lady, 'an exceedingly comely Gaboon woman' and a good cook.

One of these black trader factories is an exceedingly interesting place to stay at, for in these factories you are right down on the bed rock of the trade. On the Coast, for the greater part, the white traders are dealing with black traders, middlemen, who have procured their trade stuff from the bush natives, who collect and prepare it. Here, in the black trader factory, you see the first stage of the export part of the trade: namely the barter of the collected trade stuff between the collector and the middleman. I will not go into details regarding it. What I saw merely confirmed my opinion from my other experience, that the native is not cheated; no, not even by a fellow African trader; and I will merely here pause to sing a pæan to a very unpopular class—the black middleman as he exists on the South West Coast.

It is impossible to realise the gloom of the lives of these men in bush factories, unless you have lived in one. It is no use saying 'they know nothing better and so don't feel it', for they do know several things better, being very sociable men, fully appreciative of the joys of a Coast town, and their aim, object and end in life is, in almost every case, to get together a fortune that will enable them to live in one, give a dance twice a week, card parties most nights, and dress themselves up so that their

fellow Coast townsmen may hate them and their townswomen love them. From their own accounts of the dreadful state of trade; and the awful and unparalleled series of losses they have had, from the upsetting of canoes, the raids and robberies made on them and their goods by 'those awful bush savages'; you would, if you were of a trustful disposition, regard the black trader with an admiring awe as the man who has at last solved the great commercial problem of how to keep a shop and live by the loss. Nay, not only live, but build for himself an equivalent to a palatial residence, and keep up, not only it, but half a dozen wives, with a fine taste for dress every one of them. I am not of a trustful disposition and I accept those 'losses' with a heavy discount, and know most of the rest of them have come out of my friend the white trader's pockets. Still I can never feel the righteous indignation that I ought to feel, when I see the black trader 'down in a seaport town with his Nancy', &c., as Sir W. H. S. Gilbert classically says, because I remember those bush factories.

Mr Glass, however, was not a trader who made a fortune by losing those of other people; for he had been many years in the employ of the firm. He had risen certainly to the high post and position of charge of the Rembwé, but he was not down giddy-flying at Gaboon. His accounts of his experiences when he had been many years ago away up the still little known Nguni River, in a factory in touch with the lively Bakele were fascinating, and told vividly of the joys of first starting a factory in a wild district. The way in which your customers, for the first month or so, enjoyed themselves by trying to frighten you, the trader, out of your wits and goods, and into giving them fancy prices for things you were trading in, and for things no earthly use to you, or anyone else! The trader's existence during this period is marked by every unpleasantness save dullness; from that he is spared by the presence of a mob of noisy, dangerous, thieving savages all over his place all day; invading his cook-house, to put some nastiness into his food as a trade charm; helping themselves to portable property at large; and making themselves at home to the extent of sitting on his dining-table. At night those customers proceed to sleep all over the premises, with a view to being on hand to start shopping in the morning. Woe betide the trader if he gives in to this, and tolerates the invasion, for there is no chance of that house ever being his own again; and in addition to the local flies, &c., on the table-cloth, he will always have several big black gentlemen to share his

meals. If he raises prices, to tide over some extra row, he is a lost man; for the Africans can understand prices going up, but never prices coming down; and time being no object, they will hold back their trade. Then the district is ruined, and the trader along with it, for he cannot raise the price he gets for the things he buys.

What that trader has got to do, is to be a 'Devil man'. They always kindly said they recognised me as one, which is a great compliment. He must betray no weakness, but a character which I should describe as a compound of the best parts of those of Cardinal Richelieu, Brutus, Julius Cæsar, Prince Metternich, and Mettzofante, the latter to carry on the native language part of the business; and he must cast those customers out, not only from his house; but from his yard; and adhere to the 'No admittance except on business' principle. This causes a good deal of unpleasantness, and the trader's nights are now cheered by lively war-dances outside his stockade; the accompanying songs advertising that the customers are coming over the stockade to raid the store, and cut up the trader 'into bits like a fish'. Sometimes they do come—and then—finish; but usually they don't; and gradually settle down, and respect the trader greatly as 'a Devil man'; and do business on sound lines during the day. Over the stockade at night, by ones and twos, stealing, they will come to the end of the chapter.

At Agonjo Mr Glass, his wife, and the 'Partant pour la Syrie' vocalist used to have to take it in turns to keep watch, because it was the habit of these local 'children of nature' to sell a log or so of ebony during the day, and come and regain possession of it at night. They would then take it down to the next factory, and sell it there—similarly regaining it, and bringing it back, and re-selling it, and so on, *da capo*. Thereby it falls out that one man might live for quite a time on a few billets, with no exertion, or hard work, stealing being a beloved pastime—a kind of a sort of a game in which you only lose if you are found out.

Moonlight nights are fairly restful for the bush trader, but when it is inky black, or pouring with rain, he has got to be very much out and about, and particularly vigilant has he got to be on tornado nights—a most uncomfortable sort of weather to attend to business in, I assure you.

The journeys these bush traders make are often remarkable, and they deserve great credit for the courage and enterprise they display. Certainly they run less risk of death from fever than a white man would; but, on the other hand, their colour

gives them no protection; and their chance of getting murdered is distinctly greater; and also the white governmental powers cannot revenge their death, in the way they would the death of a white man, for these murders usually take place away in some forest region, in a district no white man has ever penetrated; and when the account of it reaches the main trading station, or the sea coast town, to whom the man belongs—for many of them are not attached to any factory, but trading on their own accounts —it is usually in the form of the statement that So-and-so died of a disease. The relatives of the deceased never believe this, but the Government naturally feel disinclined to start off on a highly expensive expedition which is next to certain in the bargain to cost a white man who goes with it his life; on a month or so's march, through trackless swamp and bush, on the off chance of finding out at the end of their quest that So-and-so did really die of a disease; or that the village where he died is utterly deserted, the natives on hearing of their approach having gone for a pic-nic in the surrounding forest.

There is a reason why the natives do not succumb every time to the temptation to kill the trader, and take his goods, and this is twofold: firstly, all trade in West Africa follows definite routes, even in the wildest parts of it; and so a village far away in the forest, but on the trade route, knows, that as a general rule twice a year, a trader will appear to purchase its rubber and ivory. If he does not appear somewhere about the expected time, that village gets uneasy. The ladies are impatient for their new clothes; the gentlemen half wild for want of tobacco; and things coming to a crisis, they make inquiries for the trader down the road, one village to another, and then, if it is found that a village has killed the trader, and stolen all his goods, there is naturally a big palaver, and things are made extremely hot, even for equatorial Africa, for that village by the tobaccoless husbands of the clothesless wives. Herein lies the trader's chief safety, the village not being an atom afraid, or disinclined to kill him, but afraid of their neighbouring villages, and disinclined to be killed by them.

But the trader is not yet safe. There is still a hole in his armour, and this is only to be stopped up in one way, namely, by wives; for you see although the village cannot safely kill him, and take all his goods, they can still safely let him die of a disease, and take part of them, passing on sufficient stuff to the other villages to keep them quiet. Now the most prevalent disease in the African bush comes out of the cooking pot, and so to

make what goes into the cooking pot—which is the important point, for earthen pots do not in themselves breed poison—safe and wholesome, you have got to have someone who is devoted to your health to attend to the cooking affairs, and who can do this like a wife? So you have a wife—one in each village up the whole of your route. I know myself one gentleman whose wives stretch over 300 miles of country, with a good wife base in a Coast town as well. This system of judiciously conducted alliances, gives the black trader a security nothing else can, because naturally he marries into influential families at each village, and all his wife's relations on the mother's side regard him as one of themselves, and look after him and his interests.

That security can lie in women, especially so many women, the so-called civilised man may ironically doubt, but the security is there, and there only, on a sound basis, for remember the position of a travelling trader's wife in a village is a position that gives the lady prestige, the discreet husband showing little favours to her family and friends, if she asks for them when he is with her; and then she has not got the bother of having a man always about the house, and liable to get all sorts of silly notions into his head if she speaks to another gentleman, and then go and impart these notions to her with a cutlass, or a kassengo, as the more domestic husband, I am assured by black ladies, is prone to.

You may now, I fear, be falling into the other adjacent error —from the wonder why any black trader survives, namely, into the wonder why any black trader gets killed, with all these safeguards, and wives. But there is yet another danger, which no quantity of wives, nor local jealousies avail to guard him through. This danger arises from the nomadic habits of the bush tribes, notably the Fan. For when a village has made up its mind to change its district, either from having made the district too hot to hold it, with quarrels with neighbouring villages; or because it has exhausted the trade stuff, *i.e.* rubber and ivory, in reach of its present situation; or because some other village has raided it, and taken away all the stuff it was saving to sell to the black trader; it resolves to give itself a final treat in the old home, and make a commercial *coup* at one fell swoop. Thus when the black trader turns up with his boxes of goods, it kills him, has some for supper, smokes the rest, and takes it and the goods, and departs to found new homes in another district.

We will now enter into the reason that induces the bush man

to collect stuff to sell among the Fans, which is the expensiveness of the ladies in the tribe. A bush Fan is bound to marry into his tribe, because over a great part of the territory occupied by them there is no other tribe handy to marry into; and a Fan residing in villages in touch with other tribes, has but little chance of getting a cheaper lady. For there is, in the Congo Français and the country adjacent to the north of it (Batanga), a regular style of aristocracy which may be summarised firstly thus: All the other tribes look down on the Fans, and the Fans look down on all the other tribes. This aristocracy has subdivisions, the M'pongwe of Gaboon are the upper circle tribe; next come the Benga of Corisco; then the Bapoka; then the Banaka. This system of aristocracy is kept up by the ladies. Thus a M'pongwe lady would not think of marrying into one of the lower tribes, so she is restricted, with many inner restrictions to her own tribe. A Benga lady would marry a M'pongwe, or a Benga, but not a Banaka, or Bapoka; and so on with the others; but not one of them would marry a Fan. As for the men, well of course they would marry any lady of any tribe, if she had a pretty face, or a good trading connection, if they were allowed to: that's just man's way.

A young Fan man has to fend for himself, and has a scratchy kind of life of it, aided only by his mother until—if he be an enterprising youth—he is able to steal a runaway wife from a neighbouring village, or if he is a quiet and steady young man, until he has amassed sufficient money to buy a wife. This he does by collecting ivory and rubber and selling it to the men who have been allotted goods by the chief of the village, from the consignment brought up by the black trader. He supports himself meanwhile by, if the situation of his village permits, fishing and selling the fish, and hunting and killing game in the forest. He keeps steadily at it in his way, reserving his roysterings until he is settled in life.

A truly careful young man does not go and buy a baby girl cheap, as soon as he has got a little money together; but works and saves on until he has got enough to buy a good, tough widow lady, who, although personally unattractive, is deeply versed in the lore of trade, and who knows exactly how much rubbish you can incorporate in a ball of india rubber, without the white trader, or the black bush factory trader, instantly detecting it.

When the Fan young man has married his wife, in a legitimate way on the cash system, he takes her round to his relations, and shows her off; and they make little presents to help the pair set

up housekeeping. But the young man cannot yet settle down, for his wife will not allow him to. She is not going to slave herself to death doing all the work of the house, &c., and so he goes on collecting, and she preparing, trade stuff, and he grows rich enough to buy other wives—some of them young children, others widows, no longer necessarily old. But it is not until he is well on in life that he gets sufficient wives, six or seven. For it takes a good time to get enough rubber to buy a lady, and he does not get a grip on the ivory trade until he has got a certain position in the village, and plantations of his own which the elephants can be discovered raiding, in which case a percentage of the ivory taken from the herd is allotted to him. Now and again he may come across a dead elephant, but that is of the nature of a windfall; and on rubber and ebony he has to depend during his early days.

These he changes with the rich men of his village for a very peculiar and interesting form of coinage—bikĕi—little iron imitation axe-heads which are tied up in bundles called ntet, ten going to one bundle, for with bikĕi must the price of a wife be paid. You cannot do so with rubber or ivory, or goods. These bikĕi pass, however, as common currency among the Fans, for other articles of trade as well, but I do not think they will pass bikĕi out of the tribe. Possibly no one else will take this form of change. Thousands of these bikĕi, done up into ntets, go to the price of a wife. I thought I saw in bikĕi a certain resemblance in underlying idea with the early Greek coins I have seen at Cambridge, made like the fore-parts of cattle; and I have little doubt that the articles of barter among the Fans before the introduction of the rubber, ebony and ivory trades, which in their districts are comparatively recent, were iron implements.

When he has surmounted his many difficulties, and dodged his relations, and married, he is seemingly a better husband than the man of a more cultured tribe. He will turn a hand to anything that does not necessitate his putting down his gun outside his village gateway. He will help chop firewood, or goat's chop, or he will carry the baby with pleasure, while his good lady does these things; and in bush villages, he always escorts her so as to be on hand in case of leopards, or other local unpleasantnesses. When inside the village he will lay down his gun, within handy reach, and build the house, tease out fibre to make game nets with, and plait baskets, or make pottery with the ladies, cheerily chatting the while.

Fan pottery, although rough and sunbaked, is artistic in

form and ornamented, for the Fan ornaments all his work; the articles made in it consist of cooking pots, palm-wine bottles, water bottles and pipes, but not all water bottles, nor all pipes are made of pottery. I wish they were, particularly the former, for they are occasionally made of beautifully plaited fibre coated with a layer of a certain gum with a vile taste, which it imparts to the water in the vessel. They say it does not do this if the vessel is soaked for two days in water, but it does, and I should think contaminates the stream it was soaked in into the bargain.

The Fan basket-work is strongly made, but very inferior to the Fjort basket-work. Their nets are, however, the finest I have ever seen. These are made mainly for catching small game, such as the beautiful little gazelles (*Ncheri*) with dark gray skins on the upper part of the body, white underneath, and satin-like in sleekness all over. Their form is very dainty, the little legs being no thicker than a man's finger, the neck long and the head ornamented with little pointed horns and broad round ears. The nets are tied on to trees in two long lines, which converge to an acute angle, the bottom part of the net lying on the ground. Then a party of men and women, accompanied by their trained dogs which have bells hung round their necks, beat the surrounding bushes, and the frightened small game rush into the nets, and become entangled. I once saw a small bush cow caught in a set of them and unable to break through, and once a leopard; he, however, took his section of the net away with him, and a good deal of vegetation and sticks to boot.

The iron-work of the Fans deserves especial notice for its excellence. The anvil is a big piece of iron which is embedded firmly in the ground. Its upper surface is flat, and pointed at both ends. The hammers are solid cones of iron, the upper part of the cones prolonged so as to give a good grip, and the blows are given directly downwards, like the blows of a pestle.

I must now speak briefly on the most important article with which the Fan deals, namely ivory. His methods of collecting this are several, and many a wild story the handles of your table knives could tell you, if their ivory has passed through Fan hands. For ivory is everywhere an evil thing before which the quest for gold sinks into a parlour game; and when its charms seize such a tribe as the Fans, 'conclusions pass their careers'.

A very common way of collecting a tooth is to kill the person who owns one. Therefore in order to prevent this catastrophe happening to you yourself, when you have one, it is held advisable, unless you are a powerful person in your own village, to

bury or sink the said tooth and say nothing about it until the trader comes into your district or you get a chance of smuggling it quietly down to him. Some of these private ivories are kept for years and years before they reach the trader's hands. And quite a third of the ivory you see coming on board a vessel to go to Europe is dark from this keeping: some teeth a lovely brown like a well-coloured meerschaum, others quite black, and gnawed by that strange little creature—much heard of, and abused, yet little known in ivory ports—the ivory rat.

This squirrel-like creature was first brought to Europe by Paul du Chaillu * and as far as I know no further specimen has been secured. I got two, but I am ashamed to say I lost them. Du Chaillu called it *Sciurus eborivorus*. Its main point, as may be imagined, is its teeth. The incisors in the upper jaw are long, and closely set together; those in the lower are still longer, and as they seem always to go in under the upper teeth, I wonder how the creature gets its mouth shut. The feet are hairless, and somewhat like those of a squirrel. The tail is long, and marked with transverse bars, and it is not carried over the back. Over the eyes, and on either side of the mouth, are very long stiff bristles. The mischief these little creatures play with buried ivory is immense, because, for some inscrutable reason, they seem to prefer the flavour of the points of the teeth, the most valuable part.

Ivory, however, that is obtained by murder is private ivory. The public ivory trade among the Fans is carried on in a way more in accordance with European ideas of a legitimate trade. The greater part of this ivory is obtained from dead elephants. There are in this region certain places where the elephants are said to go to die. A locality in one district pointed out to me as such a place, was a great swamp in the forest. A swamp that evidently was deep in the middle, for from out its dark waters no swamp plant or tree grew, and evidently its shores sloped suddenly, for the band of swamp plants round its edge was narrow. It is just possible that during the rainy season when most of the surrounding country would be under water, elephants might stray into this natural trap and get drowned, and on the drying up of the waters be discovered, and the fact being known, be regularly sought for by the natives cognisant of this.

A certain percentage of ivory collected by the Fans is from

* The French traveller and writer (1835–1903) and the first European to describe the gorilla previously known to scientists only by its skeleton. (EH)

live elephants, but I am bound to admit that their method of hunting elephants is disgracefully unsportsmanlike. A herd of elephants is discovered by rubber hunters or by depredations on plantations, and the whole village, men, women, children, babies and dogs, turn out into the forest and stalk the monsters into a suitable ravine, taking care not to scare them. When they have gradually edged the elephants on into a suitable place, they fell trees and wreathe them very roughly together with bush rope, all round an immense enclosure, still taking care not to scare the elephants into a rush. This fence is quite inadequate to stop any elephant in itself, but it is made effective by being smeared with certain things, the smell whereof the elephants detest so much that when they wander up to it, they turn back disgusted. I need hardly remark that this preparation is made by the witch doctors and its constituents a secret of theirs, and I was only able to find out some of them.

Then poisoned plantains are placed within the enclosure, and the elephants eat these and grow drowsier and drowsier; if the water supply within the enclosure is a pool it is poisoned, but if it is a running stream this cannot be done. During this time the crowd of men and women spend their days round the enclosure, ready to turn back any elephant who may attempt to break out, going to and fro to the village for their food. Their nights they spend in little bough shelters by the enclosure, watching more vigilantly than by day, as the elephants are more active at night, it being their usual feeding time.

During the whole time the witch doctor is hard at work making incantations and charms, with a view to finding out the proper time to attack the elephants. In my opinion, his decision fundamentally depends on his knowledge of the state of poisoning the animals are in, but his version is that he gets his information from the forest spirits. When, however, he has settled the day, the best hunters steal into the enclosure and take up safe positions in trees, and the outer crowd set light to the ready-built fires, and make the greatest uproar possible, and fire upon the staggering, terrified elephants as they attempt to break out. The hunters in the trees fire down on them as they rush past, the fatal point at the back of the skull being well exposed to them.

When the animals are nearly exhausted, those men who do not possess guns dash into the enclosure, and the men who do, reload and join them, and the work is then completed. One elephant hunt I chanced upon at the final stage had taken two months' preparation, and although the plan sounds safe enough,

there is really a good deal of danger left in it with all the drugging and ju-ju. There were eight elephants killed that day, but three burst through everything, sending energetic spectators flying, and squashing two men and a baby as flat as botanical specimens.

The subsequent proceedings were impressive. The whole of the people gorged themselves on the meat for days, and great chunks of it were smoked over the fires in all directions. A certain portion of the flesh of the hind leg was taken by the witch doctor for ju-ju, and was supposed to be put away by him, with certain suitable incantations, in the recesses of the forest; his idea being apparently either to give rise to more elephants, or to induce the forest spirits to bring more elephants into the district. Meanwhile the carcases were going bad, rapidly bad, and the smell for a mile round was strong enough to have taken the paint off a door. Moreover there were flies, most of the flies in West Africa, I imagine, and—but I will say no more. I thought before this experience that I had touched bottom in smells when once I spent the outside of a week in a village, on the sand bank in front of which a portly hippopotamus, who had been shot up river, got stranded, and proceeded energetically to melt into its elemental gases; but that was a passing whiff to this.

Of the method of catching game in traps I have already spoken. Such are the pursuits, sports and pastimes of my friends the Fans. I have been considerably chaffed both by whites and blacks about my partiality for this tribe, but as I like Africans in my way—not à la Sierra Leone—and these Africans have more of the qualities I like than any other tribe I have met, it is but natural that I should prefer them. They are brave and so you can respect them, which is an essential element in a friendly feeling. They are on the whole a fine race, particularly those in the mountain districts of the Sierra del Cristal, where one continually sees magnificent specimens of human beings, both male and female. Their colour is light bronze, many of the men have beards, and albinoes are rare among them. The average height in the mountain districts is five feet six to five feet eight, the difference in stature between men and women not being great.

Their countenances are very bright and expressive, and if once you have been among them, you can never mistake a Fan. But it is in their mental characteristics that their difference from the lethargic, dying-out coast tribes is most marked. The Fan is full of fire, temper, intelligence and go; very teachable,

rather difficult to manage, quick to take offence, and utterly indifferent to human life. I ought to say that other people, who should know him better than I, say he is a treacherous, thievish, murderous cannibal. I never found him treacherous; but then I never trusted him, remembering one of the aphorisms of my great teacher Captain Boler of Bonny, 'It's not safe to go among bush tribes, but if you are such a fool as to go, you needn't go and be a bigger fool still, you've done enough.' And Captain Boler's other great aphorism was: 'Never be afraid of a black man.' 'What if I can't help it?' said I. 'Don't show it,' said he. To these precepts I humbly add another: 'Never lose your head.'

My most favourite form of literature, I may remark, is accounts of mountaineering exploits, though I have never seen a glacier or a permanent snow mountain in my life. I do not care a row of pins how badly they may be written, and what form of bumble-puppy grammar and composition is employed, as long as the writer will walk along the edge of a precipice with a sheer fall of thousands of feet on one side and a sheer wall on the other; or better still crawl up an *arête* with a precipice on either. Nothing on earth would persuade me to do either of these things myself, but they remind me of bits of country I have been through where you walk along a narrow line of security with gulfs of murder looming on each side, and where in exactly the same way you are as safe as if you were in your easy chair at home, as long as you get sufficient holding ground: not on rock in the bush village inhabited by murderous cannibals, but on ideas in those men's and women's minds; and these ideas which I think I may say you will always find, give you safety. It is not advisable to play with them, or to attempt to eradicate them, because you regard them as superstitious; and never, never shoot too soon. I have never had to shoot, and hope never to have to; because in such a situation, one white alone with no troops to back him means a clean finish. But this would not discourage me if I had to start, only it makes me more inclined to walk round the obstacle, than to become a mere blood splotch against it, if this can be done without losing your self-respect, which is the mainspring of your power in West Africa.

As for flourishing about a revolver and threatening to fire, I hold it utter idiocy. I have never tried it, however, so I speak from prejudice which arises from the feeling that there is something cowardly in it. Always have your revolver ready loaded in good order, and have your hand on it when things are getting warm, and in addition have an exceedingly good bowie knife,

not a hinge knife, because with a hinge knife you have got to get it open—hard work in a country where all things go rusty in the joints—and hinge knives are liable to close on your own fingers. The best form of knife is the bowie, with a shallow half moon cut out of the back at the point end, and this depression sharpened to a cutting edge. A knife is essential, because after wading neck deep in a swamp your revolver is neither use nor ornament until you have had time to clean it. But the chances are you may go across Africa, or live years in it, and require neither.

The cannibalism of the Fans, although a prevalent habit, is no danger, I think, to white people, except as regards the bother it gives one in preventing one's black companions from getting eaten. The Fan is not a cannibal from sacrificial motives like the Negro. He does it in his common sense way. Man's flesh, he says, is good to eat, very good, and he wishes you would try it. Oh dear no, he never eats it himself, but the next door town does. He is always very much abused for eating his relations, but he really does not do this. He will eat his next door neighbour's relations and sell his own deceased to his next door neighbour in return; but he does not buy slaves and fatten them up for his table as some of the Middle Congo tribes I know of do. He has no slaves, no prisoners of war, no cemeteries, so you must draw your own conclusions. No, my friend, I will not tell you any cannibal stories. I have heard how good M. du Chaillu fared after telling you some beauties, and now you come away from the Fan village and down the Rembwé river.

CHAPTER EIGHT

Down the Rembwé to Gaboon

Getting away from Agonjo seemed as if it would be nearly as difficult as getting to it, but as the quarters were comfortable and the society fairly good, I was not anxious. Mr Glass, however, did not take things so philosophically. I was on his commercial conscience, for I had come in from the bush and there was money in me. Therefore I was a trade product—a new trade stuff that ought to be worked up and developed; and he found himself unable to do this, for although he had secured the first parcel, as it were, and got it successfully stored, yet he could not ship it, and he felt this was a reproach to him.

Many were his lamentations that the firm had not provided him with a large sailing canoe and a suitable crew to deal with this new line of trade. I did my best to comfort him, pointing out that the most enterprising firm could not be expected to provide expensive things like these, on the extremely remote chance of ladies arriving per bush at Agonjo—in fact not until the trade in them was well developed. But he refused to see it in this light and harped upon the subject, wrapped up, poor man, in a great coat and a muffler, because his ague was on him.

At this point in the affair there entered a highly dramatic figure. He came on to the scene suddenly and with much uproar, in a way that would have made his fortune in a transpontine drama. He dashed up on to the verandah, smote the frail form of Mr Glass between the shoulders, and flung his own massive one into a chair. His name was Obanjo, but he liked it pronounced Captain Johnson, and his profession was a bush and river trader on his own account. Every movement of the man was theatrical, and he used to look covertly at you every now and then to see if he had produced his impression, which was evidently intended to be that of a reckless, rollicking skipper. There was a Hallo-my-Hearty atmosphere coming off him from the top of his hat to the soles of his feet, like the scent off a flower; but it did not require a genius in judging men to see that behind and under this was a very different sort of man, and if I should ever want to engage in a wild and awful career up a West African river I shall start on it by engaging Captain Johnson. He struck me as

being one of those men, of whom I know five, whom I could rely on, that if one of them and I went into the utter bush together, one of us at least would come out alive and have made something substantial by the venture; which is a great deal more than I could say, for example, of Ngouta, who was still with me, as he desired to see the glories of Gaboon and buy a hanging lamp.

Captain Johnson wore a huge sombrero hat, a spotless singlet, and a suit of clean, well-got-up dungaree, and an uncommonly picturesque, powerful figure he cut in them, with his finely moulded, well-knit form and good-looking face, full of expression always, but always with the keen small eyes in it watching the effect his genial smiles and hearty laugh produce. The eyes were the eyes of Obanjo, the rest of the face the property of Captain Johnson. I do not mean to say that they were the eyes of a bad bold man, but you had not to look twice at them to see they belonged to a man courageous in the African manner, full of energy and resource, keenly intelligent and self-reliant, and all that sort of thing.

I left him and the refined Mr Glass together to talk over the palaver of shipping me, and they talked it at great length. Finally the price I was to pay Obanjo was settled and we proceeded to less important details. It seemed Obanjo, when up the river this time, had set about constructing a new and large trading canoe at one of his homes, in which he was just thinking of taking his goods down to Gaboon. The only drawback was this noble vessel was not finished; but that did not discourage any of us, except Mr Glass, who seemed to think the firm would debit me to his account if I got lost. However, next morning Obanjo with his vessel turned up, and saying farewell to my kind host, Mr Sanga Glass, I departed.

We left Agonjo with as much bustle and shouting and general air of brisk seamanship as Obanjo could impart to the affair, and the hopeful mind might have expected to reach somewhere important by nightfall. I did not expect that; neither, on the other hand, did I expect that after we had gone a mile and only four, as the early ballad would say, that we should pull up and anchor against a small village for the night; but this we did, the captain going ashore to see for cargo, and to get some more crew.

There were grand times ashore that night, and the captain returned on board about 2 A.M. with some rubber and pissava and two new hands whose appearance fitted them to join our

vessel; for a more villainous-looking set than our crew I never laid eye on. One enormously powerful fellow looked the incarnation of the horrid negro of buccaneer stories, and I admired Obanjo for the way he kept them in hand. We had now also acquired a small dug-out canoe as tender, and a large fishing-net.

About 4 A.M. in the moonlight we started to drop down river on the tail of the land breeze, and as I observed Obanjo wanted to sleep I offered to steer. After putting me through an examination in practical seamanship, and passing me, he gladly accepted my offer, handed over the tiller which stuck out across my bamboo staging, and went and curled himself up, falling sound asleep among the crew in less time than it takes to write. On the other nights we spent on this voyage I had no need to offer to steer; he handed over charge to me as a matter of course, and as I prefer night to day in Africa, I enjoyed it.

Indeed, much as I have enjoyed life in Africa, I do not think I ever enjoyed it to the full as I did on those nights dropping down the Rembwé. The great, black, winding river with a pathway in its midst of frosted silver where the moonlight struck it: on each side the ink-black mangrove walls, and above them the band of star and moonlit heavens that the walls of mangrove allowed one to see. Forward rose the form of our sail, idealised from bedsheetdom to glory; and the little red glow of our cooking fire gave a single note of warm colour to the cold light of the moon.

Three or four times during the second night, while I was steering along by the south bank, I found the mangrove wall thinner, and standing up, looked through the network of their roots and stems on to what seemed like plains, acres upon acres in extent, of polished silver—more specimens of those awful slime lagoons, one of which, before we reached Ndorko, had so very nearly collected me. I watched them, as we leisurely stole past with a sort of fascination. On the second night, towards the dawn, I had the great joy of seeing Mount Okoneto, away to the S.W., first showing moonlit, and then taking the colours of the dawn before they reached us down below. Ah me! give me a West African river and a canoe for sheer good pleasure. Drawbacks, you say? Well, yes, but where are there not drawbacks? The only drawbacks on those Rembwé nights were the series of horrid frights I got by steering on to tree shadows and thinking they were mud banks, or trees themselves, so black and solid did they seem. I never

roused the watch fortunately, but got her off the shadow gallantly single-handed every time, and called myself a fool instead of getting called one.

My nautical friends carp at me for getting on shadows, but I beg them to consider before they judge me, whether they have ever steered at night down a river quite unknown to them an unhandy canoe, with a bed-sheet sail, by the light of the moon. And what with my having a theory of my own regarding the proper way to take a vessel round a corner, and what with having to keep the wind in the bed-sheet where the bed-sheet would hold it, it's a wonder to me I did not cast that vessel away, or go and damage Africa.

By daylight the Rembwé scenery was certainly not so lovely, and might be slept through without a pang. It had monotony, without having enough of it to amount to grandeur. Every now and again we came to villages, each of which was situated on a heap of clay and sandy soil, presumably the end of a spit of land running out into the mangrove swamp fringing the river. Every village we saw we went alongside and had a chat with, and tried to look up cargo in the proper way.

Efforts to get a flock of goats into the canoe provide Mary Kingsley with entertainment, and an unexpected encounter.

While engaged in shouting 'Encore' to the third round, I received a considerable shock by hearing a well-modulated evidently educated voice saying in most perfect English:

'Most diverting spectacle, madam, is it not?'

Now you do not expect to hear things called 'diverting spectacles' on the Rembwé; so I turned round and saw standing on the bank against which our canoe was moored, what appeared to me to be an English gentleman who had from some misfortune gone black all over and lost his trousers and been compelled to replace them with a highly ornamental table-cloth. The rest of his wardrobe was in exquisite condition, with the usual white jean coat, white shirt and collar, very neat tie, and felt hat affected by white gentlemen out here. Taking a large and powerful cigar from his lips with one hand, he raised his hat gracefully with the other and said:

'Pray excuse me, madam.'

I said, 'Oh, please go on smoking.'

'May I?' he said, offering me a cigar-case.

'Oh, no thank you,' I replied.

'Many ladies do now,' he said, and asked me whether I 'preferred Liverpool, London, or Paris.'

I said, 'Paris; but there were nice things in both the other cities.'

'Indeed that is so,' he said; 'they have got many very decent works of art in the St George's Hall.'

I agreed, but said I thought the National Gallery preferable because there you got such fine representative series of works of early Italian schools. I felt I had got to rise to this man whoever he was, somehow, and having regained my nerve, I was coming up hand over hand to the level of his culture when Obanjo and the crew arrived, carrying goats. Obanjo dropped his goat summarily into the hold, and took off his hat with his very best bow to my new acquaintance, who acknowledged the salute with a delicious air of condescension.

'Introduce me,' said the gentleman.

'I cannot,' said Obanjo.

'I regret, madam,' said the gentleman, 'I have not brought my card-case with me. One little expects in such a remote region to require one; my name is Prince Makaga.'

I said I was similarly card-caseless for reasons identical with his own, but gave him my name and address, and Obanjo, having got all aboard, including a member of the crew, fetched by the leg, shoved off, and with many bows we and the black gentleman parted. As soon as we were out of earshot from shore 'Who is he, Obanjo?' said I. Obanjo laughed, and said he was a M'pongwe gentleman who had at one time been agent for one of the big European firms at Gaboon, and had been several times to Europe. Thinking that he could make more money on his own account, he had left the firm and started trading all round this district. At first he made a great deal of money, but a lot of his trust had recently gone bad, and he was doubtless up here now looking after some such matter. Obanjo evidently thought him too much of a lavender-kid-glove gentleman to deal with bush trade, and held it was the usual way; a man got spoilt by going to Europe. I quite agree with him on general lines, but Prince Makaga had a fine polish on him without the obvious conceit usually found in men who have been home.

I had by this time mastered the main points of incapability in our craft. A. we could not go against the wind. B. we could not go against the tide. While we were in the Rembwé there was a state we will designate as C—the tide coming one way, the wind another. With this state we could progress, backwards if the

wind came up against us too strong, but seawards if it did not, and the tide was running down. If the tide was running up, and the wind was coming down, then we went seaward, softly, softly alongside the mangrove bank, where the rip of the tide stream is least.

When, however, we got down off 'Como Point, we met there a state I will designate as *D*—a fine confused set of marine and fluvial phenomena. For away to the north the 'Como and Boqué and two other lesser, but considerable streams, were, with the Rembwé, pouring down their waters in swirling, intermingling, interclashing currents; and up against them, to make confusion worse confounded, came the tide, and the tide up the Gaboon is a swift strong thing, and irregular, and has a rise of eight feet at the springs, two-and-a-half at the neaps. The wind was lulled too, it being evening time.

Fortunately for us we arrived off the head of the Gaboon estuary in this calm, for had we had wind to deal with we should have come to an end. There were one or two wandering puffs, about the first one of which sickened our counterpane of its ambitious career as a marine sail, so it came away from its gaff and spread itself over the crew, as much as to say, 'Here, I've had enough of this sailing. I'll be a counterpane again.' We did a great deal of fine varied, spirited navigation.

A basket constructed for catching human souls in, given me as a farewell gift by a valued friend, a witch doctor, and in which I kept the few things in life I really cared for, *i.e.*, my brush, comb, tooth brush, and pocket handkerchiefs, went over the stern; while I was recovering this with my fishing line a black bag with my blouses and such essentials went away to leeward. Obanjo recovered that, but meanwhile my little portmanteau containing my papers and trade tobacco slid off to leeward; and as it also contained geological specimens of the Sierra del Cristal, a massive range of mountains, it must have hopelessly sunk had it not been for the big black, who grabbed it. All my bedding, six Equetta cloths, given me by Mr Hamilton in Opobo River before I came South, did get away successfully, but were picked up by means of the fishing line, wet but safe. After this I did not attempt any more Roman reclining couch luxuries, but stowed all my loose gear under the bamboo staging, and spent the night on the top of the stage, dozing precariously with my head on my knees.

When the morning broke, looking seaward I saw the welcome forms of König and Perroquet Islands away in the distance,

looking, as is their wont, like two lumps of cloud that have
dropped on to the broad Gaboon, and I felt that I was at last
getting near something worth reaching, *i.e.* Glass, which though
still out of sight, I knew lay away to the west of those islands on
the northern shore of the estuary.

*In Obanjo's 'unfinished canoe with an inefficient counterpane sail'
it took all day to cross the Gaboon estuary.*

Just as the night came down, however, we reached the northern shore of the Grand Gaboon at Dongila. The foreshore here is
very rocky, so we could not go close alongside but anchored out
among the rocks. At this place there is a considerable village and
a station of the Roman Catholic Mission. When we arrived a nun
was down on the shore with her school children, who were busy
catching shell-fish and generally merry-making. Obanjo went
ashore in the tender, and the holy sister kindly asked me, by
him, to come ashore and spend the night; but I was dead tired
and felt quite unfit for polite society after the long broiling hot
day and getting soaked by water that had washed on board.
Moreover I learnt she could not speak English. If I had been
able to dress up, ashore I would have gone, but as it was I wrote
her a note explaining things and thanking her.

We lay off Dongila all night, because of the tide. Obanjo
and almost all the crew stayed on shore that night, and
I rolled myself up in an Equetta cloth and went sound and happily asleep on the bamboo staging, leaving the canoe pitching
slightly. About midnight some change in the tide, or original sin
in the canoe, caused her to softly swing round a bit, and the
next news was that I was in the water. I had long expected this
to happen, so was not surprised, but highly disgusted, and
climbed on board, needless to say, streaming. So, in the darkness
of the night I got my portmanteau from the hold and thoroughly
tidied up.

The next morning we were off early, coasting along to Glass,
and safely arriving there, I attempted to look as unconcerned as
possible, and vaguely hoped Mr Hudson would be down in
Libreville; for I was nervous about meeting him, knowing that
since he had carefully deposited me in safe hands with Mme
Jacot, with many injunctions to be careful, that there were many
incidents in my career that would not meet with his approval.
Vain hope! he was on the pier. He did not approve. He had
heard of most of my goings on.

I tried to explain to him how much I had enjoyed myself and how I realised I owed it all to him; but he persisted in his opinion that my intentions and ambitions were suicidal, and took me down the Woermann Road, the ensuing Sunday, as it were on a string.

As soon as I returned to Glass I naturally went to discourse with Doctor Nassau * on Fetish. In one of these talks the Doctor mentioned that there were lakes in the centre of the Island of Corisco, and that in those lakes were quantities of fish, which fish were always and only fished by the resident ladies, at duly appointed seasons. Needless to say, I felt it a solemn duty to go and investigate personally; and equally needless to say, Doctor Nassau gave me every assistance, which took the form of lending me a small vessel called the *Lafayette*. She had been long in his possession, but of late years little used, still she was a fine seaworthy boat, so with a crew headed by the Doctor's factotum, Eveke, who was a native of the said island, together with a few friends of his, we set sail.

The off-shore breeze blows strong this morning and the tide is running out like a mill-race, so the *Lafayette* flies seaward gallantly. Libreville looks very bright and pleasing—with its red roofs and white walls amongst the surrounding wealth of dark green mango trees; but we soon leave it behind, passing along in front of the low, rolling hills, all densely clad with forests, out to Cape Clara, or Cape Joinville as some maps will have it—the end of the northern shore of the Gaboon estuary.

When we get to the Cape we find a pretty fair sea running, and Eveke, whose seamanship I am beginning to view with suspicion, lets her gybe, and I get knocked into the bottom of the boat by the boom, and stay there. There is nothing like entering into the spirit of a thing like this if you mean to enjoy it, and after all that's the wisest thing to do out here, for there's nothing between enjoying it and dying of it. The sun is broiling hot; everything one has got to sit on or catch hold of is as hot as a burning brick, and there is no cabin, nor even locker, on our craft; so I prop myself up against my collecting-box and lazily take stock of the things round me, and write.

Our cargo consists of two bags of salt, several bags and boxes of sand for ballast, several bottles of water for drinking, a

* Head of the American Presbyterian Mission in Gaboon and Batanga, and a leading authority on the religion and customs of the inhabitants of this region. (EH)

bundle of bedding—a loan from the Doctor, and a deck chair—
a loan from Mr Hudson. Owing to the *Lafayette* having no deck,
the latter is 'not required on the voyage', and is folded up. I
observe with anxiety that the cargo is not stowed in a manner
that would meet with the approval of Captain Murray, and
decide to get dunnage and do it in style the first port we call at.
Can't possibly shift cargo in this sea.

The *Lafayette* flies along before a heavy sea, and from my
position at the bottom of her I can see nothing but her big white
mainsail and her mast with its shrouds and stays standing out
clear, rocking to and fro, against the hard blue sky; and just the
white crests of the waves as they go dancing by. I have nothing
to hear save the pleasantest sounds in the world—the rustle of
the sail and the swish of the waves as they play alongside the
vessel. Now and then there is added to these the lazy, laughing
talk of the black men; and now and then an extra lively wave
throws its crest in among us.

Soon all the crew drop softly off to sleep, Eveke joining them,
so I rouse up and take the main sheet and the tiller and keep her
so. I feel as if I were being baked to a cinder, but there's no help
for it, and some of it is very pleasant. About four o'clock I see
two lumps of land on the sky-line. I wake Eveke up and he seems
surprised at my not knowing what they are. 'That's Corisco and
Banã, sir,' says he. I explain to Eveke, as I hand over the
navigation to him, that every one has not been born on Corisco,
and the fact of his having had this advantage is the reason of
his being pilot now; and I reseat myself in the bottom of the
boat and carefully look over the side, mindful of that boom
palaver.

We head for the bigger and most western bit of land, soon
seeing the details of its undulating, black-green forests. When we
get within a mile, Eveke asks me to wake up the man in front of
me, and I stir him firmly, but gently, with a chart; for I know
what waking black men leads to sometimes; and when he rouses
I order him to wake up the others, and in a few minutes they are
all more or less awake, even the man on the look-out. They wash
their mouths out with sea-water, and then re-commence their
laughing, talking and water-drinking again.

We run into a small, sandy-shored, wooded bay where, as I
find is Eveke's habit, we lower our gaff prematurely and drift, in
the proper way, leisurely towards the above, stern foremost. At
last the *Lafayette*, finding everything is left to her, says: 'Look
here, you fellows, if you don't help I won't play,' and stops and

commences to swing broadside on. So the oars—or sweeps I should call them, for we have evidently returned to fourteenth-century seamanship—are got out and in a few minutes we are bumping violently on the strand. We let go the anchor, make all snug and go ashore.

On Corisco island, Eveke takes Mary Kingsley to the house of his father, the Rev. Ibea of the Presbyterian Mission.

At the end of the avenue there is a pretty wooden house, painted white, with its doors and window-frames painted a bold bright blue. Around it are a cluster of outbuildings like it, each mounted on poles, the little church, the store, and the house for the children in the mission school. A troop of children rush out and greet Eveke effusively. One of them, I am informed, is his brother, and he commences to bubble out conversation in Benga. I send Eveke off to find his mother, thinking he will like to get his greetings with her over unobserved, and after a few minutes she comes forward to greet me—a pretty, bright-looking lady whom it is hard to believe old enough to be Eveke's mother; and not only Eveke's but the mother of a lot of strapping young women who come forward with her, and the grandmother of other strapping young women mixed up among them. Mrs Ibea insists, in the kindliest way possible, on my taking possession of her own room. Mr Ibea is away, she says, on an evangelising visit to the mainland at Cape St John (the northern extremity of Corisco Bay), intending to call at Eloby Island; so he may not be here for some days, and she promptly gives me tea and alligator pears, both exceedingly welcome.

The views from the windows of my clean and comfortable room are very beautiful. The house stands on a high promontory called Alondo Point, the turning point of the south and west sides of the island, and almost overhangs the sea. A reef of rock runs out at the foot of the cliff for about a mile, on which the sea breaks constantly. The great rollers of the South Atlantic, meeting here their first check since they left Cape Horn and the Americas, fly up in sheets of foam with a never-ending thunder. I go to bed early, thankfully observing that the gay mosquito curtain is entirely 'for dandy'—decorative and not defensive.

The obtaining of specimens of fish from the lakes in the centre of the island being my main object in visiting Corisco, I set to work by starting immediately after breakfast to the bay that

we came to last night, and which I will call Nassau Bay in future. I go along the same variegated path I came by yesterday. Eveke has slept at the village in the Bay among his relatives so as to keep an eye, he says, on the *Lafayette*. When I find him, he says that only women can catch the lake fish, and that they always catch them in certain baskets, and as these have to be made, they cannot be ready to-day.

Mary Kingsley spends the day exploring the island, and starts off next morning with Eveke and a party of women for the fishing lakes, across a recently burnt 'prairie'.

We go across this prairie into a little wood mainly made up of beautiful wild fig-trees, with their muscles showing through the skin like our own beech-trees' muscles do, only the wild fig stem is whitish-grey and most picturesquely twisted and branching. Then out of this on to another prairie, larger and unburnt. During the whole of our walk from the village we have been yelling in prolonged, intoned howls for ladies, whose presence is necessary to the legitimate carrying on of our fishing—lady representatives of each village being expected to attend and see the fish are properly divided. I cannot find there is any fetish at the bottom of this custom, and think its being restricted to the women is originally founded on the male African's aversion to work; and in the representation of the villages, on the Africans' distrust of each other.

Notably, and grievously, we howl for En-gou-ta-a-a and Engouta comes not; so we throw ourselves down on the deliciously soft, fine, golden brown grass, in the sun, and wait for the tardy, absent ones, smoking, and laughing, and sleeping, and when any of the avocations palls on any of us we rise up and howl 'Engouta'. After about two mortal hours of this, and when my companions have for some time settled down, quite reconciled, to sleep peacefully, I hear a crackle-crackle-like fusillade of miniature guns. Looking towards the place whence the sound comes I notice a cloud of bright blue smoke surmounting a rapidly advancing wall of crimson fire. I get up and mention this fact briefly to my drowsy companions, adding in the case of the more profound sleepers an enlightening kick, and make an exemplary bee-line to the bush in front of us. The others follow my example with a rapidity I should not have expected in their tribe, but, in spite of some very creditable and spirited sprint performances, three members of the party get scorched and

spent the balance of the afternoon sitting in mud-holes, comforting themselves with the balmy black slime.

A little clamber down into the wood we are in brings us to the lakes. There is a little chain of them—they are just basins in the rock strata of varying sizes, and each has a thick lining of black mud. The water is at its lowest now, as it is the end of the dry season, and the water they contain is, I think, the accumulation of rain water from wet seasons.

Most of these lakes have an encircling rim of rock, from which, if you are a fisher, you jump down into unmitigated black slime to your knees; you then waddle, and squatter, and grunt, and skylark generally, to the shallow remnant of water. If it is one of the larger lakes, you and your companions drive in two rows of stakes, cutting each other at right angles, more or less, in the centre of the lake.

This being done, the women, with the specially made baskets —affairs shaped like bed-pillows with one side open—form a line with their backs towards the banks, their faces to the water, in the enclosure; the other women go into the water by the stakes, and splash with hands and feet and sticks as hard as they can, needless to say shouting hard the while. The terrified fish fly from them into the baskets, and are scooped up by the peck. In little basins of water the stakes are not required, but the rest of the proceedings are the same, some women standing with their backs to the bank, holding their baskets' mouths just under water, and scooping up the fish flying from the beaters in the middle.

From twelve to fourteen bushels is the usual result of the day's fishing, and the fish are divided between the representatives and distributed among the villages. A tremendous fish dinner ensues in the evening, and what fish are left are smoked and kept as relishes and dainties until next fishing time comes round.

But with all this formality, after all I had gone through, and all my walks and waitings, those wretched fish were nothing and nobody else but an African mud-fish, a brute I cordially hate, for whenever I ask native fishermen for fish, they bring me him; if I start catching fish for myself, nine times in ten it's him I catch. It was a bitter disappointment, for I had looked forward to getting some strange fish, or strongly modified form, in the middle of this little sea island, in fresh-water, some twenty miles from the mainland shore. But there! it's Africa all over; presenting one with familiar objects when one least requires them.

I did not go completely round all the lakes, having to watch the fishing, and at last, finding there was only this one kind of fish to be had, and that it was getting late, I set off on my weary, long walk back to Alondo, where I found on arriving that Mrs Ibea had got tea waiting for me, and that Mr Ibea was back from his evangelising mission to Cape St John and Eloby. He is a splendidly built, square-shouldered man, a pure Benga, of the finest type, full of energy and enthusiasm. I found some difficulty in accepting his statement regarding the age of Mrs Ibea and himself, and I still think he stuck a good ten years on.

His views on native social questions I had less difficulty in accepting, more particularly those which coincide with my own. We talked about the Fan—the backbone of native, and a good big factor in white conversation, all along here.

The Fans were at this time completing a westward migration, which had brought them to the shores of the Atlantic. Mary Kingsley discusses with the Rev. Ibea the causes of fluctuations in the power and number of various West Coast tribes.

Nothing strikes one so much, in studying the degeneration of these native tribes, as the direct effect that civilisation and reformation has in hastening it. The worst enemy to the existence of the African tribe, is the one who comes to it and says:— Now you must civilise, and come to school, and leave off all those awful goings-on of yours, and settle down quietly. The tribe does so; the African is teachable and tractable; and then the ladies and some of the young men are happy and content with the excitement of European clothes and frequent Church services; but the older men and some of the bolder young men soon get bored with these things and the, to them, irksome restraints, and they go in for too much rum, or mope themselves to death, or return to their native customs.

The African treats his religion much as other men do: when he gets slightly educated, a little scientific one might say, he removes from his religion all the disagreeable parts. He promptly eliminates its equivalent Hell, represented in Fetishism by immediate and not future retribution. Then goes his rigid Sabbath-keeping, and food-restriction equivalent, and he has nothing left but the agreeable portions: dances, polygamy, and so on; and it's a very bad thing for him. I only state these things so as to urge upon people at home the importance of combining technical instruction in their mission teaching; which by instil-

ling into the African mind ideas of discipline, and providing him with manual occupation, will save him from these relapses which are now the reproach of missionary effort, and the curse and degradation of the African. I do not feel sure that one must accept Mr Ibea's opinion, and class infant marriage among the causes of tribe extinction, because this custom is in vogue among many tribes that are still swarming, and among these Fans it is in vogue as regards the women. This, I think, is the earliest stage of the custom.

Corisco Island is very rich in rubber and ebony, which is bought by the Benga native traders, and M'pongwe, and sold to the white traders at Eloby and Cocoa Beach. Those traders who know the inland tribes describe them as savage and teacherous. The Fans are coming down through this part of the country to the beach all the way along from Batanga to the Gaboon estuary. I cannot hold out much hope that they will enlighten or ameliorate the manners and customs of the older inhabitants as regards trade, but they can teach them a thing or two worth knowing in the way of activity and courtesy.

That they will suffer the same extinction that the previous migrants to the Coast have suffered, there is no reason to doubt, for they will be under similar conditions; and Mr Ibea and myself agree again, that there is something inimical to human life, black or white, in the immediate Coast region of West and South-West Africa, as far down as Congo: and the interior tribes also join us in our opinion. Many times have I, and others, been told by interior tribes that there is a certain air which comes from the sea that kills men—that is just their way of putting it. I call it Paludisme Malariæ, which is just my way of putting it, and of course I fancy that it comes from the rotting, reeking swamp land and lagoons, and not from the sea. Anyhow, white men and black feel it, and suffer and die.

CHAPTER NINE

'Stalking the Wild West African Idea'

After a rough day at sea (8 August 1895), Mary Kingsley spends a supperless and sleepless night sitting up in the little schooner. Next day they fail again to round the cape and enter Gaboon Bay, so they beach the vessel and she dosses down on a sack of seaweed in an unfinished Mission house. Next morning, the Lafayette *is almost sunk by a whale. After further adventures, they berth at Hatton and Cookson's wharf at Glass.*

Having given some account of my personal experiences among an African tribe in its original state, *i.e.*, in a state uninfluenced by European ideas and culture, I will make an attempt to give a rough sketch of the African form of thought and the difficulties of studying it, because the study of this thing is my chief motive for going to West Africa. Since 1893 I have been collecting information in its native state regarding Fetish, and I use the usual terms fetish and ju-ju because they have among us a certain fixed value—a conventional value, but a useful one.

Neither 'fetish' nor 'ju-ju' are native words. Fetish comes from the word the old Portuguese explorers used to designate the objects they thought the natives worshipped, and in which they were wise enough to recognise a certain similarity to their own little images and relics of Saints, '*Feitiço*'. Ju-ju, on the other hand, is French, and comes from the word for a toy or doll, '*jou-jou*', so it is not so applicable as the Portuguese name, for the native image is not a doll or toy, and has far more affinity to the image of a saint, inasmuch as it is not venerated for itself, or treasured because of its prettiness, but only because it is the residence, or the occasional haunt, of a spirit.

Stalking the wild West African idea is one of the most charming pursuits in the world. Quite apart from the intellectual, it has a high sporting interest; for its pursuit is as beset with difficulty and danger as grizzly bear hunting, yet the climate in which you carry on this pursuit—vile as it is—is warm, which to me is almost an essential of existence. Personally I prefer it to

elephant hunting; and I shall never forget the pleasure with which, in the forest among the Fans, I netted one reason for the advantage of possessing a white man's eye-ball, and, as I wrote it down in my water-worn notebook, saw it joined up with the reason why it is advisable to cut off big men's heads in the Niger Delta. Above all, I beg you to understand that I make no pretension to a thorough knowledge of Fetish ideas; I am only on the threshold. *'Ich weiss nicht all doch viel ist mir bekannt'*, [I don't understand everything, nevertheless I know a lot] as Faust said —and, like him after he had said it, I have got a lot to learn.

The difficulty of gaining a true conception of the savage's real idea is great and varied.

In places on the Coast where there is, or has been, much missionary influence, the trouble is greatest, for in the first case the natives carefully conceal things they fear will bring them into derision and contempt, although they still keep them in their innermost hearts; and in the second case, you have a set of traditions which are Christian in origin, though frequently altered almost beyond recognition by being kept for years in the atmosphere of the African mind. For example, there is this beautiful story now extant among the Cabindas. God made at first all men black—He always does in the African story—and then He went across a great river and called men to follow Him, and the wisest and the bravest and the best plunged into the great river and crossed it; and the water washed them white, so they are the ancestors of the white men. But the others were afraid too much, and said, 'No, we are comfortable here; we have our dances, and our tom-toms, and plenty to eat—we won't risk it, we'll stay here'; and they remained in the old place, and from them come the black men. But to this day the white men come to the bank, on the other side of the river, and call to the black men, saying, 'Come, it is better over here.' I fear there is little doubt that this story is a modified version of some parable preached to the Cabindas at the time the Jesuit Fathers had such influence among them, before they were driven out of the lower Congo regions more than a hundred years ago, for political reasons, by the Portuguese.

In the bush—where the people have been little, or not at all, in contact with European ideas—in some ways the investigation is easier; yet another set of difficulties confronts you. The difficulty that seems to occur most easily to people is the difficulty of the language. West African languages are not difficult to pick up; nevertheless, there are an awful quantity of them and they

are at the best most imperfect mediums of communication. No one who has been on the Coast can fail to recognise how inferior the native language is to the native mind behind it—and the prolixity and repetition he has therefore to employ to make his thoughts understood.

The great comfort is the wide diffusion of that peculiar language, 'trade English'; it is not only used as a means of intercommunication between whites and blacks, but between natives using two distinct languages. On the south-west Coast you find individuals in villages far from the sea, or a trading station, who know it, and this is because they have picked it up and employ it in their dealings with the coast tribes and travelling traders. It is by no means an easy language to pick up—it is not a farrago of bad words and broken phrases, but is a definite structure, has a great peculiarity in its verb forms, and employs no genders. There is no grammar of it out yet; and one of the best ways of learning it is to listen to a seasoned second mate regulating the unloading, or loading, of cargo, over the hatch of the hold. No, my Coast friends, I have *not* forgotten—but though you did not mean it helpfully, this was one of the best hints you ever gave me.

Another good way is the careful study of examples which display the highest style and the most correct diction; so I append the letter given by Mr Hutchinson as being about the best bit of trade English I know.

'To Daddy nah Tampin Office,—

Ha Daddy, do, yah, nah beg you tell dem people for me; make dem Sally-own pussin know. Do yah. Berrah well.

Ah lib nah Pademba Road—one bwoy lib dah oberside lakah dem two Doctor lib overside you Tampin office. Berrah well.

Dah bwoy head big too much—he say nah Militie Ban—he got one long long ting so so brass, someting lib dah go flip flap, dem call am key. Berrah well. Had! Dah bwoy kin blow!—she ah!—na marin, oh!—nah sun time, oh! nah evenin, oh!—nah middle night, oh!—all same—no make pussin sleep. Not ebry bit dat, more lib da! One Boney bwoy lib oberside nah he like blow bugle. When dem two woh-woh bwoy blow dem ting de nize too much too much.

When white man blow dat ting and pussin sleep he kin tap wah make dem bwoy carn do so? Dem bwoy kin blow ebry day eben Sunday dem kin blow. When ah yerry dem blow Sunday ah wish dah bugle kin go down na dem troat or dem kin blow them head-bone inside.

Do nah beg you yah tell all dem people 'bout dah ting wah dem two bwoy dah blow. Till am Amtrang Boboh hab febah bad. Till am titty carn sleep nah night. Dah nize go kill me two pickin, oh! Plabba done. Good by Daddy.

Crashey Jane.'

Now for the elementary student we will consider this letter. The complaint in Crashey Jane's letter is about two boys who are torturing her morning, noon and night, Sunday and week day, by blowing some 'long long brass ting' as well as a bugle, and the way she dwells on their staying power must bring a sympathetic pang for that black sister into the heart of many a householder in London who lives next to a ladies' school, or a family of musical tastes. 'One touch of nature' &c. 'Daddy' is not a term of low familiarity but one of esteem and respect, and the 'Tampin Office' is a respectful appellation for the Office of the 'New Era' in which this letter was once published. 'Bwoy head big too much' means that the young man is swelled with conceit because he is connected with 'Militie ban'. 'Woh woh' you will find, among all the natives in the Bights, to mean extremely bad. I think it is native, having some connection with the root Wo—meaning power, &c.; but Mr Hutchinson may be right, and it may mean 'a capacity to bring double woe'.

'Amtrang Boboh' is not the name of some uncivilised savage, as the uninitiated may think; far from it. It is Bob Armstrong —upside down, and slightly altered, and refers to the Hon. Robert Armstrong, stipendiary magistrate of Sierra Leone, &c.

'Berrah well' is a phrase used whenever the native thinks he has succeeded in putting his statement well. He sort of turns round and looks at it, says 'Berrah well', in admiration of his own art, and then proceeds.

'Pickin' are children.

'Boney bwoy' is not a local living skeleton, but a native from Bonny River.

'Sally own' is Sierra Leone.

'Blow them head-bone inside' means, blow the top off their heads.

I have a collection of trade English letters and documents, for it is a language that I regard as exceedingly charming, and it really requires study, as you will see by reading Crashey Jane's epistle without the aid of a dictionary. It is, moreover, a language that will take you unexpectedly far in Africa, and if you do not understand it, land you in some pretty situations.

One important point that you must remember is that the African is logically right in his answer to such a question as 'You have not cleaned this lamp?'—he says, 'Yes, sah'—which means, 'yes, I have not cleaned the lamp'. It does not mean a denial to your accusation; he always uses this form, and it is liable to confuse you at first, as are many other of the phrases, such as 'I look him, I no see him'; this means 'I have been searching for the thing but have not found it'; if he really meant he had looked upon the object but had been unable to get to it, he would say: 'I look him, I no catch him', &c.

The difficulty of the language is, however, far less than the whole set of difficulties with your own mind. Unless you can make it pliant enough to follow the African idea step by step, however much care you may take, you will not bag your game. I heard an account the other day—I have forgotten where—of a representative of her Majesty in Africa who went out for a day's antelope shooting. There were plenty of antelope about, and he stalked them with great care; but always, just before he got within shot of the game, they saw something and bolted. Knowing he and the boy behind him had been making no sound and could not have been seen, he stalked on, but always with the same result; until happening to look round, he saw the boy behind him was supporting the dignity of the Empire at large, and this representative of it in particular, by steadfastly holding aloft the consular flag. Well, if you go hunting the African idea with the flag of your own religion or opinions floating ostentatiously over you, you will similarly get a very poor bag.

A few hints as to your mental outfit when starting on this sport may be useful. Before starting for West Africa, burn all your notions about sun-myths and worship of the elemental forces. My own opinion is you had better also burn the notion, although it is fashionable, that human beings got their first notion of the origin of the soul from dreams.

I went out with my mind full of the deductions of every book on Ethnology, German or English, that I had read during fifteen years—and being a good Cambridge person, I was particularly confident that from Mr Frazer's book, *The Golden Bough*, I had got a semi-universal key to the underlying idea of native custom and belief. But I soon found this was very far from being the case. His idea is a true key to a certain quantity of facts, but in West Africa only to a limited quantity.

I do not say, do not read Ethnology—by all means do so; and above all things read, until you know it by heart, *Primitive*

Culture, by Dr E. B. Tylor, regarding which book I may say that I have never found a fact that flew in the face of the carefully made, broad-minded deductions of this greatest of Ethnologists. In addition, you must know your Westermarck on *Human Marriage*, and your Waitz *Anthropologie*, and your Topinard—not that you need expect to go measuring people's skulls and chests as this last named authority expects you to do, for no self-respecting person black or white likes that sort of thing from the hands of an utter stranger, and if you attempt it you'll get yourself disliked in West Africa. Add to this the knowledge of all A. B. Ellis's works; Burton's *Anatomy of Melancholy;* Pliny's *Natural History;* and as much of Aristotle as possible. If you have a good knowledge of the Greek and Latin classics, I think it would be an immense advantage; an advantage I do not possess, for my classical knowledge is scrappy, and in place of it I have a knowledge of Red Indian dogma: a dogma by the way that seems to me much nearer the African in type than Asiatic forms of dogma.

Armed with these instruments of observation, with a little industry and care you should in the mill of your mind be able to make the varied tangled rag-bag of facts that you will soon become possessed of into a paper. And then I advise you to lay the results of your collection before some great thinker and he will write upon it the opinion that his greater and clearer vision makes him more fit to form.

However good may be the outfit for your work that you take with you, you will have, at first, great difficulty in realising that it is possible for the people you are among really to believe things in the way they do. And you cannot associate with them long before you must recognise that these Africans have often a remarkable mental acuteness and a large share of common sense; that there is nothing really 'child-like' in their form of mind at all. Observe them further and you will find they are not a flighty-minded, mystical set of people in the least. They are not dreamers, or poets, and you will observe, and I hope observe closely—for to my mind this is the most important difference between their make of mind and our own—that they are notably deficient in all mechanical arts: they have never made, unless under white direction and instruction, a single fourteenth-rate piece of cloth, pottery, a tool or machine, house, road, bridge, picture or statue; that a written language of their own construction they none of them possess.

A careful study of the things a man, black or white fails to do,

whether for good or evil, usually gives you a truer knowledge of the man than the things he succeeds in doing. When you fully realise this acuteness on one hand, and this mechanical incapacity on the other, which exist in the people you are studying, you can go ahead. Only, I beseech you, go ahead carefully. When you have found the easy key that opens the reason underlying a series of facts, as for example, these: a Benga spits on your hand as a greeting; you see a man who has been marching regardless through the broiling sun all the forenoon, with a heavy load, on entering a village and having put down his load, elaborately steal round in the shelter of the houses, instead of crossing the street; you come across a tribe that cuts its dead up into small pieces and scatters them broadcast, and another tribe that thinks a white man's eye-ball is a most desirable thing to be possessed of—do not, when you have found this key, drop your collecting work, and go home with a shriek of 'I know all about Fetish', because you don't, for the key to the above facts will not open the reason why it is regarded advisable to kill a person who is making Ikung; or why you should avoid at night a cotton tree that has red earth at its roots; or why combings of hair and paring of nails should be taken care of; or why a speck of blood that may fall from your flesh should be cut out of wood—if it has fallen on that—and destroyed, and if it has fallen on the ground stamped and rubbed into the soil with great care. This set requires another key entirely.

I must warn you also that your own mind requires protection when you send it stalking the savage idea through the tangled forests, the dark caves, the swamps and the fogs of the Ethiopian intellect. The best protection lies in recognising the untrustworthiness of human evidence regarding the unseen, and also the seen, when it is viewed by a person who has in his mind an explanation of the phenomenon before it occurs. For example, taken a person who, believing in ghosts, sees a white figure in a churchyard, bolts home, has fits, and on revival states he has seen a ghost, and gives details. He has seen a ghost and therefore he is telling the truth. Another person who does not believe in ghosts sees the thing, flies at it and finds its component parts are boy and bed-sheet.

I warn you that, with all precaution, the study of African metaphysics is bad for the brain, when you go and carry it on among all the weird, often unaccountable surroundings, and depressing scenery of the Land of the Shadow of Death—a land that stretches from Goree to Loanda.

The fascination of the African point of view is as sure to linger in your mind as the malaria in your body. The truth is, the study of natural phenomena knocks the bottom out of any man's conceit if it is done honestly and not by selecting only those facts that fit in with his pre-conceived or ingrafted notions. And, to my mind, the wisest way is to get into the state of mind of an old marine engineer who oils and sees that every screw and bolt of his engines is clean and well watched, and who loves them as living things, caressing and scolding them himself, defending them, with stormy language, against the aspersions of the silly, uninformed outside world, which persists in regarding them as mere machines, a thing his superior intelligence and experience knows they are not. Even animistic-minded I got awfully sat upon the other day in Cameroon by a superior but kindred spirit, in the form of a First Engineer. I had thoughtlessly repeated some scandalous gossip against the character of a naphtha launch in the river. 'Stuff!' said he furiously; 'she's all right, and she'd go from June to January if those blithering fools would let her alone.' Of course I apologised.

The religious ideas of the Negroes, *i.e.*, the West Africans in the district from the Gambia to the Cameroon region, say roughly to the Rio del Rey (for the Bakwiri appear to have more of the Bantu form of idea than the Negro, although physically they seem nearer the latter), differ very considerably from the religious ideas of the Bantu South-West Coast tribes. The Bantu is vague on religious subjects; he gives one accustomed to the Negro the impression that he once had the same set of ideas, but has forgotten half of them, and those that he possesses have not got that hold on him that the corresponding or super-imposed Christian ideas have over the true Negro; although he is quite as keen on the subject of witchcraft, and his witchcraft differs far less from the witchcraft of the Negro than his religious ideas do.

The god, in the sense we use the word, is in essence the same in all of the Bantu tribes I have met with on the Coast: a non-interfering and therefore a negligible quantity. He varies his name: Anzambi, Anyambi, Nyambi, Nzambi, Anzam, Nyam, Ukuku, Suku and Nzam, but a better investigation shows that Nzam of the Fans is practically identical with Suku south of the Congo in the Bihe country, and so on.

They regard their god as the creator of man, plants, animals, and the earth, and they hold that having made them, he takes no further interest in the affair. But not so the crowd of spirits with

which the universe is peopled, they take only too much interest and the Bantu wishes they would not and is perpetually saying so in his prayers, a large percentage whereof amounts to 'Go away, we don't want you.' 'Come not into this house, this village, or its plantations.' He knows from experience that the spirits pay little heed to these objurgations, and as they are the people who must be attended to, he develops a cult whereby they may be managed, used and understood. This cult is what we call witchcraft.

As I am not here writing a complete work on Fetish I will leave Nzam on one side, and turn to the inferior spirits. These are almost all malevolent; sometimes they can be coaxed into having creditable feelings, like generosity and gratitude, but you can never trust them. No, not even if you are yourself a well-established medicine man. Indeed they are particularly dangerous to medicine men, just as lions are to lion tamers, and many a professional gentleman, in the full bloom of his practice, gets eaten up by his own particular familiar which he has to keep in his own inside whenever he has not sent it off into other people's.

I am indebted to the Reverend Doctor Nassau for a great quantity of valuable information regarding Bantu religious ideas—information which no one is so competent to give as he, for no one else knows the West Coast Bantu tribes with the same thoroughness and sympathy. He has lived among them since 1851, and is perfectly conversant with their languages and culture, and he brings to bear upon the study of them a singularly clear, powerful, and highly-educated intelligence.

He says the origin of these spirits is vague—some of them come into existence by the authority of Anzam, others are self-existent—many are distinctly the souls of departed human beings, 'which in the future which is all around them' retain their human wants and feelings, and the Doctor assures me he has heard dying people with their last breath threatening to return as spirits to revenge themselves upon their living enemies. He could not tell me if there was any duration set upon the existence as spirits of these human souls, but two Congo Français natives, of different tribes, Benga and Igalwa, told me that when a family had quite died out, after a time its spirits died too. Some, but by no means all, of these spirits of human origin, as is the case among the Negro Effiks, undergo reincarnation. The Doctor told me he once knew a man whose plantations were devastated by an elephant. He advised that the beast

should be shot, but the man said he dare not because the spirit of his dead father had passed into the elephant.

Their number is infinite and their powers as varied as human imagination can make them; classifying them is therefore a difficult work, but Doctor Nassau thinks this may be done fairly completely into:

1. Human disembodied spirits – *Manu*.
2. Vague beings, well described by our word ghosts: *Abambo*.
3. Beings something like dryads, who resent intrusion into their territory, on to their rock, past their promontory, or tree. When passing the residence of one of these beings, the traveller must go by silently, or with some cabalistic invocation, with bowed or bared head, and deposit some symbol of an offering or tribute even if it be only a pebble. You occasionally come across great trees that have fallen across a path that have quite little heaps of pebbles, small shells, &c., upon them deposited by previous passers-by. This class is called *Ombwiri*.
4. Beings who are the agents in causing sickness, and either aid or hinder human plans – *Mionde*.
5. There seems to be, the Doctor says, another class of spirits somewhat akin to the ancient Lares and Penates, who especially belong to the household, and descend by inheritance with the family. In their honour are secretly kept a bundle of finger, or other, bones, nail-clippings, eyes, brains, &c., accumulated from deceased members of successive generations.

Dr Nassau says 'secretly', and he refers to this custom being existent in non-cannibal tribes. I saw bundles of this character among the cannibal Fans, and among the non-cannibal Adooma, openly hanging up in the thatch of the sleeping apartment.

6. He also says there may be a sixth class, which may, however, only be a function of any of the other classes—namely, those that enter into any animal body, generally a leopard. Sometimes the spirits of living human beings do this, and the animal is then guided by human intelligence, and will exercise its strength for the purposes of its temporary human possessor. In other cases it is a non-human soul that enters into the animal, as in the case of Ukuku.

Spirits are not easily classified by their functions because those of different class may be employed in identical undertakings. Thus one witch-doctor may have, I find, particular influence over one class of spirit and another over another class; yet they will both engage to do identical work. But in spite of this I do not see how you can classify spirits otherwise than by their

functions; you cannot weigh and measure them, and it is only a few that show themselves in corporeal form.

There are characteristics that all the authorities seem agreed on, and one is that individual spirits in the same class vary in power: some are strong of their sort, some weak.

They are all to a certain extent limited in the nature of their power; there is no one spirit that can do all things; their efficiency only runs in certain lines of action and all of them are capable of being influenced, and made subservient to human wishes, by proper incantations. This latter characteristic is of course to human advantage, but it has its disadvantages, for you can never really trust a spirit, even if you have paid a considerable sum to a most distinguished medicine man to get a powerful one put up in a ju-ju, or monde, as it is called in several tribes.

The method of making these charms is much the same among Bantu and Negroes, so I here confine myself to the Bantu. This similarity of procedure naturally arises from the same underlying idea existing in the two races.

You call in the medicine man, the 'oganga', as he is commonly called in Congo Français tribes. After a variety of ceremonies and processes, the spirit is induced to localise itself in some object subject to the will of the possessor. The things most frequently used are antelopes' horns, the large snail-shells, and large nut-shells, according to Doctor Nassau. Among the Fan I found the most frequent charm-case was in the shape of a little sausage, made very neatly of pineapple fibre, the contents being the residence of the spirit or power, and the outside coloured red to flatter and please him—for spirits always like red.

The substance put inside charms is all manner of nastiness, usually on the sea coast having a high percentage of fowl dung.

The nature of the substance depends on the spirit it is intended to be attractive to—attractive enough to induce it to leave its present abode and come and reside in the charm.

In addition to this attractive substance I find there are other materials inserted which have relation towards the work the spirit will be wanted to do for its owner. For example, charms made either to influence a person to be well disposed towards the owner, or the still larger class made with intent to work evil on other human beings against whom the owner has a grudge, must have in them some portion of the person to be dealt with—his hair, blood, nail-parings, &c.—or, failing that, his or her most intimate belonging, something that has got his smell in—a piece of his old waist-cloth for example.

This ability to obtain power over people by means of their blood, hair, nails, &c., is universally diffused; you will find it down in Devon, and away in far Cathay, and the Chinese, I am told, have in some parts of their empire little ovens to burn their nail- and hair-clippings in. The fear of these latter belongings falling into the hands of evilly-disposed persons is ever present to the West Africans. The Igalwa and other tribes will allow no one but a trusted friend to do their hair, and bits of nails and hair are carefully burnt or thrown away into a river; and blood, even that from a small cut or a fit of nose-bleeding, is most carefully covered up and stamped out if it has fallen on the earth. Dr Nassau says, 'If it falls on the side of a canoe, or a tree the place is carefully cut out and the chip destroyed.' Blood from a wound on a woman is held in high horror. This has probably something to do with the drawing of blood constituting grounds of divorce among the Igalwa. A Fan told me that a man in the village, who was so weak from some cause or other that he could hardly crawl about, had fallen into this state by seeing the blood of a woman who had been killed by a falling tree. The underlying idea regarding blood is of course the old one that the blood is the life.

The life in Africa means a spirit, hence the liberated blood is the liberated spirit, and liberated spirits are always whipping into people who do not want them. In the case of the young Fan, the opinion held was that the weak spirit of the woman had got into him. I could not help being reminded of the saying one often hears from a person in England who has seen some tragedy, —'I cannot get the horror of it out of my eyes.' This 'horror' would mean to an African a spirit coming from the thing itself.

Charms are made for every occupation and desire in life— loving, hating, buying, selling, fishing, planting, travelling, hunting, &c., and although they are usually in the form of things filled with a mixture in which the spirit nestles, yet there are other kinds; for example, a great love charm is made of the water the lover has washed in, and this, mingled with the drink of the loved one, is held to soften the hardest heart. Of a similar nature is the friendship-compelling charm I know of on the Ivory Coast, which I have been told is used also in the Batanga regions. This is obtained on the death of a person you know really cared for you—like your father or mother, for example—by cutting off the head and suspending it over a heap of chalk, as the white earth that you find in river beds is called here, then letting it drip as long as it will and using this saturated chalk to mix in

among the food of anyone you wish should think kindly of you and trust you. This charm, a Bassa man said to me, 'was good too much for the white trader', and made him give you 'good price too much' for palm oil, &c., and that statement revived my sympathy for a friend who once said to me that when he used first to come to the Coast he had 'pretty well had the inside raked up out of him' from the sickness caused by the charms that his local cook administered to him in the interest of the cook's friends. That man keeps an Accra cook now, and I trust lives a life of healthy, icy, unemotional calm.

Some kinds of charms, such as those to prevent your getting drowned, shot, seen by elephants, &c., are worn on a bracelet or necklace. A new-born child starts with a health-knot tied round the wrist, neck or loins, and throughout the rest of its life its collection of charms goes on increasing. This collection does not, however, attain inconvenient dimensions, owing to the failure of some of the charms to work.

That is the worst of charms and prayers. The thing you wish of them may, and frequently does, happen in a strikingly direct way, but other times it does not. In Africa this is held to arise from the bad character of the spirits; their gross ingratitude and fickleness. You may have taken every care of a spirit for years, given it food and other offerings that you wanted for yourself, wrapped it up in your cloth on chilly nights and gone cold, put it in the only dry spot in the canoe, and so on, and yet after all this, the wretched thing will be capable of being got at by your rival or enemy and lured away, leaving you only the case it once lived in.

Finding, we will say, that you have been upset and half-drowned, and your canoe-load of goods lost three times in a week, that your paddles are always breaking, and the amount of snags in the river and so on is abnormal, you judge that your canoe-charm has stopped. Then you go to the medicine man who supplied you with it and complain. He says it was a perfectly good charm when he sold it you and he never had any complaints before, but he will investigate the affair; when he has done so, he either says the spirit has been lured away from the home he prepared for it by incantations and presents from other people, or that he finds the spirit is dead; it has been killed by a more powerful spirit of its class, which is in the pay of some enemy of yours.

In all cases the little thing you kept the spirit in is no use now, and only fit to sell to a white man as 'a big curio!' and the sooner

you let him have sufficient money to procure you a fresh and still more powerful spirit—necessarily more expensive—the safer it will be for you, particularly as your misfortunes distinctly point to someone being desirous of your death. You of course grumble, but seeing the thing in his light you pay up, and the medicine man goes busily to work with incantations, dances, looking into mirrors or basins of still water, and concoctions of messes to make you a new protecting charm.

Human eye-balls, particularly of white men, I have already said are a great charm. Dr Nassau says he has known graves rifled for them. This, I fancy, is to secure the 'man that lives in your eyes' for the service of the village, and naturally the white man, being regarded as a superior being, would be of high value if enlisted into its service. A similar idea of the possibility of gaining possession of the spirit of a dead man obtains among the Negroes, and the heads of important chiefs in the Calabar districts are usually cut off from the body on burial and kept secretly for fear the head, and thereby the spirit, of the dead chief, should be stolen from the town. If it [the head] were stolen it would be not only a great advantage to its new possessor, but a great danger to the chief's old town, because it would know all the peculiar ju-ju relating to [the town]. For each town has a peculiar one, kept exceedingly secret, in addition to the general ju-jus, and this secret one would then be in the hands of the new owners of the spirit. It is for similar reasons that brave General MacCarthy's head was treasured by the Ashantees, and so on.

Charms are not all worn upon the body, some go to the plantations, and are hung there, ensuring an unhappy and swift end for the thief who comes stealing. Some are hung round the bows of the canoe, others over the doorway of the house, to prevent evil spirits from coming in—a sort of tame watch-dog spirit.

The entrances to the long street-shaped villages are frequently closed with a fence of saplings and this sapling fence you will see hung with fetish charms to prevent evil spirits from entering the village; and sometimes in addition to charms you will see the fence wreathed with leaves and flowers. I tried to find out whether these leaves were for the residence or amusement of the protecting spirits, or whether they were traps for the evil spirits attempting to enter the town. Both reasons were given me, the latter most definitely.

Frequently a sapling is tied horizontally near the ground

across the entrance. Dr Nassau could not tell me why, but says it must never be trodden on. When the smallpox, a dire pestilence in these regions, is raging, or when there is war, these gateways are sprinkled with the blood of sacrifices, and for these sacrifices and for the payments of heavy blood fines, &c., goats and sheep are kept. They are rarely eaten for ordinary purposes, and these West Coast Africans have all a perfect horror of the idea of drinking milk, holding this custom to be a filthy habit, and saying so in unmitigated language.

The villagers eat the meat of the sacrifice, that having nothing to do with the sacrifice to the spirits, which is the blood, for the blood is the life.

Beside the few spirits that the Bantu regards himself as having got under control in his charms, he has to worship the uncontrolled army of the air. This he does by sacrifice and incantation.

The sacrifice is the usual killing of something valuable as an offering to the spirits. The value of the offering in these S.W. Coast regions has certainly a regular relationship to the value of the favour required of the spirits. Some favours are worth a dish of plantains, some a fowl, some a goat and some a human being, though human sacrifice is very rare in Congo Français, the killing of people being nine times in ten a witchcraft palaver.

In some part of the long single street of most villages there is built a low hut in which charms are hung, and by which grows a consecrated plant, a lily, a euphorbia or a fig. In some tribes a rudely carved figure, generally female, is set up as an idol before which offerings are laid. I saw at Egaja two figures about 2 feet 6 inches high, in the house placed at my disposal. They were left in it during my occupation, save that the rolls of cloth (their power) which were round their necks, were removed by the owner chief; of the significance of these rolls I will speak elsewhere.

Incantations may be divided into two classes, supplications analogous to our idea of prayers, and certain cabalistic words and phrases. The supplications are addresses to the higher spirits. Some are made even to Anzam himself, but the spirit of the new moon is that most commonly addressed to keep the lower spirits from molesting.

Regarding the cabalistic words and phrases, things which had long given me great trouble to get any comprehension of, Doctor Nassau gave me great help. He says some of these phrases and words are coined by the person himself, others are archaisms handed down from ancestors and believed to possess an efficacy,

though their actual meaning is forgotten. He says they are used at any time as defence from evil, when a person is startled, sneezes or stumbles. Among these I think I ought to class that peculiar form of friendly farewell or greeting which the Doctor poetically calls a 'blown blessing' and the natives Ibata. I thought the three times it was given to me that it was just spitting on the hand. Practically it is so, but the Doctor says the spitting is accidental, a by-product I suppose. The method consists in taking the right hand in both yours, turning it palm upwards, bending your head low over it, and saying with great energy and a violent propulsion of the breath, Ibata.

Idols are comparatively rare in Congo Français, but where they are used the people have the same idea about them as the true Negroes have, namely, that they are things which spirits reside in, or haunt, but not in their corporeal nature adorable. The resident spirit in them and in the charms and plants, which are also regarded as residences of spirits, has to be placated with offerings of food and other sacrifices. You will see in the Fetish huts above mentioned dishes of plantain and fish left till they rot. Dr Nassau says the life or essence of the food only is eaten by the spirit, the form of the vegetable or flesh being left to be removed when its life is gone out. The Calabar Negroes told me that the spirits often take the forms of lizards—which abound in this country—and come and eat the food, and they always seem to doubt whether the offered food has reached its proper destination unless some animal has eaten it. But for one thing, as I have said before, the true Negro is more definite in his ideas, and his gods and spirits very practical individuals, whereas the Bantu are vaguer, and moreover there are not so many lizards in Congo Français, so perhaps the native metaphysician is forced to be more spiritual in his ideas about his sacrifice.

In cases of emergency a fowl with its blood is laid at the door of the Fetish hut, or when pestilence is expected, or an attack by enemies, or a great man or woman is very ill, goats and sheep are sacrificed and the blood put in the Fetish hut as well as on the gateways of the village. These sacrifices among the Fan are made with a very peculiar-shaped knife, a fine specimen of which I secured by the kindness of Captain Davies; it is shaped like the head of a hornbill and is quite unlike the knives in common use among the tribes, which are either long, leaf-shaped blades sharpened along both edges, or broad, trowel-shaped, almost triangular daggers. All Fan knives are fine weapons, superior to the knives of all other Coast tribes I have met with,

but the sacrifice knife is distinctly peculiar. It is perfectly adapted for killing animals by a blow behind the head, at the top of the spine, and this is the way I have seen it used.

I found to my great interest the same superstition in Congo Français that I met with first in the Oil Rivers. Its meaning I am unable to fully account for, but I believe it to be a form of sacrifice. In Calabar each individual has a certain forbidden thing or things. These things are either forms of food, or the method of eating. In Calabar this prohibition is called Ibet* and when, in consequence of the influence of white culture, a man gives up his Ibet, he is regarded by good sound ju-juists as leading an irregular and dissipated life, and even the unintentional breaking of the Ibet is regarded as very dangerous. For example, in buying a slave the purchaser always inquires what is the slave's Ibet, because if the slave were given his Ibet to eat, he would get ill; again, once when staying with my esteemed friend Miss Mary Slessor at Okÿon, there arrived among her crowd of patients a small boy with a very 'sick foot'. On being asked from what it had arisen, instead of getting the usual answer, 'picked up medicine on the road', the boy said he had broken his Ibet. Miss Slessor told me that shortly after a child is born some of the elderly female relatives meet together and find out, by their magic, what the child's Ibet during life is to be. When they have done so, it is made known and he has to keep to it.

Special days are set apart by each individual; on these days he eats only the smallest quantity and plainest quality of food. No one must eat with him, nor any dog, fowl, &c., feed off the crumbs, nor anyone watch him while eating. I suspect on this day the Ibet is eaten, but I have not verified this, only getting, from an untrustworthy source, a statement that supported it.

Dr Nassau told me that among Congo Français tribes certain rites are performed for children during infancy or youth, in which a prohibition ['Orunda'] is laid upon the child as regards the eating of some particular article of food, or the doing of certain acts. Anything may be an Orunda provided only that it is connected with food; I have been able to find no definite ground for the selection of it. The Doctor said, for example, that 'once when on a boat journey, and camped in the forest for the noon-day meal, the crew of four had no meat. They needed it. I had a chicken but ate only a portion, and gave the rest to the

* Mary Kingsley says elsewhere that the drinking of unboiled water is her own *ibet*. (EH)

crew. Three men ate it with their manioc meal, the fourth would not touch it. It was his Orunda.' 'On another journey,' said the Doctor, 'instead of all my crew leaving me respectfully alone in the canoe to have my lunch and going ashore to have theirs, one of them stayed behind in the canoe, and I found his Orunda was only to eat over water when on a journey by water.' 'At another place, a chief at whose village we once anchored in a small steamer when a glass of rum was given him, had a piece of cloth held up before his mouth that the people might not see him drink, which was his Orunda.'

The word Orunda means prohibition, the Doctor says. In Effik I found the word Ibet meant a command—a law—an abstinence.

CHAPTER TEN

The World of the Spirit

It is exceedingly interesting to compare the ideas of the Negroes with those of the Bantu. At present I have a more definite knowledge of the former, but I have gained sufficient knowledge of the West Coast Bantu to be able to commence a regular comparative study of these two analogous, but by no means identical, sets of ideas.

One thing about Negro and Bantu races is very certain, and that is that their lives are dominated by a profound belief in witchcraft and its effects.

Among both alike the rule is that death is regarded as a direct consequence of the witchcraft of some malevolent human being, acting by means of spirits, over which he has, by some means or another, obtained control.

To all rules there are exceptions. Among the Calabar Negroes, who are definite in their opinions, I found two classes of exceptions. The first arises from their belief in a bush-soul. They believe every man has four souls: *a*, the soul that survives death; *b*, the shadow on the path; *c*, the dream-soul; *d*, the bush-soul.

This bush-soul is always in the form of an animal in the forest —never of a plant. Sometimes when a man sickens it is because his bush-soul is angry at being neglected, and a witch-doctor is called in, who, having diagnosed this as being the cause of the complaint, advises the administration of some kind of offering to the offended one. When you wander about in the forests of the Calabar region, you will frequently see little dwarf huts with these offerings in them. You must not confuse these huts with those of similar construction you are continually seeing in plantations, or near roads, which refer to quite other affairs. These offerings, in the little huts in the forest, are placed where your bush-soul was last seen. Unfortunately, you are compelled to call in a doctor, which is an expense, but you cannot see your own bush-soul, unless you are an Ebumtup, a sort of second-sighter.

Ebumtupism is rare, and if you do happen to possess this gift, it is discovered by the presiding elders during your initiation to the secret society of your tribe. When it is discovered, the

presiding elders strongly advise that you should enter the medical profession and become a witch-doctor, as this profession is a paying one, although the training for it is dreadfully expensive to your parents, for it has to be carried on by the established witch-doctor. Your parents, if you are discovered to be an Ebumtup, usually make sacrifices after the way of parents, black or white, and you proceed with your studies.

But to return to the bush-soul of an ordinary person. If the offering in the hut works well on the bush-soul, the patient recovers, but if it does not, he dies. Diseases arising from derangements in the temper of the bush-soul, however, even when treated by the most eminent practitioners, are very apt to be intractable, because it never realises that by injuring you it endangers its own existence. For when its human owner dies, the bush-soul can no longer find a good place, and goes mad, rushing to and fro—if it sees a fire it rushes into it; if it sees a lot of people it rushes among them, until it is killed, and when it is killed it is 'finish' for it, as M. Pichault would say, for it is not an immortal soul.

The bush-souls of a family are usually the same for a man and for his sons, for a mother and for her daughters. Sometimes, however, I am told all the children take the mother's, sometimes all take the father's. They may be almost any kind of animal, sometimes they are leopards, sometimes fish, or tortoises, and so on.

There is another peculiarity about the bush-soul, and that is that it is on its account that old people are held in such esteem among the Calabar tribes. For, however bad these old people's personal record may have been, the fact of their longevity demonstrates the possession of powerful and astute bush-souls. On the other hand, a man may be a quiet, respectable citizen, devoted to peace and a whole skin, and yet he may have a sadly flighty disreputable bush-soul which will get itself killed or damaged and cause him death or continual ill-health.

There is another way by which a man dies apart from the action of bush-souls or witchcraft; he may have had a bad illness from some cause in his previous life and, when reincarnated, part of this disease may get reincarnated with him and then he will ultimately die of it. There is no medicine of any avail against these reincarnated diseases.

The idea of reincarnation is very strong in the Niger Delta tribes. It exists, as far as I have been able to find out, throughout all Africa, but usually only in scattered cases, as it were; but

in the Delta, most—I think I may say all—human souls of the 'surviving soul' class are regarded as returning to the earth again, and undergoing a reincarnation shortly after the due burial of the soul.

These two exceptions from the rule of all deaths and sickness being caused by witchcraft are, however, of minor importance, for infinitely the larger proportion of death and sickness is held to arise from witchcraft itself, more particularly among the Bantu.

Witchcraft acts in two ways, namely, witching something out of a man, or witching something into him. The former method is used by both Negro and Bantu, but is decidedly more common among the Negroes, where the witches are continually setting traps to catch the soul that wanders from the body when a man is sleeping; and when they have caught this soul, they tie it up over the canoe fire and its owner sickens as the soul shrivels.

This is merely a regular line of business, and not an affair of individual hate or revenge. The witch does not care whose dream-soul gets into the trap, and will restore it on payment. Also witch-doctors, men of unblemished professional reputation, will keep asylums for lost souls, *i.e.*, souls who have been out wandering and found on their return to their body that their place has been filled up by a Sisa, a low class soul I will speak of later. These doctors keep souls and administer them to patients who are short of the article.

But there are other witches, either wicked on their own account, or hired by people who are moved by some hatred to individuals, and then the trap is carefully set and baited for the soul of the particular man they wish to injure, and concealed in the bait at the bottom of the pot are knives and sharp hooks which tear and damage the soul, either killing it outright, or mauling it so that it causes its owner sickness on its return to him. I knew the case of a Kruman who for several nights had smelt in his dreams the savoury smell of smoked crawfish seasoned with red peppers. He became anxious, and the headman decided some witch had set a trap baited with this dainty for his dream-soul, with intent to do him grievous bodily harm, and great trouble was taken for the next few nights to prevent this soul of his from straying abroad.

My attention was drawn to the case by snorts, snores and flumps on the Kruman's part of even more than usual violence, and I went to see what was up with the man, mentally deciding that what he wanted was a dose of my pet pill. I found him

under a blanket and his nose and mouth tied over with a handkerchief. It was a sweltering hot night and the man was as wet with sweat as if he had been dragged through a river, so I suggested his muzzle should be removed; and then being informed of the state of affairs regarding his soul, I of course did not interfere.

The witching of things into a man is far the most frequent method among the Bantu, hence the prevalence among them of the post-mortem examination—a practice I never found among the Negroes.

The idea of the majority of deaths arising from witchcraft is, I believe, quite true if you will read witchcraft as poison. In a dull sort of way sometimes the black man understands it so too, as is shown by his very generally regarding the best remedy for witching as being a brisk purgative and emetic, accompanied of course with suitable ceremonies.

The belief in witchcraft is the cause of more African deaths than anything else. It has killed and still kills more men and women than the slave-trade. Its only rival is perhaps the small-pox, the Grand Kraw-Kraw as the Krumen graphically call it.

At almost every death a suspicion of witchcraft arises. The witch-doctor is called in, and proceeds to find out the guilty person. Then woe to the unpopular men, the weak women and the slaves; for on some of them will fall the accusation that means ordeal by poison, or fire, followed, if these point to guilt, as from their nature they usually do, by a terrible death: slow roasting alive—mutilation by degrees before the throat is mercifully cut—tying to stakes at low tide that the high tide may come and drown—and any other death human ingenuity and hate can devise.

The terror in which witchcraft is held is interesting in spite of all its horror. I have seen mild, gentle men and women turned by it, in a moment, to incarnate fiends, ready to rend and destroy those who a second before were nearest and dearest to them. Terrible is the fear that falls like a spell upon a village when a big man, or big woman, is just known to be dead. The very men catch their breaths and grow grey round the lips, and then every one, particularly those belonging to the household of the deceased, goes in for the most demonstrative exhibition of grief. Long, low howls creep up out of the first silence—those blood-curdling, infinitely melancholy, wailing howls—once heard, never to be forgotten.

The men tear off their clothes and wear only the most filthy

rags; women, particularly the widows, take off ornaments and almost all dress; their faces are painted white with chalk, their heads are shaven, and they sit crouched on the earth in the house, in the attitude of abasement, the hands resting on the shoulders, palm downwards, not crossed across the breast, unless they are going into the street.

Meanwhile the witch-doctor has been sent for, if he is not already present, and he sets to work in different ways to find out who are the persons guilty of causing the death.

Whether the methods vary with the tribe, or with the individual witch-doctor, I cannot absolutely say, but I think largely with the latter.

Among the Benga I saw a witch-doctor going round a village ringing a small bell which was to stop ringing outside the hut of the guilty. Among the Cabindas (Fjort) I saw, at different times, two witch-doctors trying to find witches, one by means of taking on and off the lid of a small basket while he repeated the names of all the people in the village. When the lid refused to come off at the name of a person, that person was doomed. The other Cabinda doctor first tried throwing nuts upon the ground, also repeating names. That method apparently failed. Then he resorted to another, rubbing the flattened palms of his hands against each other. When the palms refused to meet at a name, and his hands flew about wildly, he had got his man.

The accused person, if he denies the guilt, and does not claim the ordeal, is tortured until he not only acknowledges his guilt but names his accomplices in the murder, for remember this witchcraft is murder in the African eyes. It is not just producing the parlour tricks of modern spiritualists.

If he claims the ordeal, as he usually does, he usually has to take a poison drink. Among all the Bantu tribes I know this is made from Sass wood (sass = bad; sass water = rough water; sass surf = bad surf, &c.), and is a decoction of the freshly pulled bark of a great hardwood forest tree, which has a tall unbranched stem, terminating in a crown of branches bearing small leaves. Among the Calabar tribes the ordeal drink is of two kinds: one made from the Calabar bean, the other, the great ju-ju drink Mbiam, which is used also in taking oaths.

In both the sass-wood and Calabar bean drink, the only chance for the accused lies in squaring the witch-doctor, so that in the case of the sass-wood drink it is allowed to settle before administration, and in the bean that you get a very heavy dose, both arrangements tending to produce the immediate emetic

effect indicative of innocence. If this effect does not come on quickly you die a miserable death from the effects of the poison interrupted by the means taken to kill you as soon as it is decided from the absence of violent sickness that you are guilty.

The Mbiam is not poisonous, nor is its use confined, as the use of the bean is, entirely to witch palaver; but it is the most respected and dreaded of all oaths, and from its decision there is but one appeal, the appeal open to all condemned persons, but rarely made—the appeal to Long ju-ju. This Long ju-ju means almost certain death, and before it a severe frightening that is worse to a Negro mind than mere physical torture.

The Mbiam oath formula I was able to secure in the upper districts of the Calabar. One form of it runs thus, and it is recited before swallowing the drink made of filth and blood:

If I have been guilty of this crime,
If I have gone and sought the sick one's hurt,
If I have sent another to seek the sick one's hurt,
If I have employed anyone to make charms or to cook bush,
Or to put anything in the road,
Or to touch his cloth,
Or to touch his yams,
Or to touch his goats,
Or to touch his fowl,
Or to touch his children,
If I have prayed for his hurt,
If I have thought to hurt him in my heart,
If I have any intention to hurt him,
If I ever, at any time, do any of these things (recite in full),
Or employ others to do these things (recite in full)
Then, Mbiam! Thou deal with me.

This form I give was for use when a man was sick, and things were generally going badly with him, for it is not customary in cases of disease to wait until death occurs before making an accusation of witchcraft. In the case of Mbiam being administered after a death, this long and complicated oath would be worded to meet the case most carefully, the future intention clauses being omitted. In all cases, whenever it is used, the greatest care is taken that the oath be recited in full, oath-takers being sadly prone to kiss their thumb, as it were, particularly ladies who are taking Mbiam for accusations of adultery, in conjunction with the boiling oil ordeal. Indeed, so unreliable is

this class of offenders, or let us rather say this class of suspected persons, that someone usually says the oath for them.

From the penalty and inconveniences of these accusations of witchcraft there is but one escape, namely flight to a sanctuary. There are several sanctuaries in Congo Français. The great one in the Calabar district is at Omon. Thither mothers of twins, widows, thieves and slaves fly, and if they reach it are safe. But an attempt at flight is a confession of guilt; no one is quite certain the accusation will fall on him, or her, and hopes for the best until it is generally too late. Moreover, flying anywhere beyond a day's march, is difficult work in West Africa. So the killing goes on and it is no uncommon thing for ten or more people to be destroyed for one man's sickness or death; and thus over immense tracts of country the death-rate exceeds the birth-rate. Indeed some of the smaller tribes have thus been almost wiped out. In the Calabar district I have heard of entire villages taking the bean voluntarily because another village had accused it *en bloc* of witchcraft. It amounts almost to a mania with these people. Miss Slessor has frequently told me how, during a quarrel, one person has accused another of witchcraft, and the accused has bolted off in a towering rage and swallowed the bean.

The witch-doctor is not always the cause of people being subjected to the ordeal or torture. In Calabar and the Okÿon districts all the widows of a dead man are subjected to ordeal.

They have to go the next night after the death, before an assemblage of chiefs and the general surrounding crowd, to a cleared space where there is a fire burning. A fowl is tied to the right hand of each widow, and should that fowl fail to cluck at the sight of the fire the woman is held guilty of having bewitched her husband and is dealt with accordingly.

Among the Bantu, although the killing among the wives from the accusation of witchcraft is high, some of them being almost certain to fall victims, yet there is not the wholesale slaughter of women and slaves sent down with the soul of the dead that there is among the Negroes.

Dr Nassau told me of an interesting case which had come under his notice. Once he met a native heathen Akele chief who showed him a string of shells, horns and wild cats' tails which he said could turn aside bullets. Although the Doctor is well known as a dead shot, the Akele dared him, in a friendly way, to shoot at him with a rifle, and to try him the Doctor pointed the

rifle at him, at the distance of a few paces, but the Akele never quailed, and 'of course,' said the Doctor, 'I did not fire'. Two years after, that same man when hunting was charged by a wounded elephant and pierced by its tusks. His attendants drove off the beast, and the fearfully lacerated man survived just long enough to accuse one of his women and some slaves of having bewitched his gun and thus caused his death, and on this accusation four people were killed.

In doubtful cases of death, *i.e.*, in all cases not arising from actual violence, when blood shows in the killing, the Bantu of the S.W. Coast make post-mortem examinations. Notably common is this practice among the Cameroons and Batanga region tribes. The body is cut open to find in the entrails some sign of the path of the injected witch.

I am informed that it is the lung that is most usually eaten by the spirit. If the deceased is a witch-doctor it is thought, as I have mentioned before, that his familiar spirit has eaten him internally, and he is opened with a view of securing and destroying his witch. In 1893 I saw in a village in Kacongo five unpleasant-looking objects stuck on sticks. They were the livers and lungs, and in fact the plucks, of witch-doctors, and the inhabitants informed me they were the witches that had been found in them on post-mortems and then been secured.

Again in 1893 I came across another instance of the post-mortem practice. A woman had dropped down dead on a factory beach at Corisco Bay. The natives could not make it out at all. They were irritated about her conduct: 'She no sick, she no complain, she no nothing, and then she go die one time.'

The post-mortem showed a burst aneurism. The native verdict was 'She done witch herself', *i.e.*, she was a witch eaten by her own familiar.

The general opinion held by people living near a river is that the spirit of a witch can take the form of a crocodile to do its work in; those who live away from large rivers or in districts like Congo Français, where crocodiles are not very savage, hold that the witch takes on the form of a leopard. Still the crocodile spirit form is believed in in Congo Français, and to a greater extent in Kacongo, because here the crocodiles of the Congo are very ferocious and numerous, taking as heavy a toll in human life as they do in the delta of the Niger and the estuaries of the Sierra Leone and Sherboro' Rivers.

One witch-doctor I know in Kacongo had a strange professional method. When, by means of his hand rubbings, &c., he had got

hold of a witch or a bewitched one, he always gave the unfortunate an emetic and always found several lively young crocodiles in the consequence. The stories of the natives in this region abound in accounts of people who have been carried off by witch crocodiles, and kept in places underground for years. I often wonder whether this idea may not have arisen from the well-known habit of the crocodile of burying its prey on the bank. Sometimes it will take off a limb of its victim at once, but frequently it buries the body whole for a few days before eating it. The body is always buried if it is left to the crocodile.

I have a most profound respect for the whole medical profession, but I am bound to confess that the African representatives of it are a little empirical in their methods of treatment. The African doctor is not always a witch-doctor in the bargain, but he is usually. Lady doctors abound. They are a bit dangerous in pharmacy, but they do not often venture on surgery, so on the whole they are safer, for African surgery is heroic. Dr Nassau cited the worst case of it I know of. A man had been accidentally shot in the chest by another man with a gun on the Ogowé. The native doctor who was called in made a perpendicular incision into the man's chest, extending down to the last rib; he then cut diagonally across, and actually lifted the wall of the chest, and groped about among the vitals for the bullet which he successfully extracted. Patient died. No anæsthetic was employed.

I came across a minor operation. A man had broken the ulna of the left arm. The native doctor got a piece—a very nice piece —of bamboo, drove it in through the muscles and integuments from the wrist to the elbow, then encased the limb in plantain leaves, and bound it round, tightly and neatly, needless to say with tie-tie. The arm and hand when I saw it, some six or seven months after the operation, was quite useless, and was withering away.

Many of their methods, however, are better. The Dualla medicos are truly great on poultices for extracting foreign substances, such as bits of iron cooking-pot—a very frequent form of foreign substance in a man out here, owing to their being generally used as bullets. Almost incredible stories are told by black and white of the efficacy of these poultices; one case I heard from a reliable source of a man who had been shot with fragments of iron pot in the thigh. The white doctor extracted several pieces and said he had got all out, but the man still went on suffering, and could not walk, so, at his request, a native doctor was called in, and he applied his poultice. In a

few minutes he removed it, and on its face were two pieces of jagged iron pot. Probably they had been in the poultice when it was applied, anyhow the patient recovered rapidly.

Baths accompanied by massage are much esteemed. The baths are sometimes of hot water with a few herbs thrown in, sometimes they are made by digging a hole in the earth and putting into it a quantity of herbs, and bruised cardamoms, and peppers. Boiling water is then plentifully poured over these and the patient is placed in the bath and is covered over with the par-boiled green stuff; a coating of clay is then placed over all, leaving just the head sticking out. The patient remains in this bath for a period of a few hours, up to a day and a half, and when taken out is well rubbed and kneaded. This form of bath I saw used by the M'pongwe and Igalwas, and it is undoubtedly good for many diseases, notably for that curse of the Coast, rheumatism, which afflicts black and white alike. Rubbing and kneading and hot baths are, I think, the best native remedies, and the plaster of grains-of-paradise pounded up, and mixed with clay, and applied to the forehead as a remedy for malarial headache, or brow ague, is often very useful, but apart from these, I have never seen, in any of these herbal remedies, any trace of a really valuable drug.

The Calabar natives are notably behindhand in their medical methods, depending more on ju-ju than the Bantus. In a case of rheumatism, for example, instead of ordering the hot bath, the local practitioner will 'woka' his patient and extract from the painful part, even when it has not been wounded, pieces of iron pot, millepedes, &c., and, in cases of dysentery, bundles of shred-up palm-leaves. These things, he asserts, have been by witchcraft inserted into the patient.

The strangest thing, however, that I ever heard of being witched into a man I was told of by a most intelligent Igalwa, a Christian and a very trustworthy man, and his statement was attested by another man, equally reliable, but not a Christian. They said that a relation of theirs had been witched two years previously. An emetic was administered, and there appeared upon the scene a strange little animal which grew with visible rapidity. An hour after its coming to light it crawled about, got out of its basin and then flew away. I tried my best to identify the species, but the nearest thing I could get to it was that it was like a small bat. It had bat's wings, but then it had a body and tail like a lizard, which was distracting of it, to a naturalist. This thing, they said, had been given to the man when it was

'small small', (*i.e.*, very small) in some drink or food, and if it had been left undisturbed by that emetic, it would have grown up inside the man, killing him by feeding on his vitals. There was no want of information or verbal testimony in the case, but I should have felt more sure about the affair if I could have got that thing in a bottle of pure alcohol. The only other case of this winged lizard I heard of was at Batanga, when a witch-doctor had been opened and a winged, lizard-like thing found in his inside, which, Batanga said, was his power.

Dying in West Africa, particularly in the Niger Delta, is made very unpleasant for the native by his friends and relations.

When a person is insensible, violent means are taken to recall the spirit to the body. Pepper is forced up the nose and into the eyes. The mouth is propped open with a stick. The shredded fibres of the outside of the oil-nut are set alight and held under the nose, and the whole crowd of friends and relations with whom the stifling hot hut is tightly packed yell the dying man's name at the top of their voices, in a way that makes them hoarse for days, just as if they were calling to a person lost in the bush or to a person struggling and being torn or lured away from them. 'Hi, hi, don't you hear? Come back, come back. See here. This is your place,' &c.

Among the Okÿon tribes especial care is taken in the case of a woman dying and leaving a child over six months old. The underlying idea is that the spirit of the mother is sure to come back and fetch the child, and in order to pacify her and prevent the child dying, it is brought in and held just in front of the dead body of the mother and then gradually carried away behind her where she cannot see it, and the person holding the child makes it cry out and says, 'See, your child is here, you are going to have it with you all right'. Then the child is hastily smuggled out of the hut, while a bunch of plantains is put in with the body of the woman and bound up with the funeral binding clothes.

Very young children they do not attempt to keep, but throw them away in the bush alive, as all children are thrown who have not arrived in this world in the way considered orthodox, or who cut their teeth in an improper way. Twins are killed among all the Niger Delta tribes, and in districts out of English control the mother is killed too, except in Omon, where the sanctuary is.

There twin mothers and their children are exiled to an island in the Cross River. They have to remain on the island and if any

man goes across and marries one of them he has to remain on the island too. This twin-killing is a widely diffused custom among the Negro tribes.

The terror with which twins are regarded in the Niger Delta is exceedingly strange and real. When I had the honour of being with Miss Slessor at Okÿon, the first twins in that district were saved with their mother from immolation owing entirely to Miss Slessor's great influence with the natives and her own unbounded courage and energy. The mother in this case was a slave woman —an Eboe, the most expensive and valuable of slaves. She was the property of a big woman who had always treated her—as indeed most slaves are treated in Calabar—with great kindness and consideration, but when these two children arrived all was changed; immediately she was subjected to torrents of virulent abuse, her things were torn from her, her English china basins, possessions she valued most highly, were smashed, her clothes were torn, and she was driven out as an unclean thing. Had it not been for the fear of incurring Miss Slessor's anger, she would, at this point, have been killed with her children, and the bodies thrown into the bush.

As it was, she was hounded out of the village. The rest of her possessions were jammed into an empty gin-case and cast to her. No one would touch her, as they might not touch to kill. Miss Slessor had heard of the twins' arrival and had started off, barefooted and bareheaded, at that pace she can go down a bush path. By the time she had gone four miles she met the procession, the woman coming to her and all the rest of the village yelling and howling behind her. On the top of her head was the gin-case, into which the children had been stuffed, on the top of them the woman's big brass skillet, and on the top of that her two market calabashes. Needless to say, on arriving Miss Slessor took charge of affairs, relieving the unfortunate, weak, staggering woman from her load and carrying it herself, for no one else would touch it, or anything belonging to those awful twin things, and they started back together to Miss Slessor's house in the forest-clearing, saved by that tact which, coupled with her courage, has given Miss Slessor an influence and a power among the Negroes unmatched in its way by that of any other white.

She did not take the twins and their mother down the village path to her own house, for though had she done so the people of Okÿon would not have prevented her, yet so polluted would the path have been, and so dangerous to pass down, that they would have been compelled to cut another, no light task in that bit of

forest, I assure you. So Miss Slessor stood waiting in the broiling
sun, in the hot season's height, while a path was being cut to
enable her just to get through to her own grounds. The natives
worked away hard, knowing that it saved the polluting of a long
stretch of market road, and when it was finished Miss Slessor
went to her own house by it and attended with all kindness,
promptness and skill, to the woman and children.

I arrived in the middle of this affair for my first meeting with
Miss Slessor, and things at Okÿon were rather crowded, one way
and another, that afternoon. All the attention one of the children wanted—the boy, for there was a boy and a girl—was burying, for the people who had crammed them into the box had
utterly smashed the child's head. The other child was alive, and
is still a member of that household of rescued children all of
whom owe their lives to Miss Slessor. There are among them
twins from other districts, and delicate children who must have
died had they been left in their villages, and a very wonderful
young lady, very plump and very pretty, aged about four. Her
mother died a few days after her birth, so the child was taken
and thrown into the bush, by the side of the road that led to the
market. This was done one market-day some distance from the
Okÿon town. This particular market is held every ninth day,
and on the succeeding market-day some women from the village
by the side of Miss Slessor's house happened to pass along the
path and heard the child feebly crying: they came into Miss
Slessor's yard in the evening, and sat chatting over the day's
shopping, &c., and casually mentioned in the way of conversation that they had heard the child crying, and that it was rather
remarkable it should be still alive.

Needless to say, Miss Slessor was off, and had that waif home.
It was truly in an awful state, but just alive. In a marvellous
way it had been left by leopards and snakes, with which this bit
of forest abounds, and, more marvellous still, the driver ants had
not scented it. Other ants had considerably eaten into it one way
and another; nose, eyes, &c., were swarming with them and
flies; the cartilage of the nose and part of the upper lip had
been absolutely eaten into, but in spite of this she is now one of
the prettiest black children I have ever seen, which is saying a
good deal, for Negro children are very pretty with their round
faces, their large mouths not yet coarsened by heavy lips, their
beautifully shaped flat little ears and their immense melancholy
deer-like eyes, and above these charms they possess that of being
fairly quiet. This child is not an object of terror, like the twin

children; it was just thrown away because no one would be bothered to rear it, but when Miss Slessor had had all the trouble of it the natives had no objection to pet and play with it, calling it 'the child of wonder', because of its survival.

With the twin baby it was very different. They would not touch it and only approached it after some days, and then only when it was held by Miss Slessor or me. If either of us wanted to do or get something, and we handed over the bundle to one of the house children to hold, there was a stampede of men and women off the verandah, out of the yard and over the fence, if need be, that was exceedingly comic, but most convincing as to the reality of the terror and horror in which they held the thing. Even its own mother could not be trusted with the child; she would have killed it. She never betrayed the slightest desire to have it with her, and after a few days' nursing and feeding up she was anxious to go back to her mistress, who, being an enlightened woman, was willing to have her if she came without the child.

The main horror is undoubtedly of the child, the mother being killed more as a punishment for having been so intimately mixed up in bringing the curse, danger and horror into the village than for anything else.

The woman went back by the road that had been cut for her coming, and would have to live for the rest of her life an outcast, and for a long time in a state of isolation, in a hut of her own into which no one would enter, neither would anyone eat or drink with her, nor partake of the food or water she had cooked or fetched. She would lead the life of a leper, working in the plantation by day, and going into her lonely hut at night, shunned and cursed. I tried to find out whether there was any set period for this quarantine, and all I could arrive at was that if—and a very considerable if—a man were to marry her and she were subsequently to present to society an acceptable infant, she would be to a certain extent socially rehabilitated, but she would always be a woman with a past—a thing the African, to his credit be it said, has no taste for.

I have tried to find out the reason of this widely diffused custom which is the cause of such a pitiful waste of life; for in addition to the mother and children being killed it often leads to other people, totally unconcerned in the affair, being killed by the relatives of the sufferer on the suspicion of having caused the calamity by witchcraft, and until one gets hold of the underlying idea, and can destroy that, the custom will be hard to stamp out

in a district like the great Niger Delta. But I have never been able to hunt it down, though I am sure it is there, and a very quaint idea it undoubtedly is. The usual answer is, 'It was the custom of our fathers', but that always and only means, 'We don't intend to tell'.

Another explanation is that the dislike is grounded on the idea that it is like the lower animals. The teeth-filing I think undoubtedly does arise from this; you often hear a native of tribes that go in for filing or knocking out teeth say contemptuously of those who do not follow the custom, 'Those men have teeth all same for one with dog.' Although I grant that when you are a Niger Delta native you have to be a little careful for fear of being taken for one of the lower animals, just as seedy young men with us object to carrying paper parcels for fear of being taken for tailors, still this idea does not explain the terror, the abject terror, with which twins are regarded, nor the conviction that their existence and proximity bring down on all diseases, difficulties and disaster.

Affiliated to this custom of twin-killing, and having, I suspect, the same underlying idea, is the custom common in Negro and Bantu tribes of throwing away the body of a woman who has died in her confinement without the child being born, burning everything belonging to her, and blotting out her name and memory. The name of such a woman is never mentioned after the catastrophe, and the body is thrown far away into the bush, not near the path, where the bodies of little children are thrown in order that their souls may choose a new mother from the women who pass by.

Funeral customs vary considerably between the Negro and Bantu, and I never yet found among the Bantu those unpleasant death-charms which are in vogue in the Niger Delta. One of these is the custom of the nearest relatives sitting round the body during the time—an awesome long time considering the climate—that elapses before burial under the house floor, the assembled relatives sniffing frequently and powerfully at the body. The young children are brought in and held over it so that they can sniff too.

I was once in a canoe with four men and women and three children, and a corpse came towards us on the current. My companions paddled towards it with enthusiasm and getting it against the side of the canoe, dipped their calabashes into the water round the corpse, and drank calabash after calabash, until they had got their back teeth under water and then they

emptied, in that fine swallow-or-choke and hang-the-spilling style of theirs, calabashes of water into the children until the unfortunate infants fairly overflowed.

'Good death-charm,' they said to me. 'I shouldn't wonder if it were,' said I, 'paddle away,' for I was frightened lest these people, who are, barring their manners and customs, kindly and affectionate, should have the corpse on board and take it home to their families and make a decoction for home consumption, and it was an unpleasant corpse—smallpox and all that sort of thing, you know. I am told this custom occurs in the Niger estuaries and in the Old Calabar regions. I was in Bantu regions, but my companions were not pure Bantu.

The Calabar people, when the consular eye is off them, bury under the house. In the case of a great chief the head is cut off and buried with great secrecy somewhere else, for reasons I have already stated. The body is buried a few days after death, but the really important part of the funeral is the burying of the spirit, and this is the thing that causes all the West Africans, Negro and Bantu alike, great worry, trouble and expense. For the spirit, no matter what its late owner may have been, is malevolent—all native-made spirits are. The family have to get together a considerable amount of wealth to carry out this burial of the spirit, so between the body-burying and the spirit-burying a considerable time usually elapses; maybe a year, maybe more.

The custom of keeping the affair open until the big funeral can be made obtains also in Cabinda and Loango, but there, instead of burying the body in the meantime, it is placed upon a platform of wood, and slow fires kept going underneath to dry it, a mat roof being usually erected over it to keep off rain. When sufficiently dried, it is wrapped in clothes and put into a coffin, until the money to finish the affair is ready. The Duallas are more tied down; their death-dances must be celebrated, I am informed, on the third, seventh and ninth day after death. On these days the spirit is supposed to be particularly present in its old home. In all the other cases, I should remark, the spirit does not leave the home until its devil is made and if this is delayed too long he naturally becomes fractious.

Among the Congo Français tribes there are many different kinds of burial—as the cannibalistic of the Fan. I may remark, however, that they tell me themselves that it is considered decent to bury a relative, even if you subsequently dig him up and dispose of the body to the neighbours. Then there is the earth-burial of the Igalwas and M'pongwe, and the beating into

unrecognisable pulp of the body which, I am told on good native authority, is the method of several Upper Ogowé tribes, including the Adoomas. I had no opportunity of making quiet researches on burial customs when I was above Njoli, because I was so busy trying to avoid qualifying for a burial myself; so I am not quite sure whether this method is the general one among these little-known tribes, as I am told by native traders, who have it among them that it is—or whether it is reserved for the bodies of people believed to have been possessed of dangerous souls.

Destroying the body by beating up, or by cutting up, is a widely diffused custom in West Africa in the case of dangerous souls, and is universally followed with those that have contained wanderer-souls, *i.e.*, those souls which keep turning up in the successive infants of a family. A child dies, then another child comes to the same father or mother, and that dies, after giving the usual trouble and expense. A third arrives and if that dies, the worm—the father, I mean—turns, and if he is still desirous of more children, he just breaks one of the legs of the body before throwing it in the bush.

This he thinks will act as a warning to the wanderer-soul and give it to understand that if it will persist in coming into his family, it must settle down there and give up its flighty ways. If a fourth child arrives in the family, 'it usually limps', and if it dies, the justly irritated parent cuts its body up carefully into very small pieces, and scatters them, doing away with the soul altogether.

The uniform custom among both Negroes and Bantus is that widows who escape execution on the charge of having witched the husband to death, shall remain in a state of filth and abasement, not even removing vermin from themselves, until after the soul-burial is complete—the soul of the dead man being regarded as hanging about them and liable to be injured. Therefore, also to the end of preventing his soul from getting damaged, they are confined to their huts; this latter restriction is not rigidly enforced, but it is held theoretically to be the correct thing.

They maintain the attitude of grief and abasement, sitting on the ground, eating but little food, and that of a coarse kind. In Calabar their legal rights over property, such as slaves, are meanwhile considerably in abeyance, and they are put to great expense during the time the spirit is awaiting burial. They have to keep watch, two at a time, in the hut, when the body is buried,

keeping lights burning, and they have to pay out of their separate estate for the entertainment of all the friends of the deceased who come to pay him compliment; and if he has been an important man, a big man, the whole district will come, not in a squadron, but just when it suits them, exactly as if they were calling on a live friend. Thus it often happens that even a big woman is bankrupt by the expense.

It is not only the widows that remain, either theoretically or practically, unwashed; all the mourners do. The Ibibios seem to me to wear the deepest crape in the form of accumulated dirt, and all the African tribes I have met have peculiar forms of hair cutting—shaving the entire head, not shaving it at all, shaving half of it &c.—when in mourning.

The period of the duration of wearing mourning is, I believe, in all West Coast tribes, that which elapses between the death and the burial of the soul. I believe a more thorough knowledge would show us that there is among the Bantu also a fixed time for the lingering of the soul on earth after death, but we have not got sufficient evidence on the point yet. The only thing we know is that it is not proper for the widow to re-marry while his soul is still in her vicinity.

Among the Calabar tribes the burial of the spirit liberates the woman. Among the Tschwi she requires special ceremonies on her own account. In Togoland, among the Ewe people, I know the period is between five and six weeks, during which time the widow remains in the hut, armed with a good stout stick, as a precaution against the ghost of her husband, so as to ward off attacks should he be ill-tempered. After these six weeks the widow can come out of the hut, but as his ghost has not permanently gone hence, and is apt to revisit the neighbourhood for the next six months, she has to be taken care of during this period. Then, after certain ceremonies, she is free to marry again. So I conclude the period of mourning, in all tribes, is that period during which the soul remains round its old possessions, whether these tribes have a definite soul-burial or devil-making or not.

The ideas connected with the under-world to which the ghost goes are exceedingly interesting. The Negroes and Bantus are at one on these subjects in one particular only, and that is that no marriages take place there. The Tschwis say that this under-world, Srahmandazi, is just the same as this world in all other particulars, save that it is dimmer, a veritable shadow-land where men have not the joys of life, but only the shadow of the

joy. Hence, says the Tschwi proverb, 'One day in this world is worth a year in Srahmandazi.'

The Tschwis, with their usual definiteness in this sort of detail, know all about their Srahmandazi. Its entrance is just east of the middle Volta, and the way down is difficult to follow, and when the sun sets on this world it rises on Srahmandazi. The Bantus are vague on this important and interesting point. The Benga, for example, although holding the absence of marriage there, do not take steps to meet the case as the Tschwis do, and kill a supply of wives to take down with them. This reason for killing wives at a funeral is another instance that, however strange and cruel a custom may be here in West Africa, however much it may at first appear to be the flower of a rootless superstition, you will find on close investigation that it has some root in a religious idea, and a common-sense element.

The common-sense element in the killing of wives and slaves among both the Tschwi and the Calabar tribes consists in the fact that it discourages poisoning. A Calabar chief elaborately explained to me that the rigorous putting down of killing at funerals that was being carried on by the Government not only landed a man in the next world as a wretched pauper, but added an additional chance to his going there prematurely, for his wives and slaves, no longer restrained by the prospect of being killed at his death and sent off with him would, on very slight aggravation, put 'bush in his chop'. It is sad to think of this thorn being added to the rose-leaves of a West Coast chief's life, as there are 99·9 per cent. of thorns in it already.

I came across a similar case on the Gold Coast, when a chief complained to me of the way the Government were preserving vermin, in the shape of witches, in the districts under its surveillance. You were no longer allowed to destroy them as of old, and therefore the vermin were destroying the game; for, said he, the witches here live almost entirely on the blood they suck from children at night. They used, in old days, to do this furtively, and do so now where native custom is unchecked; but in districts where the Government says that witchcraft is utter nonsense, and killing its proficients utter murder which will be dealt with accordingly, the witch flourishes exceedingly, and blackmails the fathers and mothers of families, threatening that if they are not bought off they will have their child's blood; and if they are not paid, the child dies away gradually—poison again, most likely.

I often think it must be the common-sense element in fetish

customs that enables them to survive, in the strange way they do, in the minds of Africans who have been long under European influence and education. In witching, for example, every intelligent native knows there is a lot of poison in the affair, but the explanation he gives you will not usually display this knowledge, and it was not until I found the wide diffusion of the idea of the advisability of administering an emetic to the bewitched person, that I began to suspect my black friends of sound judgment.

The good ju-juist will tell you all things act by means of their life, which means their power, their spirit. Dr Nassau tells me the efficacy of drugs is held to depend on their benevolent spirits, which, on being put into the body, drive away the malevolent disease-causing spirits—a leucocytes-versus pathogenic-bacteria sort of influence, I suppose. On this same idea also depends the custom of the appeal to ordeal, the working of which is supposed to be spiritual. Nevertheless, the intelligent native, believing all the time in this factor, squares the common-sense factor by bribing the witch-doctor who makes the ordeal drink.

The feeling regarding the importance of funeral observances is quite Greek in its intensity. Given a duly educated African, I am sure that he would grasp the true inwardness of the *Antigone* far and away better than any European now living can. A pathetic story which bears on this feeling was told me some time ago by Miss Slessor when she was stationed at Creek Town. An old blind slave woman was found in the bush, and brought into the mission. She was in a deplorable state, utterly neglected and starving, her feet torn by thorns and full of jiggers, and so on. Every care was taken of her and she soon revived and began to crawl about, but her whole mind was set on one thing with a passion that had made her alike indifferent to her past sufferings and to her present advantages. What she wanted was a bit, only a little bit, of white cloth.

Now, I may remark, white cloth is anathema to the Missions, for it is used for ju-ju offerings, and a rule has to be made against its being given to the unconverted, or the missionary becomes an accessory before the fact to pagan practices, so white cloth the old woman was told she could not have, she had been given plenty of garments for her own use and that was enough. The old woman, however, kept on pleading and saying the spirit of her dead mistress kept coming to her asking and crying for white cloth, and white cloth she must get for her, and so at last, finding it was not to be got at the Mission station, she stole away one day, unobserved, and wandered off into the bush, from

which she never again reappeared, doubtless falling a victim to
the many leopards that haunted hereabouts.

To provide a proper burial for the dead relation is the great
duty of a Negro's life, its only rival in his mind is the desire to
have a burial of his own. But, in a good Negro, this passion will
go under before the other, and he will risk his very life to do it.
He may know, surely and well, that killing slaves and women at
a dead brother's grave means hanging for him when their Big
Consul knows of it, but in the Delta he will do it. On the Coast
Leeward and Windward, he will spend every penny he possesses
and, on top, if need be, go and pawn himself, his wives or his
children into slavery to give a deceased relation a proper
funeral.

Among the Tschwi the slaves and women killed are to form
for the dead a retinue, and riches wherewith to start life in
Srahmandazi, where there are markets and towns and all things
as on this earth, and so the Tschwi would have little difficulty
in replacing human beings at funerals with gold-dust, cloth and
other forms of riches, and this is already done in districts under
white influence. But in the Delta there is no under-world to live
in, the souls shortly after reaching the under-world being
forwarded back to this, in new babies, and the wealth that is
sent down with a man serves as an indication as to what class of
baby the soul is to be repacked and sent up in.

As wealth in the Delta consists of women and slaves, I do not
believe the under-world gods of the Niger would understand the
status of a chief who arrived before them, let us say, with ten
puncheons of palm oil, and four hundred yards of crimson figured
velvet; they would say, 'Oh! very good as far as it goes, but
where is your real estate? The chances are you are only a trade
slave boy and have stolen these things'; and in consequence of
this, killing at funerals will be a custom exceedingly difficult to
stamp out in these regions. Try and imagine yourself how abhorrent it must be to send down a dear and honoured relative
to the danger of his being returned to this world shortly as a
slave. There is no doubt a certain idea among the Negroes that
some souls may get a rise in status on their next incarnation.
You often hear a woman saying she will be a man next time, a
slave he will be a freeman, and so on, but how or why some souls
obtain promotion I have not yet sufficient evidence to show. I
think a little more investigation will place this important point
in my possession. I once said to a Calabar man, 'But surely it
would be easy for a man's friends to cheat; they could send down

a chief's outfit with a man, though he was only a small man here?'

'No,' said he, 'the other souls would tell on him, and then he would get sent up as a dog or some beast as a punishment.'

My first conception of the prevalence of the incarnation idea was also gained from a Delta Negro. I said, 'Why in the world do you throw away in the bush the bodies of your dead slaves? Where I have been they tie a string to the leg of a dead slave and when they bury him bring the string to the top and fix it to a peg, with the owner's name on, and then when the owner dies he has that slave again down below.'

'They be fool men,' said he, and he went on to explain that the ghost of that slave would be almost immediately back on earth again growing up ready to work for someone else, and would not wait for its last owner's soul down below, and out of the luxuriant jungle of information that followed I gathered that no man's soul dallies below long, and also that a soul returning to a family, a thing ensured by certain ju-jus, was identified. The new babies as they arrive in the family are shown a selection of small articles belonging to deceased members whose souls are still absent; the thing the child catches hold of identifies him. 'Why he's Uncle John, see! he knows his own pipe'; or 'That's cousin Emma, see! she knows her market calabash', and so on.

As I have dwelt on the repellent view of Negro funeral custom, I must in justice to them cite their better view. There is a custom that I missed much on going south of Calabar, for it is a pretty one. Outside the villages in the Calabar districts, by the sides of the most frequented roads, you will see erections of boughs. I do not think these are intended for huts, but for beds, for they are very like the Calabar type of bed, only made in wood instead of clay. Over them a roof of mats is put, to furnish a protection against rain.

These shelters—graves or fetish huts they are wrongly called by Europeans—are made by driving four longish stout poles into the ground while at the height of about three feet or so four more poles are tied so as to make a skeleton platform which is filled in with withies and made flat. Another set of five poles is tied above, and to these the roof is affixed. On the platform, is placed the bedding belonging to the deceased, the undercloth, counterpane, &c., and at the head are laid the pillows, bolster-shaped and stuffed with cotton-tree fluff, or shredded palm-leaves, and covered with some gaily-coloured cotton cloth. In

every case I have seen—and they amount to hundreds, for you cannot take an hour's walk even from Duke Town without coming upon a dozen or so of these erections—the pillows are placed so that the person lying on the bed would look towards the village.

On the roof and on the bed, and underneath it on the ground, are placed the household utensils that belonged to the deceased; the calabashes, the basins, the spoons cut out of wood, and the boughten iron ones, as we should say in Devon, and on the stakes are hung the other little possessions; there is one I know of made for the ghost of a poor girl who died, on to the stakes of which are hung the dolls and the little pin-cushions, &c., given her by a kind missionary.

Food is set out at these places and spirit poured over them from time to time, and sometimes, though not often, pieces of new cloth are laid on them. Most of the things are deliberately damaged before they are put on the home for the spirit; I do not think this is to prevent them from being stolen, because all are not damaged sufficiently to make them useless. There was a beautifully made spoon with a burnt-in pattern on one of these places when I left Calabar to go South, and on my return, some six months after, it was still there. On another there was a very handsome pair of market calabashes, also much decorated, that were only just chipped and in better repair than many in use in Calabar markets, and I make no doubt the spoon and they are still lying rotting among the *débris* of the pillows, &c. These places are only attended to during the time the spirit is awaiting burial, as they are regarded merely as a resting-place for it while it is awaiting this ceremony. The body is not buried near them, I may remark.

In spite, however, of the care that is taken to bury spirits, a considerable percentage from various causes—poverty of the relations, the deceased being a stranger in the land, accidental death in some unknown part of the forest or the surf—remain unburied, and hang about to the common danger of the village they may choose to haunt. Many devices are resorted to, to purify the villages from these spirits. One which was in use in Creek Town, Calabar, to within a few years ago, and which I am informed is still customary in some interior villages, was very ingenious, and believed to work well by those who employed it.

In the houses were set up Nbakim—large, grotesque images carved of wood and hung about with cloth strips and gew-gaws.

Every November in Creek Town (I was told by some authorities it was every second November) there was a sort of festival held. Offerings of food and spirits were placed before these images; a band of people accompanied by the rest of the population used to make a thorough round of the town, up and down each street and round every house, dancing, singing, screaming and tom-toming, in fact making all the noise they knew how to—and a Calabar Effik is very gifted in the power of making noise. After this had been done for what was regarded as a sufficient time, the images were taken out of the houses, the crowd still making a terrific row, and were then thrown into the river, and the town was regarded as being cleared of spirits.

The rationale of the affair is this. The wandering spirits are attracted by the images, and take shelter among their rags, like earwigs or something of that kind. The *charivari* is to drive any of the spirits who might be away from their shelters back into them. The shouting of the mob is to keep the spirits from venturing out again while they are being carried to the river. The throwing of the images, rags and all, into the river, is to destroy the spirits or at least send them elsewhere. They did not go and pour boiling water on their earwig-traps, as wicked white men do, but they meant the same thing, and when this was over they made and set up new images for fresh spirits who might come into the town, and these were kept and tended as before, until the next N'dok ceremony came round.

It is owing to the spiritual view which the African takes of existence at large that ceremonial observances form the greater part of even his common-law procedure.

There is, both among the Negro and Bantu, a recognised code of law, founded on principles of true but merciless justice. It is not often employed, because of the difficulty and the danger to the individual who appeals to it, should that individual be unbacked by power, but nevertheless the code exists.

The laws against adultery are, theoretically, exceedingly severe. The punishment is death, and this is sometimes carried out. The other day King Bell in Cameroon flogged one of his wives to death, and the German Government have deposed and deported him, for you cannot do that sort of thing with impunity within a stone's throw of a Government head-quarters. But as a general rule all along the Coast the death penalty for murder or adultery is commuted to a fine, or you can send a substitute to be killed for you, if you are rich. This is frequently done, because

it is cheaper, if you have a seedy slave, to give him to be killed in your stead than to pay a fine which is often enormous.

The adultery itself is often only a matter of laying your hand, even in self-defence from a virago, on a woman—or brushing against her in the path. These accusations of adultery are, next to witchcraft, the great social danger to the West Coast native, and they are often made merely from motives of extortion or spite, and without an atom of truth in them.

It is customary for a chief to put his wives frequently to ordeal on this point, and this is almost always done after there has been a big devil-making, or a dance, which his family have been gracing with their presence. The usual method of applying the ordeal is by boiling palm-oil—a pot is nearly filled with the oil, which is brought to the boil over a fire; when it is seething, the woman to be tried is brought out in front of it. She first dips her hands into water, and then has administered to her the Mbiam oath, saying or having said for her that long elaborate formula, in a form adjusted to meet the case. Then she plunges her hand into the boiling oil for an instant, and shakes the oil off with all possible rapidity, and the next woman comes forward and goes through the same performance, and so on.

Next day, the hands of the women are examined, and those found blistered are adjudged guilty, and punished. In order to escape heavy punishment the woman will accuse some man of having hustled against her, or sat down on a bench beside her, and so on, and the accused man has to pay up. If he does not, in the Calabar district, Egbo will come and 'eat the adultery', and there won't be much of that man's earthly goods left. Sometimes the accusation is volunteered by the woman, and frequently the husband and wife conspire together and cook up a case against a man for the sake of getting the damages. There is nothing that ensures a man an unblemished character in West Africa, save the possession of sufficient power to make it risky work for people to cast slurs on it.

The ownership of children is a great source of palaver. The law among Negroes and Bantus is that the children of a free woman belong to her. The children of slave wives are the only children the father has absolute power over, if he is the legal owner of the slave woman. If, as is frequently the case, a free man marries a slave woman who belongs to another man, all her children are the absolute property of her owner, not her husband; and the owner of the woman can take them and sell them, or do whatsoever he chooses with them, unless the free man father

redeems them, as he usually does, although the woman may still remain the absolute property of the owner, recallable by him at any time.

This law is the cause of the most brain-spraining palavers that come before the white authorities. There is naturally no statute of limitations in West Africa, because the African does not care a row of pins about time. The wily A. will let his slave woman live with B. without claiming the redemption fees as they become due—letting them stand over, as it were, at compound interest. All the male as well as the female children of the first generation are A.'s property, and all the female children of these children are his property even unto the second and third generation and away into eternity. A. may die before he puts in his claim, in which case the ownership passes on into the hands of his heir or assignees, who may foreclose at once, on entering into their heritage, or may again let things accumulate for their heirs.

Anyhow, sooner or later the foreclosure comes and then there is trouble. X., Y., Z., &c., free men, have married some of the original A.'s slave woman's descendants. They have either bought them right out, or kept on conscientiously redeeming children of theirs as they arrived. Of course A., or his heirs, contend that X., Y., Z., &c. have been wasting time and money by so doing, because the people X., Y., Z. have paid the money to had no legal title to the women. Of course X., Y., Z. contend that their particular woman, or her ancestress, was duly redeemed from the legal owner.

Remember there is no documentary evidence available, and squads of equally reliable and oldest inhabitants are swearing hard-all both ways. Just realise this, and that your Government says that whenever native law is not blood-stained it must be supported, and you may be able to realise the giddy mazes of a native palaver, which if you continuously attempt to follow with the determination that justice shall be duly administered, will for certain lay you low with an attack of fever.

The law of ownership is not all in favour of the owner, masters being responsible for damage done by their slaves, and this law falls very heavily and expensively on the owner of a bad slave. Indeed, when one lives out here and sees the surrounding conditions of this state of culture, the conviction grows on you that, morally speaking, the African is far from being the brutal fiend he is often painted, a creature that loves cruelty and blood for their own sake. The African does not; and though his culture does not contain our institutions, lunatic asylums, prisons,

workhouses, hospitals, &c., he has to deal with the same classes of people who require these things. So with them he deals by means of his equivalent institutions, slavery, the lash and death. You have just as much right, my logical friend, to call the West Coast Chief hard names for his habit of using brass bars, heads of tobacco and so on, in place of sixpenny pieces, as you have to abuse him for clubbing an inveterate thief. It's deplorably low of him, I own, but by what alternative plan of government his can be replaced I do not quite see, under existing conditions.

In religious affairs, the affairs which lead him into the majority of his iniquities, his real sin consists in believing too much. In his witchcraft, the sin is the same. Toleration means indifference, I believe, among all men. The African is not indifferent on the subject of witchcraft, and I do not see how one can expect him to be. Put yourself in his place and imagine you have got hold of a man or woman who has been placing a live crocodile or a catawumpus of some kind into your own or a valued relative's, or fellow-townsman's inside, so that it may eat up valuable viscera, and cause you or your friend suffering and death. How would you feel? A little like lynching your captive, I fancy.

I confess that the more I know of the West Coast Africans the more I like them. I own I think them fools of the first water for their power of believing in things; but I fancy I have analogous feelings towards even my fellow-countrymen when they go and violently believe in something that I cannot quite swallow.

CHAPTER ELEVEN

Gods, Devils and Secret Societies

However much some of the African's mental attributes get under-rated, I am sure there are others of them for which he gets more credit than he deserves. One of these is his imagination. It strikes the new-comer with awe, and frequently fills him with rage, when he first meets it; but as he matures and gets used to the African, he sees the string. For the African fancy is not the 'aërial fancy flying free', mentioned by our poets, but merely the aërial of the theatre suspended by a wire or cord. The wire that supports the African's fancy may be a very thin, small fact indeed, or in some cases merely his incapacity to distinguish between animate and inanimate objects, which give rise to his idea that everything is possessed of a soul.

Everything has a soul to him, and to make confusion worse confounded, he usually believes in the existence of matter apart from its soul. But there is little he won't believe in, if it comes to that; and I have a feeling of thankfulness that Buddhism, Theosophy and above all Atheism, which chases its tail and proves that nothing can be proved, have not yet been given the African to believe in. He would believe the whole lot if he had the chance, and his mind is in a pretty muddle as it is. I dare say I speak with irritation, but I have suffered much from the African's mind muddle.

The African's want of making it clear in his language whether he is referring to an animate or inanimate thing, has landed me in many a dilemma, and his foolishness in not having a male and female gender in his languages amounts to a nuisance, and has nearly, at one fell swoop, turned my hairs gray, and brought them in sorrow to the grave. For example, I am a most lady-like old person and yet get constantly called 'Sir'. I hasten to assure you I never even wear a masculine collar and tie, and as for encasing the more earthward extremities of my anatomy in— you know what I mean—well, I would rather perish on a public scaffold. The other day, circumstances having got beyond my control during the afternoon, I arrived in the evening in a saturated condition at a white settlement, and wishing to get accommodation for myself and my men, I made my way to the

factory of a firm from whose representatives I have always
received great and most courteous help. The agent in charge was
not at home, and his steward-boy said, 'Massa live for Mr B's
house.' 'Go tell him I live for come from,' &c., said I, and 'I fit
for want place for my men.' I had nothing to write on, or with,
and I thought the steward-boy could carry this little message to
its destination without dropping any of it, as Mr B.'s house was
close by; but I was wrong. Off he went, and soon returned with
the note I here give a copy of:

'DEAR OLD MAN,

You must be in a deuce of a mess after the tornado. Just
help yourself to a set of my dry things. The shirts are in the
bottom drawer, the trousers are in the box under the bed, and
then come over here to the sing-song. My leg is dickey or I'd
come across. Yours, &c.'

Had there been any smelling salts or sal volatile in this sub-
division of the Ethiopian region I should have forthwith fainted
on reading this, but I well knew there was not, so I blushed
until the steam from my soaking clothes (for I truly was 'in a
deuce of a mess') went up in a cloud and then, just as I was I
went 'across' and appeared before the author of that awful note.
When he came round, he said it had taken seven years' growth
out of him, and was intensely apologetic. I remarked it had very
nearly taken thirty years' growth out of me, and he said the
steward boy had merely informed him that 'White man live for
come from X', a place where he knew there was another factory
belonging to his firm, and he naturally thought it was the agent
from X who had come across.

You rarely, indeed I believe never, find an African with a gift
for picturesque descriptions of scenery. The nearest approach
to it I ever got was from my cook when we were on Mungo mah
Lobeh. He proudly boasted he had been on a mountain, up
Cameroon River, with a German officer, and on that mountain,
'If you fall down one side you die, if you fall down other side
you die.'

But I will not go into the subject of African languages here,
but only remark of them that although they are elaborate
enough to produce, for their users, nearly every shade of erroneous statement, they are not, save perhaps M'pongwe, elaborate enough to enable a native to state his exact thought. Some
of them are very dependent on gesture. When I was with the

Fans they frequently said, 'We will go to the fire so that we can see what they say,' when my question had to be decided after dark, and the inhabitants of Fernando Po, the Bubis, are quite unable to converse with each other unless they have sufficient light to see the accompanying gestures of the conversation. In all cases I feel sure the African's intelligence is far ahead of his language.

The African is usually great at dreams, and has them very noisily; but he does not seem to me to attach immense importance to them, certainly not so much as the Red Indian does. I doubt whether there is much real ground for supposing that from dreams came man's first conception of the spirit world, and I think the origin of man's religious belief lies in man's misfortunes.

There can be little doubt that the very earliest human beings found, as their descendants still find, their plans frustrated, let them plan ever so wisely and carefully; they must have seen their companions overtaken by death and disaster, arising both from things they could see and from things they could not see. The distinction between these two classes of phenomena is not so definitely recognised by savages or animals as it is by the more cultured races of humanity. I doubt whether a savage depends on his five senses alone to teach him what the world is made of, any more than a Fellow of the Royal Society does. From this method of viewing nature I feel sure that the general idea arose —which you find in all early cultures—that death was always the consequence of the action of some malignant spirit, and that there is no accidental or natural death, as we call it; and death is, after all, the most impressive attribute of life.

If a man were knocked on the head with a club, or shot with an arrow, the cause of death is clearly the malignancy of the person using these weapons; and so it is easy to think that a man killed by a fallen tree, or by the upsetting of a canoe in the surf, or in an eddy in the river, is also the victim of some being using these things as weapons.

A man having thus gained a belief that there are more than human actors in life's tragedy, the idea that disease is also a manifestation of some invisible being's wrath and power seems to me natural and easy; and he knows you can get another man for a consideration to kill or harm a third party, and so he thinks that, for a consideration, you can also get one of these superhuman beings, which we call gods or devils, but which the African regards in another light, to do so.

A certain set of men and women then specialise off to study how these spirits can be managed, and so arises a priesthood; and the priests, or medicine men as they are called in their earliest forms, gradually, for their own ends, elaborate and wrap round their profession with ritual and mystery.

The savage is also conscious of another great set of phenomena which, he soon learns, take no interest in human affairs. The sun which rises and sets, the moon which changes, the tides which come and go—what do they care? Nothing; and what is more, sacrifice to them what you may, you cannot get them to care about you and your affairs, and so the savage turns his attention to those other spirits that do take only too much interest, as is proved by those unexpected catastrophes; and, as their actions show, these spirits are all malignant, so he deals with them just as he would deal with a bad man whom he was desirous of managing. He flatters and fees them, he deprives himself of riches to give to them as sacrifices, believing they will relish it all the more because it gives him pain of some sort to give it to them. He holds that they think it will be advisable for them to encourage him to continue the giving by occasionally doing what he asks them. Naturally he never feels sure of them; he sees that you may sacrifice to a god for years, you may wrap him up—or more properly speaking, the object in which he resides—in your only cloth on chilly nights while you shiver yourself; you and your children, and your mother, and your sister and her children, may go hungry that food may rot upon his shrine; and yet, in some hour of dire necessity, the power will not come and save you—because he has been lured away by some richer gifts than yours.

The African fully knows the liability of his fetish to fail, but he equally fully knows its power. One, to me, grandly tragic instance of this I learnt at Opobo. There was a very great Fetish doctor there, universally admired and trusted, who lived out on the land at the mouth of the Great River. One day he himself fell sick, and he made ju-ju against the sickness; but it held on, and he grew worse. He made more ju-ju of greater power, but again in vain, and then he made the greatest ju-ju man can make, and it availed nought, and he knew he was dying; and so, with his remaining strength, he broke up and dishonoured and destroyed all the Fetishes in which the spirits lived, and cast them out into the surf and died like a man.

Then horror came upon the people when they knew he had done this, and they burnt his house and all things belonging to

him, and cried upon the spirits not to forsake them, not to lay
this one man's deadly sin at their doors. I rather doubt whether
those spirits have come round yet, for Dr Tompstone wrote to
me that last November, just when their yearly plays were in full
swing, to make sure of having fine weather for them, Opobo
'called in a noted consultant from up river and,' says the Doctor
with a gracious sympathy for a fellow medical man, 'it has rained
in torrents ever since. It is very rough on him, as I believe he did
his best and sacrificed large numbers of fowls.'

In connection with the gods of West Africa I may remark that
in almost all the series of native tradition there, you will find
accounts of a time when there was direct intercourse between
the gods or spirits that live in the sky, and men. That intercourse
is always said to have been cut off by some human error; for
example, the Fernando Po people say that once upon a time
there was no trouble or serious disturbance upon earth because
there was a ladder, made like the one you get palm-nuts with,
'only long, long'; and this ladder reached from earth to heaven
so the gods could go up and down it and attend personally
to mundane affairs. But one day a cripple boy started to go
up the ladder, and he had got a long way up when his mother
saw him, and went up in pursuit. The gods, horrified at
the prospect of having boys and women invading heaven,
threw down the ladder, and have since left humanity severely
alone.

No trace of sun-worship have I ever found. The firmament is,
I believe, always the great indifferent and neglected god. The
African thinks this god has great power if he would only exert it,
and when things go very badly with him, when the river rises
higher than usual and sweeps away his home and his plantations;
when the smallpox stalks through the land, and day and night
the corpses float down the river past him, and he finds them
jammed among his canoes that are tied to the beach, and chok-
ing up his fish traps; and then when at last the death-wail over
its victims goes up night and day from his own village, he will
rise up and call upon his great god in the terror maddened by
despair, that he may hear and restrain the evil workings of these
lesser devils; but he evidently finds, as Peer Gynt says, '*Nein, er
hört nicht. Er is taub wie gewöhnlich*' [No, he does not hear. As
usual he is deaf] for there is no organised cult for Anzam.

Accounts of apparitions abound in all the West Coast districts, and although the African holds them all in high horror
and terror, he does not see anything supernatural in his 'Duppy'.

It is a horrid thing to happen on, but there is nothing strange about it, and he is ten thousand times more frightened than puzzled over the affair. He does not want to 'investigate' to see whether there is anything in it. He wants to get clear away, and make ju-ju against it, 'one time'.

These apparitions have a great variety of form, for, firstly, there are all the true spirits, nature spirits; secondly, the spirits of human beings—these human spirits are held to exist before as well as during and after bodily life; thirdly, the spirits of things. Probably the most horrid of class one is the Tschwi's Sasabonsum. He lives in the forest, in or under those great silk-cotton trees around the roots of which the earth is red. This coloured earth identifies a silk-cotton tree as being the residence of a Sasabonsum, as its colour is held to arise from the blood it whips off him as he goes down to his under-world home after a night's carnage. All silk-cotton trees are suspected because they are held to be the roosts for Duppies. But the red earth ones are feared with a great fear, and no one makes a path by them, or a camp near them at night.

Sasabonsum is a friend of witches. He is of enormous size, and of a red colour. He wears his hair straight and he waylays unprotected wayfarers in the forest at night, and in all districts except that of Apollonia he eats them. Round Apollonia he only sucks their blood. Natives of this district after meeting him have crawled home and given an account of his appearance, and then expired.

Ellis says he is believed to be implacable, and when angered can never be mollified or propitiated, but it is certain that human victims are constantly sacrificed to him in districts beyond white control; in districts under it, the equivalent value of a human sacrifice in sheep and goats is offered to him. In Ashantee he has priests, and of course human sacrifice. Away among the Daho-meyan tribes—where he has kept his habits but got another name, and seems to have crystallised from a class into an indivi-dual—the usual way in which a god develops—he has priests and priestesses, and they are holy terrors; but among the Tschwi, Sasabonsum is mainly dealt with by witches, and people desirous of possessing the power of becoming witches.

A description follows of the procedure adopted by a witch in order to obtain control of a suhman, a spirit which takes up its abode in a particular charm and will encompass the death of anyone designated by its master.

The quantity of charms among the Negroes, as among the Bantu, verges on infinity. Most of them are procured from *suhman* holders, but not all. I fancy a *suhman* wears himself out in making charms, for you will sometimes come across 'dead' ones that you may buy. These dead ones are *ehsuhman* (pl.) who have failed several times to work because the spirit has left them; whereas a live charm is treasured, and treated as a sentient thing. A man I know had a bundle of feathers with a porcupine tail in their midst, and he used always to squirt out of his mouth a little rum over it when he was drinking.

As a rule the person who has a *suhman* keeps the fact pretty quiet, for the possession of such an article would lead half the catastrophes in his district, from the decease of pigs, fowls, and babies, to fires, &c., to be accredited to him, which would lead to his neighbours making 'witch palaver' over him, and he would have to undergo poison-ordeal and other unpleasantness to clear his character. He, however, always keeps a special day in his *suhman*'s honour, and should he be powerful, as a king or big chief, he will keep this day openly. King Kwoffi Karri Kari, whom we fought with in 1874, used to make a big day for his *suhman*, which was kept in a box covered with gold plates, and he sacrificed a human victim to it every Tuesday, with general festivities and dances in its honour.

I should remark that Sasabonsum is married. His wife, or more properly speaking his female form, is called Srahmantin. She is far less malignant than the male form. Her name comes from Srahman—ghost or spirit; the termination 'tin' is an abbreviation of *tsintsin*—tall. She is of immense height, and white; perhaps this idea is derived from the white stem of the silk-cotton trees wherein she invariably abides. Her method of dealing with the solitary wayfarer is no doubt inconvenient to him, but it is kinder than her husband's ways, for she does not kill and eat him, as Sasabonsum does, but merely detains him some months while she teaches him all about the forest: what herbs are good to eat, or to cure disease; where the game come to drink, and what they say to each other, and so forth. I often wish I knew this lady, for the grim, grand African forests are like a great library, in which, so far, I can do little more than look at the pictures, although I am now busily learning the alphabet of their language, so that I may some day read what these pictures mean.

Do not go away with the idea, I beg, that goddesses, as a general rule, are better than gods. They are not. There are

stories about them which I could—I mean I could not—tell you. There is one belonging also to the Tschwi. She lives at Moree, a village five miles from Cape Coast. She is, as is usual with deities, human in shape and colossal in size, and as is not usual with deities, she is covered with hair from head to foot—short white hair like a goat. Her abode is on the path to surf-cursed Anamabu near the sea-beach, and her name is Aynfwa; a worshipper of hers has only got to mention the name of a person he wishes dead when passing her abode and Aynfwa does the rest. She is the goddess of all albinoes, who are said to be more frequent in occurrence round Moree than elsewhere. Ellis says that in 1886, when he was there, they were 1 per cent. of the entire population. These albinoes are, *ipso facto*, her priests and priestesses, and in old days an albino had only to name anywhere a person Aynfwa wished for, and that person was forthwith killed.

I think I may safely say that every dangerous place in West Africa is regarded as the residence of a god—rocks and whirl-pools in the rivers—swamps 'no man fit to pass'—and naturally, the surf. Along the Gold Coast, at every place where you have to land through the surf, it fairly swarms with gods. A little experience with the said surf inclines you to think, as the dab-blers in spiritualism say, 'that there is something in it'. I will back this West Coast surf—'the Calemma', as we call it down South—against any other malevolent abomination, barring only the English climate.

There was a bad man once on the Gold Coast who had ill-used his men, and when they took him out through the surf to go aboard the ship that was to take him home, there was the usual catastrophe, which no one thought much of, only saying 'It was hard on B. just as he was going home', until the body of B. came ashore, and then, in the clothes, were found three iron shark hooks, with lots of line attached, wherewith the men had held B. back from shore, and played him like a fish, until the surf beat the life out of him

There is one thing about the surf that I do not understand, and that is why witches always walk stark naked along the beach by it at night, and eat sea crabs the while. That such is a confirmed habit of theirs is certain; and they tell me that while doing this the witches emit a bright light, and also that there is a certain medicine, which, if you have it with you, you can throw over the witch, and then he, or she, will remain blazing until morning time, running to and fro, crying out wildly, in front of

the white, breaking, thundering surf wall, and when the dawn comes the fire burns the witch right up, leaving only a grey ash —and palaver set in this world and the next for that witch.

A highly-esteemed native minister told me when I was at Cape Coast last, that a fortnight before, he had been away in the Apollonia district on mission work. One evening he and a friend were walking along the beach and the night was dark, so that you could see only the surf. It is never too dark to see that, it seems to have light in itself. They saw a flame coming towards them, and after a moment's doubt they knew it was a witch, and feeling frightened, hid themselves among the bushes that edge the sandy shore. As they watched, it came straight on and passed them, and they saw it disappear in the distance. My informant laughed at himself, and very wisely said, 'One has not got to believe those things here, one has in Apollonia.'

To the surf and its spirits the sea-board-dwelling Tschwís bring women who have had children and widows, both after a period of eight days from the birth of the child, or the death of the husband.

The Tschwis hold that there is a definite earthly existence belonging to each soul of a human kind. Let us say, for example, a soul has a thirty years' bodily existence belonging to it. Well, suppose that soul's body gets killed off at twenty-five, its remaining five years it has to spend, if it is left alone, in knocking about its old haunts, homes and wives. In this state it is called a Sisa, and is a nuisance. It will cause sickness. It will throw stones. It will pull off roofs, and it will play the very mischief with its wives' subsequent husbands, all because, not having reached its full term of life, it has not learnt its way down the dark and difficult path to Srahmandazi, the entrance to which is across the Volta River to the N.E. This knowledge of the path to Srahmandazi is a thing that grows gradually on a man's immortal soul (the other three souls are not immortal), and naturally not having been allowed to complete his life, his knowledge is imperfect.

A man's soul, however, can be taught the way, if necessary, in the funeral 'custom' made by his relatives and the priests; but in a case of an incompletelifeonearthsoul, as a German would say, when it does arrive in the land of Insrah (pl.) it is in a weak and feeble state from the difficulties of its journey, whereas a soul that has lived out its allotted span of life goes straightway off to Srahmandazi as soon as its 'custom' or 'devil' is made and gives its surviving relatives no further trouble.

Before closing these observations on Srahmandazi I will give the best account of that land that I am at present able to. Some day perhaps I may share the fate of the Oxford Professor in *In the Wrong Paradise* and go there myself, but so far my information is second-hand. It is like this world. There are towns and villages, rivers, mountains, bush, plantations, and markets. When the sun rises here it sets in Srahmandazi. It has its pleasures and its pains, not necessarily retributive or rewarding, but dim. All souls in it grow forward or backward into the prime of life and remain there, some informants say; others say that each inhabitant remains there at the same age as he was, when he quitted the world above. This latter view is most like the South West one. The former is possibly only an attempt to make Srahmandazi into a heaven in conformation with Christian teaching, which it is not, any more than it is a hell.

I have much curious information regarding its flora and fauna. A great deal of both is seemingly indigenous, and then there are the souls of great human beings, the Asrahmanfo, and the souls of all the human beings, animals and things sent down with them. I have had great and highly abstruse controversies with Ethiopian theologians on the question of what happens to the soul of the soul of things, when the Asrahmanfo kills these for his support in Srahmandazi. But as nothing since the Middle Ages has approached these controversies in confusion of idea and worthlessness of ultimate deductions arrived at, I will not inflict them on you here. The ghosts do not seem to leave off their interest in mundane affairs, for they not only have local palavers, but try palavers left over from their earthly existence; and when there is an outbreak of sickness in a Fantee town or village, and several inhabitants die off, the opinion is often held that there is a big palaver going on down in Srahmandazi and that the spirits are sending up on earth for witnesses, subpœnaing them as it were. Medicine men or priests are called in to find out what particular earthly grievance can be the subject of the ghost palaver, and when they have ascertained this they take the evidence of every one in the town on this affair, as it were on commission, and transmit the information to the court sitting in Srahmandazi. This prevents the living being incommoded by personal journeys down below and although the priests have their fee, it is cheaper in the end, because the witnesses' funeral expenses would fall heavier still.

Although far more elaborated and thought out than any other African under-world I have ever come across, the Tschwi

Srahmandazi may be taken as a type of all the African under-
worlds. The Bantu's idea of a future life is a life spent in much
such a place. As far as I can make out there is no definite idea of
eternity. I have even come across cases in which doubt was
thrown on the present existence of the Creating God, but I
think this has arisen from attempts having been made to introduce concise conceptions into the African mind, conceptions
that are quite foreign to its true nature and which alarm and
worry it. You never get the strange idea of the difference between
time and eternity—the idea I mean, that they are different
things—in the African that one frequently gets in cultured
Europeans; and as for the human soul, the African always believes 'that still the spirit is whole, and life and death but
shadows of the soul'.

Apparitions are by no means always of human soul origin. All
the Tschwis and the Ewe gods, for example, have the habit of
appearing pretty regularly to their priests, and occasionally to
the laity, like Sasabonsum; but it is only to priests that these
appearances are harmless or beneficial. The effect of Sasabonsum's appearance to the layman I have cited above, and I
could give many other examples of the bad effects of those of
other gods, but will only now mention Tando, the Hater, the
chief god of the Northern Tschwis, the Ashantees, &c. He is
terribly malicious, human in shape, and though not quite white,
is decidedly lighter in complexion than the chief god of the
Southern Tschwis, Bobowissi. His hair is lank, and he carries a
native sword and wears a long robe. His well-selected messengers
are those awful driver ants (Inkran) which it is not orthodox to
molest in Tando's territories. He uses as his weapons lightning,
tempest and disease, but the last is the most favourite one.

There is absolutely no trick too mean or venomous for Tando.
For example, he has a way of appearing near a village he has a
grudge against in the form of a male child, and wanders about
crying bitterly, until some kind-hearted, unsuspecting villager
comes and takes him in and feeds him. Then he develops a con-
tagious disease that clears that village out.

This form of appearance and subsequent conduct is, unhap-
pily, not rigidly confined to Tando, but is used by many spirits
as a method of collecting arrears in taxes in the way of sacrifices.
I have found traces of it among Bantu gods or spirits, and it
gives rise to a general hesitation in West Africa to take care of
waifs and strays of unexplained origin.

Other things beside gods and human spirits have the habit of becoming incarnate. Once I had to sit waiting a long time at an apparently perfectly clear bush path, because in front of us a spear's ghost used to fly across the path about that time in the afternoon, and if anyone was struck by it they died. A certain spring I know of is haunted by the ghost of a pitcher. Many ladies when they have gone alone to fill their pitchers in the evening time at this forest spring have noticed a very fine pitcher standing there ready filled, and thinking exchange is no robbery, or at any rate they would risk it if it were, have left their own pitcher and taken the better looking one; but always as soon as they have come within sight of the village huts, the new pitcher has crumbled into dust, and the water in it been spilt on the ground; and the worst of it is, when they have returned to fetch their own discarded pitcher, they find it also shattered into pieces.

There is also another class of apparition, of which I have met with two instances, one among pure Negroes (Okÿon); the other among pure Bantu (Kangwe). I will give the Bantu version of the affair, because at Okÿon the incident had happened a good time before the details were told me, and in the Bantu case they had happened the previous evening. But there was very little difference in the main facts of the case, and it was an important thing because in both cases the underlying idea was sacrificial.

The woman who told me was an exceedingly intelligent, shrewd, reliable person. She had been to the factory with some trade, and had got a good price for it, and so was in a good temper on her return home in the evening. She got out of her canoe and leaving her slave boy to bring up the things, walked to her house, which was the ordinary house of a prosperous Igalwa native, having two distinct rooms in it, and a separate cook-house close by in a clean, sandy yard. She trod on some nastiness in the yard, and going into the cookhouse found the slave girls round a very small and inefficient fire, trying to cook the evening meal. She blew them up for not having a proper fire; they said the wood was wet, and would not burn. She said they lied, and she would see to them later, and she went into the chamber she used for a sleeping apartment, and trod on something more on the floor in the dark; those good-for-nothing hussies of slaves had not lit her palm-oil lamp, and mentally forming the opinion that they had been out flirting during her absence, and resolving to teach them well the iniquity of such

conduct, she sat down on her bed into a lot of messy stuff of a clammy, damp nature. Now this fairly roused her, for she is a notable housewife, who keeps her house and slaves in exceedingly good order. So dismissing from her mind the commercial consideration she had intended to gloat over when she came into her room, she called Ingremina and others in a tone that brought those young ladies on the spot. She asked them how they dared forget to light her lamp; they said they had not, but the lamp in the room must have gone out like the other lamps had, after burning dim and spluttering. They further said they had not been out, but had been sitting round the fire trying to make it burn properly. She duly whacked and pulled the ears of all within reach. I say within reach for she is not very active, weighing, I am sure, upwards of eighteen stone. Then she went back into her room and got out her beautiful English paraffin lamp, which she keeps in a box, and taking it into the cookhouse, picked up a bit of wood from the hissing, spluttering fire, and lit it. When she picked up the wood she noticed that it was covered with the same sticky abomination she had met before that evening, and it smelt of the same faint smell she had noticed as soon as she had reached her house, and by now the whole air seemed oppressive with it.

As soon as the lamp was alight she saw what the stuff was, namely, blood. Blood was everywhere, the rest of the sticks in the fire had it on them, it sizzled at the burning ends, and ran off the other in rills. There were pools of it about her clean, sandy yard. Her own room was reeking, the bed, the stools, the floor; it trickled down the door-post; coagulated on the lintel. She herself was smeared with it from the things she had come in contact with in the dark, and the slaves seemed to have been sitting in pools of it. The things she picked up off the table and shelf left rims of it behind them; there was more in the skillets, and the oil in the open palm-oil lamps had a film of it floating on the oil. Investigation showed that the whole of the rest of her house was in a similar mess. The good lady gave a complete catalogue of the household furniture and its condition, which I need not give here. The slave girls when the light came were terrified at what they saw, and she called in the aristocracy of the village, and asked them their opinion on the blood palaver. They said they could make nothing of it at first, but subsequently formed the opinion that it meant something was going to happen, and suggested with the kind, helpful cheerfulness of relatives and friends, that they should not wonder if it were a

prophecy of her own death. This view irritated the already tried lady, and she sent them about their business, and started the slaves on house-cleaning. The blood cleaned up all right when you were about it, but kept on turning up in other places, and in the one you had just cleaned as soon as you left off and went elsewhere; and the morning came and found things in much the same state until 'before suntime', say about 10 o'clock, when it faded away.

I cautiously tried to get my stately, touchy dowager duchess to explain how it was that there was such a lot of blood, and how it was it got into the house. She just said 'it had to go somewhere', and refused to give rational explanations as *Chambers's Journal* does after telling a good ghost story. I found afterwards that it was quite decided it was a case of 'blood come before', and at Okÿon, Miss Slessor told me, in regard to the similar case there, that this was the opinion held regarding the phenomenon.

It is always held uncanny in Africa if a person dies without shedding blood. You see, the blood is the life, and if you see it come out, you know the going of the thing, as it were. If you do not, it is mysterious. At Okÿon, a few days after the blood appeared, a nephew of the person whose house it came into was killed while felling a tree in the forest; a bough struck him and broke his neck, without shedding a drop of blood, and this bore out the theory, for the blood having 'to go somewhere' came before. In the Bantu case I did not hear of such a supporting incident happening.

Certain African ideas about blood puzzle me. I was told by a Batanga friend, a resident white trader, that a short time previously a man was convicted of theft by the natives of a village close to him. The hands and feet of the criminal were tied together, and he was flung into the river. He got himself free, and swam to the other bank, and went for bush. He was recaptured, and a stone tied to his neck, and in again he was thrown. The second time he got free and ashore, and was recaptured, and the chief then, most regretfully, ordered that he was to be knocked on the head before being thrown in for a third time.

This time palaver set, but the chief knew that he would die himself, by spitting the blood he had spilt, from his own lungs, before the year was out. I inquired about the chief when I passed this place, more than eighteen months after, and learnt from a native that the chief was dead, and that he had died in

this way. The objection thus was not to shedding blood in a general way, but to the shedding in the course of judicial execution. There may be some idea of this kind underlying the ingenious and awful ways the Negroes have of killing thieves, by tying them to stakes in the rivers, or down on to paths for the driver ants to kill and eat, but this is only conjecture.

I cannot close this brief notice of native ideas without mentioning the secret societies; but to go fully into this branch of the subject would require volumes, for every tribe has its secret society. The Poorah of Sierra Leone, the Oru of Lagos, the Egbo of Calabar, the Yasi of the Igalwa, the Ukuku of the M'pongwe, the Ikun of the Bakele, and the Lukuku of the Bachilangi, Baluba, are some of the most powerful secret societies on the West African Coast.

These secret societies are not essentially religious, their action is mainly judicial, and their particularly presiding spirit is not a god or devil in our sense of the word. The ritual differs for each in its detail, but there are broad lines of agreement between them. There are societies both for men and for women, but no mixed societies for both sexes. Those that I have mentioned above are all male, and women are utterly forbidden to participate in the rites or become acquainted with their secrets, for one of the chief duties of these societies is to keep the women in order; and besides this reason it is undoubtedly held that women are bad for certain forms of ju-ju, even when these forms are not directly connected, as far as I can find out, with the secret society.

For example, the other day a chief up the Mungo River deliberately destroyed his ju-ju by showing it to his women. It was a great ju-ju, but expensive to keep up, requiring sacrifices of slaves and goats, so what with trade being bad, fall in the price of oil and ivory and so on, he felt he could not afford that ju-ju, and so destroyed its power, so as to prevent its harming him when he neglected it. Probably the destructive action of women is not only the idea of their inferiority—for had inferiority been the point, that chief would have laid his ju-ju with dogs, or pigs—but arises from the undoubted fact that women are notably deficient in real reverence for authority, as is demonstrated by the way they continually treat that of their husbands.

The general rule with these secret societies is to admit the young free people at an age of about eight to ten years, the boys entering the male, the girls the female society. Both societies are rigidly kept apart. A man who attempts to penetrate the

female mysteries would be as surely killed as a woman who might attempt to investigate the male mysteries; still I came, in 1893, across an amusing case which demonstrates the inextinguishable thirst for knowledge, so long as that knowledge is forbidden, which characterises our sex.

It was in the district just south of Big Batanga. The male society had been very hard on the ladies for some time, and one day one star-like intellect among the latter told her next-door neighbour, in strict confidence, that she did not believe Ikun was a spirit at all, but only old So-and-so dressed up in leaves. This rank heresy spread rapidly, in strict confidence, among the ladies at large, and they used to assemble together in the house of the foundress of the theory, secretly of course, because husbands down there are hasty with the cutlass and the kassengo, and they talked the matter over. Somehow or other, this came to the ears of the men. Whether the ladies got too emancipated and winked when Ikun was mentioned, or asked how Mr So-and-so was this morning, in a pointed way, after an Ikun manifestation, I do not know; some people told me this was so, but others, who, I fear, were right, considering the acknowledged slowness of men in putting two and two together, and the treachery of women towards each other, said that a woman had told a man that she had heard some of the other women were going on in this heretical way.

Anyhow, the men knew, and were much alarmed; scepticism had spread by now to such an extent that nothing short of burning or drowning all the women could stamp it out and reintroduce the proper sense of awe into the female side of society, and after a good deal of consideration the men saw, for men are undoubtedly more gifted in foresight than our sex, that it was no particular use reintroducing this awe if there was no female half of society to be impressed by it. It was a brain-spraining problem for the men all round, for it is clear society cannot be kept together without some superhuman aid to help to keep the feminine portion of it within bounds.

Grave councils were held, and it was decided that the woman at whose house these treasonable meetings were held should be sent away early one morning on a trading mission to the nearest factory, a job she readily undertook; and while the other women were away in the plantation or at the spring, certain men entered her house secretly and dug a big chamber out in the floor of the hut, and one of them, dressed as Ikun, and provided with refreshments for the day, got into this chamber, and

the whole affair was covered over carefully and the floor re-sanded.

That afternoon there was a big manifestation of Ikun. He came in the most terrible form, his howls were awful, and he finally went dancing away into the bush as the night came down. The ladies had just taken the common-sense precaution of removing all goats, sheep, fowls, &c., into enclosed premises, for, like all his kind, he seizes and holds any property he may come across in the street, but there was evidently no emotional thrill in the female mind regarding him, and when the leading lady returned home in the evening the other ladies strolled into their leader's hut to hear about what new cotton prints, beads, and things Mr—— had got at his factory by the last steamer from Europe, and interesting kindred subjects bearing on Mr——.

When they had threshed these matters out, the conversation turned on to religion, and what fools those men had been making of themselves all the afternoon with their Ikun. No sooner was his name uttered than a venomous howl, terminating in squeals of rage and impatience, came from the ground beneath them. They stared at each other for one second, and then, feeling that something was tearing its way up through the floor, they left for the interior of Africa with one accord. Ikun gave chase as soon as he got free, but what with being half-stifled and a bit cramped in the legs, and much encumbered with his vegetable decorations, the ladies got clear away and no arrests were made—but society was saved. Scepticism became in the twinkling of an eye a thing of the past.

Ikun has the peculiar habit of coming in from the sea in a canoe. The heads of his society always see him first, and go out to meet him in their canoes, and bring him in his Jack-in-the-Green dress ashore; meanwhile all the women dash about driving into enclosures ducks, chickens, children, sheep and goats, and then conceal themselves. He is the only member of his class I have ever heard of that comes in from the sea; they usually come out of the bush like Egbo and Yasi, and his dress is bush any-how. There is another peculiarity of Ikun, which is that he has a peculiar way of taking payment for a thing which all his fellow secret societies and spirits also supply, namely, the power of becoming rich.

For example, a man desires this power, so he goes to someone known to possess Ikun, and inquires of him if he will let him have a certain quantity of his power, say, enough to ensure his becoming a thousand-pound-a-yearer. The man who possesses

the power says that for this quantity of the power the applicant must pay the lives of fifty of his blood relations. All these lives the man must take himself, from time to time, secretly, as occasion offers; and the spirits of the murdered go to Ikun in the under-world and work for him as slaves, and as they go down, so every undertaking of the murderer turns out profitably, and he gradually grows richer and richer.

It is a dangerous practice in this world, because when your neighbours notice how your relatives are going off, and how you are getting on, they are apt to say you are making Ikun; whereupon they descend on you and kill you, and collar your hard-earned wealth, and have a dance in the evening; but I am assured that if you succeed in killing off your relations, unnoticed, up to the proper amount, there is no eternal unpleasantness awaiting you personally as there would be in Europe if you made a deal with the devil. Whether this arises from a lack of moral perception of the iniquity of this sort of thing in the African, or from the difficulty of imagining—with only the African's allowance of imagination—a greater hell than existence in a West African village under native law, I must leave to psychologists.

The great point of agreement between all these West African secret societies lies in the methods of initiation.

The boy, if he belongs to a tribe that goes in for tattooing, is tattooed, and is handed over to instructors in the societies' secrets and formulæ. He lives, with the other boys of his tribe undergoing initiation, usually under the rule of several instructors, and for the space of one year. He lives always in the forest, and is naked and smeared with clay.

The boys are exercised so as to become inured to hardship: in some districts, they make raids so as to perfect themselves in this useful accomplishment. They always take a new name, and are supposed by the initiation process to become new beings in the magic wood, and on their return to their village at the end of their course, they pretend to have entirely forgotten their life before they entered the wood; but this pretence is not kept up beyond the period of festivities given to welcome them home. They all learn; to a certain extent, a new language, a secret language only understood by the initiated.

The same removal from home and instruction from initiated members is also observed with the girls. However, in their case, it is not always a forest-grove they are secluded in, sometimes it it is done in huts. Among the Grain Coast tribes, however, the

girls go into a magic wood until they are married. Should they have to leave the wood for any temporary reason, they must smear themselves with white clay. A similar custom holds good in Okÿon, Calabar district, where, should a girl have to leave the fattening-house, she must be covered with white clay. I believe this fattening-house custom in Calabar is not only for fattening up the women to improve their appearance, but an initiatory custom as well, although the main intention is now, undoubtedly, fattening, and the girl is constantly fed with fat-producing foods, such as fou-fou soaked in palm oil. I am told, but I think wrongly, that the white clay with which a Calabar girl is kept covered while in the fattening-house, putting on an extra coating of it should she come outside, is to assist in the fattening process by preventing perspiration.

The duration of the period of seclusion varies somewhat. San Salvador boys are six months in the wood. Cameroon boys are twelve months. In most districts the girls are betrothed in infancy, and they go into the wood or initiatory hut for a few months before marriage. In this case the time seems to vary with the circumstances of the individual; not so with the boys, for whom each tribal society has a duly appointed course terminating at a duly appointed time; but sometimes, as among some of the Yoruba tribes, the boy has to remain under the rule of the presiding elders of the society, painted white, and wearing only a bit of grass cloth, if he wears anything, until he has killed a man. Then he is held to have attained man's estate by having demonstrated his courage and also by having secured for himself the soul of the man he has killed as a spirit slave.

The initiation of boys into a few of the elementary dogmas of the secret society by no means composes the entire work of the society. All of them are judicial, and taken on the whole they do an immense amount of good. The methods are frequently a little quaint. Rushing about the streets disguised under masks and drapery, with an imitation tail swinging behind you, while you lash out at every one you meet with a whip or cutlass, is not a European way of keeping the peace, or perhaps I should say maintaining the dignity of the law. But discipline must be maintained, and this is the West African way of doing it.

Egbo has the most grades of initiation, except perhaps Poorah, and it exercises jurisdiction over all classes of crime except witchcraft. Any Effik man who desires to become an influential person in the tribe must buy himself into as high a grade of Egbo as he can afford, and these grades are expensive, £1,500 or

£1,000 English being required for the higher steps, I am informed. But it is worth it to a great trader, as an influential Effik necessarily is, for he can call out his own class of Egbo and send it against those of his debtors who may be of lower grades, and as the Egbo methods of delivering its orders to pay up consist in placing Egbo at a man's doorway, and until it removes itself from that doorway the man dare not venture outside his house, it is most successful.

Last February I was making my way back towards Duke Town—late, as usual; I was just by a town on the Qwa River. As I was hurrying onward I heard a terrific uproar accompanied by drums in the thick bush into which, after a brief interval of open ground, the path turned. I became cautious and alarmed, and hid in some dense bush as the men making the noise approached. I saw it was some ju-ju affair. They had a sort of box which they carried on poles, and their dresses were peculiar, and abnormally ample over the upper part of the body. They were prancing about in an ecstatic way round the box, which had one end open, beating their drums and shouting. They were fairly close to me, but fortunately turned their attention to another bit of undergrowth, or that evening they would have landed another kind of thing to what they were after.

The bushes they selected they surrounded, and evidently did their best to induce something to come out of them and go into their box arrangement. I was every bit as anxious as they were that they should succeed, and succeed rapidly, for you know there are a nasty lot of snakes and things in general, not to mention driver ants, about that Calabar bush, that do not make it at all pleasant to go sitting about in. However, presently they got this something into their box and rejoiced exceedingly, and departed staggering under the weight. I gave them a good start, and then made the best of my way home; and all that night Duke Town howled, and sang, and thumped its tom-toms unceasingly; for I was told Egbo had come into the town.

Egbo is very coy, even for a secret society spirit, and seems to loathe publicity; but when he is ensconced in this ark he utters sententious observations on the subject of current politics, and his word is law. The voice that comes out of the ark is very strange, and unlike a human voice. I heard it shortly after Egbo had been secured. I expect, from what I saw, that there was some person in that ark all the time, but I do not know. It is more than I can do to understand my ju-ju details at present, let alone explain them on rational lines.

I hear that there is a tribe on the slave coast who have been proved to keep a small child in the drum that is the residence of their chief spirit, and that when the child grows too large to go in it is killed, and another one that has in the meantime been trained by the priests takes the place of the dead one, until it, in its turn, grows too big and is killed, and so on. I expect this killing of the children is not sacrificial, but arises entirely from the fact that as ex-kings are dangerous to the body politic, therefore still more dangerous would ex-gods be.

Very little is known by outsiders regarding Egbo compared to what there must be to be known, owing to a want of interest or to a sense of inability on the part of most white people to make head or tail out of what seems to them a horrid pagan practice or a farrago of nonsense.

After dealing with other secret societies, Mary Kingsley comes to leopard societies, which she maintains fall into a different category, though a man may belong to both.

These other societies [leopard societies] are practically murder societies, and their practices usually include cannibalism, which is not an essential part of the rites of the great tribal societies, Yasi or Egbo. In the Calabar district I was informed by natives that there was a society of which the last entered member has to provide, for the entertainment of the other members, the body of a relative of his own, and sacrificial cannibalism is always breaking out, or perhaps I should say being discovered, by the white authorities in the Niger Delta. There was the great outburst of it at Brass, early last year, and the one chronicled in the *Liverpool Mercury* for August 13th, 1895, as occurring at Sierra Leone. This account is worth quoting. It describes the hanging by the authorities of three murderers, and states the incidents, which took place in the Imperi country behind Free Town.

One of the chief murderers was a man named Jowe, who had formerly been a Sunday-school teacher in Sierra Leone. He pleaded in extenuation of his offence that he had been compelled to join the society. The others said they committed the murders in order to obtain certain parts of the body for ju-ju purposes, the leg, the hand, the heart, &c. The *Mercury* goes on to give the statement of the Reverend Father Bomy of the Roman Catholic Mission.

'He said he was at Bromtu, where the St Joseph Mission has

a station, when a man was brought down from the Imperi country in a boat. The poor fellow was in a dreadful state, and was brought to the station for medical treatment. He said he was working on his farm, when he was suddenly pounced upon from behind. A number of sharp instruments were driven into the back of his neck. He presented a fearful sight, having wounds all over his body supposed to have been inflicted by the claws of the leopard, but in reality they were stabs from sharp-pointed knives. The native, who was a powerfully-built man, called out, and his cries attracting the attention of his relations, the leopards made off. The poor fellow died at Bromtu from the injuries. It was only his splendid physique that kept him alive until his arrival at the Mission.'

These things are known and acknowledged to have taken place in a colony like Sierra Leone, which has had unequalled opportunities of becoming christianised for more than one hundred years, and now has more than one hundred and thirty places of Christian worship in it.

Sometimes, instead of the three-pronged forks, there are fixed in the paws of the leopard skin sharp-pointed cutting knives, the skin being made into a sort of glove into which the hand of the human leopard fits. In one skin I saw down south this was most ingeniously done. The knives were shaped like the leopard's claws, curved, sharp-pointed, and with cutting edges underneath, and I am told the American Mendi Mission, which works in the Sierra Leone districts, have got a similar skin in their possession. In Calabar and Libreville, these murders used to be very common right in close to the white settlements; but in Calabar white jurisdiction is now too much feared for them to be carried on near it, and in Libreville the making of the 'Boulevard' between that town and Glass has cleared the custom out from its great haunt along by the swamp path that was formerly there. In the districts I know where human leopardism occurs (from Bonny to Congo Belge) the victims are killed to provide human flesh for certain secret societies who eat it as one of their rites. Sometimes it is used by a man playing a lone hand to kill an enemy.

The ju-ju parts of the leopard are the whiskers. You cannot get a skin from a native with them on, and gay, reckless young hunters wear them stuck in their hair and swagger tremendously while the elders shake their heads and keep a keen eye on their subsequent conduct.

I must say the African leopard is an audacious animal. I

really think, taken as a whole, he is the most lovely animal I have ever seen; only seeing him, in the one way you can gain a full idea of his beauty, namely in his native forest, is not an unmixed joy to a person, like myself, of a nervous disposition. I may remark that my nervousness regarding the big game of Africa is of a rather peculiar kind. I can confidently say I am not afraid of any wild animal—until I see it—and then—well I will yield to nobody in terror; fortunately as I say my terror is a special variety; fortunately because no one can manage their own terror. You can suppress alarm, excitement, fear, fright, and all those small-fry emotions, but the real terror is as dependent on the inner make of you as the colour of your eyes, or the shape of your nose; and when terror ascends its throne in my mind I become preternaturally artful, and intelligent to an extent utterly foreign to my true nature, and save, in the case of close quarters with bad big animals, a feeling of rage against some unknown person that such things as leopards, elephants, crocodiles, &c., should be allowed out loose in that disgracefully dangerous way, I do not think much about it at the time. Whenever I have come across an awful animal in the forest and I know it has seen me I take Jerome's advice, and instead of relying on the power of the human eye rely upon that of the human leg, and effect a masterly retreat in the face of the enemy. If I know it has not seen me I sink in my tracks and keep an eye on it, hoping that it will go away soon.

Thus I once came upon a leopard. I had got caught in a tornado in a dense forest. The massive, mighty trees were waving like a wheat-field in an autumn gale in England, and I dare say a field mouse in a wheat-field in a gale would have heard much the same uproar. The tornado shrieked like ten thousand vengeful demons. The great trees creaked and groaned and strained against it and their bush-rope cables groaned and smacked like whips, and ever and anon a thundering crash with snaps like pistol shots told that they and their mighty tree had strained and struggled in vain. The fierce rain came in a roar, tearing to shreds the leaves and blossoms and deluging everything.

I was making bad weather of it, and climbing up over a lot of rocks out of a gully bottom where I had been half drowned in a stream, and on getting my head to the level of a block of rock I observed right in front of my eyes, broadside on, maybe a yard off, certainly not more, a big leopard. He was crouching on the ground, with his magnificent head thrown back and his eyes

shut. His fore-paws were spread out in front of him and he lashed the ground with his tail, and I grieve to say, in face of that awful danger—I don't mean me, but the tornado—that depraved creature swore, softly, but repeatedly and profoundly.

I did not get all these facts up in one glance, for no sooner did I see him than I ducked under the rocks, and remembered thankfully that leopards are said to have no power of smell. But I heard his observation on the weather, and the flip-flap of his tail on the ground. Every now and then I cautiously took a look at him with one eye round a rock-edge, and he remained in the same position. My feelings tell me he remained there twelve months, but my calmer judgment puts the time down at twenty minutes; and at last, on taking another cautious peep, I saw he was gone. At the time I wished I knew exactly where, but I do not care about that detail now, for I saw no more of him.

He had moved off in one of those weird lulls which you get in a tornado, when for a few seconds the wild herd of hurrying winds seem to have lost themselves, and wander round crying and wailing like lost souls, until their common rage seizes them again and they rush back to their work of destruction. It was an immense pleasure to have seen the great creature like that. He was so evidently enraged and baffled by the uproar and dazzled by the floods of lightning that swept down into the deepest recesses of the forest, showing at one second every detail of twig, leaf, branch and stone round you, and then leaving you in a sort of swirling dark until the next flash came; this, and the great conglomerate roar of the wind, rain and thunder, was enough to bewilder any living thing.

I have never hurt a leopard intentionally; I am habitually kind to animals, and besides I do not think it is ladylike to go shooting things with a gun. Twice, however, I have been in collision with them. On one occasion a big leopard had attacked a dog, who, with her family, was occupying a broken-down hut next to mine. The dog was a half-bred boarhound, and a savage brute on her own account. I, being roused by the uproar, rushed out into the feeble moonlight, thinking she was having one of her habitual turns-up with other dogs, and I saw a whirling mass of animal matter within a yard of me. I fired two mushroom-shaped native stools in rapid succession into the brown of it, and the meeting broke up into a leopard and a dog. The leopard crouched, I think to spring on me. I can see its great, beautiful, lambent eyes still, and I seized an earthen water-cooler and flung it straight at them.

It was a noble shot; it burst on the leopard's head like a shell and the leopard went for bush one time. Twenty minutes after people began to drop in cautiously and inquire if anything was the matter, and I civilly asked them to go and ask the leopard in the bush, but they firmly refused. We found the dog had got her shoulder slit open as if by a blow from a cutlass, and the leopard had evidently seized the dog by the scruff of her neck, but owing to the loose folds of skin no bones were broken and she got round all right after much ointment from me, which she paid me for with several bites. Do not mistake this for a sporting adventure. I no more thought it was a leopard than that it was a lotus when I joined the fight.

My other leopard was also after a dog. Leopards always come after dogs, because once upon a time the leopard and the dog were great friends, and the leopard went out one day and left her whelps in charge of the dog, and the dog went out flirting, and a snake came and killed the whelps, so there is ill-feeling to this day between the two.

In addition to the secret society and the leopard society, there are in the Delta some ju-jus held only by a few great chiefs. The one in Bonny has a complete language to itself, and there is one in Duke Town so powerful that should you desire the death of any person you have only to go and name him before it. 'These ju-jus are very swift and sure.' I would rather drink than fight with any of them—yes, far.

CHAPTER TWELVE

'The Throne of Thunder'

After returning from Corisco I remained a few weeks in Gaboon, and then regretfully left on the *Niger*. My regrets, I should say, arose from leaving the charms and interests of Congo Français, and had nothing whatever to do with taking passage on one of the most comfortable ships of all those which call on the Coast.

The *Niger* was homeward-bound when I joined her, and in due course arrived in Cameroon River, and I was once again under the dominion of Germany. It would be a very interesting thing to compare the various forms of European government in Africa—English, French, German, Portuguese and Spanish; but to do so with any justice would occupy more space than I have at my disposal, for the subject is extremely intricate. Each of these forms of government have their good points and their bad. Each of them are dealing with bits of Africa differing from each other—in the nature of their inhabitants and their formation, and so on—so I will not enter into any comparison of them here, but merely remark that, on the whole, German colonial methods in Africa are more akin to English than to French, and that Germany has one of the main English faults in an emphasised state—namely, a want of due appreciation of the work of the men who serve her in Africa.

Time after time I have come across cases of German officers in Cameroon who have done their country good and noble service, and who yet, on their return to the Fatherland they have loved so well, have found, not only a want of due reward, but worse. When the flush of enthusiasm for colonial enterprise dies out in Germany—as it may die out in the face of the want of profit from her colonies, arising from a too heavy expenditure of money on them—the sin of her ingratitude to those men who have served her in Cameroon will find her out, and no longer will her best and bravest sons risk their honour in her service.

From the deck of the *Niger* I found myself again confronted with my great temptation—the magnificent Mungo Mah Lobeh—the Throne of Thunder. Now it is none of my business to go up mountains. There's next to no fish on them in West Africa, and precious little good rank fetish, as the population

on them is sparse—the African, like myself, abhorring cool
air. Nevertheless, I feel quite sure that no white man has ever
looked on the great Peak of Cameroon without a desire arising
in his mind to ascend it and know in detail the highest point on
the western side of the continent, and indeed one of the highest
points in all Africa.

So great is the majesty and charm of this mountain that the
temptation of it is as great to me to-day as it was on the first day
I saw it, when I was feeling my way down the West Coast of
Africa on the s.s. *Lagos* in 1893, and it revealed itself by good
chance from its surf-washed plinth to its sky-scraping summit.
Certainly it is most striking when you see it first, as I first saw
it, after coasting for weeks along the low shores and mangrove-
fringed rivers of the Niger Delta. Suddenly, right up out of the
sea, rises the great mountain to its 13,760 feet, while close at
hand, to westward, towers the lovely island mass of Fernando
Po to 10,190 feet. But every time you pass it by its beauty
grows on you with greater and greater force, though it is never
twice the same. Sometimes it is wreathed with indigo-black
tornado clouds, sometimes crested with snow, sometimes softly
gorgeous with gold, green, and rose-coloured vapours tinted by
the setting sun, sometimes completely swathed in dense cloud
so that you cannot see it at all; but when you once know it is
there it is all the same, and you bow down and worship.

There are only two distinct peaks to this glorious thing that
geologists brutally call the volcanic intrusive mass of the
Cameroon Mountains, viz., Big Cameroon and Little Cameroon.
The latter, Mungo Mah Etindeh, has not yet been scaled, although it is only 5,820 feet. One reason for this is doubtless that
the few people in fever-stricken, over-worked West Africa who
are able to go up mountains, naturally try for the adjacent Big
Cameroon; the other reason is that Mungo Mah Etindeh, to
which Burton refers as 'the awful form of Little Cameroon', is
mostly sheer cliff, and is from foot to summit clothed in an
almost impenetrable forest.

*On 20 September 1895 Mary Kingsley with a small party left
Victoria and tramped up the beginnings of a new road under
construction from Ambas Bay to Buea.*

The whole scheme of colour is indescribably rich and full in
tone. The very earth is a velvety red brown, and the butterflies
—which abound—show themselves off in the sunlight, in their

canary-coloured, crimson, and peacock-blue liveries, to perfection. After five minutes' experience of the road I envy those butterflies. I do not believe there is a more lovely road in this world, and besides, it's a noble and enterprising thing of a Government to go and make it, considering the climate and the country; but to get any genuine pleasure out of it, it is requisite to hover in a bird- or butterfly-like way, for of all the truly awful things to walk on, that road, when I was on it, was the worst.

Of course this arose from its not being finished, not having its top on in fact: the bit that was finished, and had got its top on, for half a mile beyond the bridge, you could go over in a Bath chair. The rest of it made you fit for one for the rest of your natural life, for it was one mass of broken lava rock, and here and there leviathan tree-stumps that had been partially blown up with gunpowder.

When we near the forest end of the road, it comes on to rain heavily, and I see a little house on the left-hand side, and a European engineer superintending a group of very cheerful natives felling timber. He most kindly invites me to take shelter, saying it cannot rain as heavily as this for long. My men also announce a desire for water, and so I sit down and chat with the engineer under the shelter of his verandah, while the men go to the water-hole, some twenty minutes off.

I presently see one of my men sitting right in the middle of the road on a rock, totally unsheltered, and a feeling of shame comes over me in the face of this black man's aquatic courage. Besides, there is no use delaying. Into the rain I go, and off we start. I may remark I subsequently found that my aquatic underling was drunk. I conscientiously attempt to keep dry, by hold-up an umbrella, knowing that though hopeless it is the proper thing to do.

We leave the road about fifty yards above the hut, turning into the unbroken forest on the right-hand side, and following a narrow, slippery, muddy, root-beset bush-path that was a comfort after the road. Presently we come to a lovely mountain torrent flying down over red-brown rocks in white foam; exquisitely lovely, and only a shade damper than the rest of things. Seeing this I solemnly fold up my umbrella and give it to Kefalla.

Now we are evidently dealing with a foot-hillside, but the rain is too thick for one to see two yards in any direction, and we seem to be in a ghost-land forest, for the great palms and red-woods rise up in the mist before us, and fade out in the mist

behind, as we pass on. The rocks which edge and strew the path at our feet are covered with exquisite ferns and mosses—all the most delicate shades of green imaginable, and here and there of absolute gold colour, looking as if some ray of sunshine had lingered too long playing on the earth, and had got shut off from heaven by the mist, and so lay nestling among the rocks until it might rejoin the sun.

The path now becomes an absolute torrent, with mud-thickened water, which cascades round one's ankles in a sportive way, and round one's knees in the hollows in the path. Five seconds after abandoning the umbrella I am wet through, but it is not uncomfortable at this temperature, something like that of a cucumber frame with the lights on, if you can clear your mind of all prejudice, as Dr Johnson says, and forget the risk of fever which saturation entails.

On we go, the path underneath the water seems a pretty equal mixture of rock and mud, but they are not evenly distributed. Plantations full of weeds show up on either side of us, and we are evidently now on the top of a foot-hill. I suspect a fine view of the sea could be obtained from here, if you have an atmosphere that is less than 99¾ per cent. of water. As it is, a white sheet—or more properly speaking, considering its soft, stuffy woolliness, a white blanket—is stretched across the landscape to the south-west, where the sea would show.

We go down-hill now, the water rushing into the back of my shoes for a change. The path is fringed by a high, sugar-cane-like grass which hangs across it in a lackadaisical way, swishing you in the face and cutting like a knife whenever you catch its edge, and pouring continually insidious rills of water down one's neck. It does not matter. The whole Atlantic could not get more water on to me than I have already got. Ever and again I stop and wring out some of it from my skirts, for it is weighty. One would not imagine that anything could come down in the way of water thicker than the rain, but it can. When one is on the top of the hills, a cold breeze comes through the mist chilling one to the bone, and bending the heads of the palm trees, sends down from them water by the bucketful with a slap; hitting or missing you as the case may be.

Both myself and my men are by now getting anxious for our 'chop', and they tell me, 'We look them big hut soon'. Soon we do look them big hut, but with faces of undisguised horror, for the big hut consists of a few charred roof-mats, &c., lying on the ground. There has been a fire in that simple savage home.

Continuing on their way, they shelter in the house of an African bible-reader, where Mary Kingsley spends so cold, wet, noisy and comfortless a night that even the perusal of Dr Günther on fishes proves no anodyne.

No watchman is required to wake you in the morning on the top of a Cameroon foot-hill by 5.30, because about 4 AM the dank chill that comes before the dawn does so most effectively. One old chief turned up early out of the mist and dashed me a bottle of palm wine; he says he wants to dash me a fowl, but I decline, and accept two eggs, and give him four heads of tobacco.

The whole place is swathed in thick white mist through which my audience arrive. But I am firm with them, and shut up the doors and windows and disregard their bangings on them while I am dressing, or rather redressing. The mission teachers get in with my tea, and sit and smoke and spit while I have my breakfast. Give me cannibal Fans!

It is pouring with rain again now, and we go down the steep hillock to the path we came along yesterday, keep it until we come to where the old path cuts it, and then turn up to the right following the old path's course and leave Buana without a pang of regret. Our road goes N.E. Oh, the mud of it! Not the clearish cascades of yesterday but sticky, slippery mud, intensely sticky, and intensely slippery. The narrow path which is filled by this, is V-shaped underneath from wear, and I soon find the safest way is right through the deepest mud in the middle.

The white mist shuts off all details beyond ten yards in any direction. All we can see, as we first turn up the path, is a patch of kokos of tremendous size on our right. After this comes weedy plantation, and stretches of sword grass hanging across the road. The country is not so level as—or rather, I should say, more acutely unlevel than—that we came over yesterday. On we go, patiently doing our mud pulling through the valleys; toiling up a hillside among lumps of rock and stretches of forest, for we are now beyond Buana's plantations; and skirting the summit of the hill only to descend into another valley. Evidently this is a succession of foot-hills of the great mountain and we are not on its true face yet. As we go on they become more and more abrupt in form, the valleys mere narrow ravines.

My men and I flounder about; thrice one of them, load and all, goes down with a squidge and a crash into the side grass, and says 'damn!' with quite the European accent; as a rule, how-

ever, we go on in single file, my shoes giving out a mellifluous squidge, and their naked feet a squish, squash. The men take it very good temperedly, and sing in between accidents; I do not feel much like singing myself, particularly at one awful spot, which was the exception to the rule that ground at acute angles forms the best going. This exception was a long slippery slide down into a ravine with a long, perfectly glassy slope up out of it.

I remember one of my tutors saying, 'Always when on a long march assume the attitude you feel most inclined to, as it is less tiring.' There could not be the least shadow of a doubt about your inclinations as to attitude here, nor to giving way to them, so we arrive at the bottom of that ravine in a fine confused heap. As for going up out of it, it was not mere inclination—it was passion that possessed you. What you wanted to do was to plant your nose against the hill-side and wave your normally earth-ward extremities in the air, particularly when you were near the middle of the slope, or close to the top. Two of the boys gave way to this impulse; I, of course, did not, but when I felt it coming on like a sort of fit, flung myself sideways into the dense bush that edges the path, and when it had passed off, scrambled out and had another try at the slide.

After this we have a stretch of rocky forest, and pass by a widening in the path which I am told is a place where men blow, i.e., rest, and then pass through another a little further on, which is Buea's bush market. Then through an opening in the great war-hedge of Buea, a growing stockade some fifteen feet high, the lower part of it wattled. Close by is a cross put up to mark the spot where that gallant young German officer fell last January twelvemonth, when on the first expedition to open up this side of the mountain.

At the sides of the path here grow banks of bergamot and balsam, returning good for evil and smiling sweetly as we crush them. Thank goodness we are in forest now, and we seem to have done with the sword-grass. The rocks are covered with moss and ferns, and the mist curling and wandering about among the stems is very lovely. I have to pause in life's pleasures because I want to measure one of the large earthworms, which, with smaller sealing-wax-red worms, are crawling about the path. He was eleven inches and three-quarters. He detained me some time getting this information, because he was so nervous during the operation.

The soil up here, about 2,500 feet above sea-level, though rock-laden is exceedingly rich, and the higher we go there is

more bergamot, native indigo, with its under-leaf dark blue, and lovely coleuses with red markings on their upper leaves, and crimson linings. I, as an ichthyologist, am in the wrong paradise. What a region this would be for a botanist!

The country is gloriously lovely if one could only see it for the rain and mist; but one only gets dim hints of its beauty when some cold draughts of wind come down from the great mountains and seem to push open the mist-veil as with spirit hands, and then in a minute let it fall together again. I do not expect to reach Buea within regulation time, but at 11.30 my men say 'we close in', and then, coming along a forested hill and down a ravine, we find ourselves facing a rushing river, wherein a squad of black soldiers are washing clothes, with the assistance of a squad of black ladies, with much uproar and sky-larking.

I hesitate on the bank. I am in an awful mess—mud-caked skirts, and blood-stained hands and face. Shall I make an exhibition of myself and wash here, or make an exhibition of myself by going unwashed to that unknown German officer who is in charge of the station? Naturally I wash here, standing in the river and swishing the mud out of my skirts; and then wading across to the other bank, I wring out my skirts, but what is life without a towel? The ground on the further side of the river is cleared of bush, and only bears a heavy crop of balsam; a few steps onwards bring me in view of a corrugated iron-roofed, plank-sided house, in front of which, towards the great mountain which now towers up into the mist, is a low clearing with a quadrangle of native huts—the barracks.

I receive a most kindly welcome from a fair, grey-eyed German gentleman, only unfortunately I see my efforts to appear before him clean and tidy have been quite unavailing, for he views my appearance with unmixed horror, and suggests an instant hot bath. I decline. Men can be trying! How in the world is anyone going to take a bath in a house with no doors, and only very sketchy wooden window-shutters?

The German officer is building the house quickly, as Ollendorff would say, but he has not yet got to such luxuries as doors, and so uses army blankets strung across the doorway; and he has got up temporary wooden shutters to keep the worst of the rain out, and across his own room's window he has a frame covered with greased paper. Thank goodness he has made a table, and a bench, and a washhand-stand out of planks for his spare room, which he kindly places at my disposal; and the Fatherland has evidently stood him an iron bedstead and a mattress for it.

But the Fatherland is not spoiling or cosseting this man to an extent that will enervate him in the least.

I get the loads brought into my room, where they steam and distil rills of water onto the bare floor, and then, barricading the door-blankets and the window-shutters, I dispossess myself of the German territory I have acquired during the last twenty-four hours, and my portmanteau having kept fairly watertight, I appear as a reasonable being before society—*i.e.*, Herr Liebert, the German officer—and hunt up my boys to get me tea. This being done, I go out on the verandah and discourse.

The mist clears off in the evening about five, and the surrounding scenery is at last visible. The great S.E. face of Mungo Mah Lobeh looks awfully steep when you know you have got to go up it. This station at Buea is 3,000 feet above sea-level, which explains the hills we have had to come up. The mountain wall when viewed from Buea is very grand, although it lacks snow-cap or glacier, and the highest summits of Mungo are not visible because we are too close under them, but its enormous bulk and its isolation make it highly impressive. The forest runs up it in a great band above Buea, then sends up great tongues into the grass belt above.

At 7.30 a heavy tornado comes rolling down upon us. Masses of indigo cloud with livid lightning flashing in the van, roll out from over the wall of the great crater above; then with that malevolence peculiar to the tornado it sees all the soldiers and their wives and children sitting happily in the barrack yard, howling in a minor key and beating their beloved tom-toms, so it comes and sits flump down on them with deluges of water, and sends its lightning running over the ground in livid streams of living death. Oh they are nice things are tornadoes! I wonder what they will be like when we are up in their home; up atop of that precious wall? I had no idea Mungo was so steep. If I had—well, I am in for it now!

No one stirring till six, when people come out of the huts, and stretch themselves and proceed to begin the day, in the African's usual perfunctory, listless way. My crew are worse than the rest. I go and hunt cook out. He props open one eye, with difficulty, and yawns a yawn that nearly cuts his head in two. I wake him up with a shock, by saying I mean to go on up today, and want my chop, and to start one time. He goes off and announces my horrible intention to the others.

Kefalla soon arrives upon the scene full of argument, 'You

no sabe this be Sunday, Ma?' says he in a tone that tells he considers this settles the matter. I 'sabe' unconcernedly; Kefalla scratches his head for other argument, but he has opened with his heavy artillery; which being repulsed throws his rear lines into confusion. Bum, the head man, then turns up, sound asleep inside, but quite ready to come. Bum, I find, is always ready to do what he is told, but has no more original ideas in his head than there are in a chair leg. Kefalla, however, by scratching other parts of his anatomy diligently, has now another argument ready, the two Bakwiris are sick with abdominal trouble that requires rum and rest, and one of the other boys has hot foot.

Herr Liebert now appears upon the scene, and says I can have some of his labourers, who are now more or less idle, because he cannot get about much with his bad foot to direct them, so I give the Bakwiris and the two hot foot cases 'books' to take down to Herr von Lucke [the Vice-Governor of Cameroon in Victoria] who will pay them off for me, and seeing that they have each a good day's rations of rice, beef, &c., eliminate them from the party.

In addition to the labourers, I am to have as a guide Sasu, a black sergeant, who went up the Peak with the officers of the *Hyæna*, and I get my breakfast, and then hang about watching my men getting ready very slowly to start. Off we get about 8, and start with all good wishes, and grim prophecies, from Herr Liebert.

These prove justified, and they are forced by the bad going to return to the Station and seek another route which leads them, after further trials, to the rain-forest on the higher slopes of the mountain.

Imagine a vast, seemingly limitless cathedral with its countless columns covered, nay, composed of the most exquisite dark-green, large-fronded moss, with here and there a delicate fern embedded in it as an extra decoration. The white, gauze-like mist comes down from the upper mountain towards us: creeping, twining round, and streaming through the moss-covered tree columns—long bands of it reaching along sinuous, but evenly, for fifty and sixty feet or more, and then ending in a puff like the smoke of a gun. Soon, however, all the mist-streams coalesce and make the atmosphere all their own, wrapping us round in a clammy, chill embrace; it is not that wool-blanket, smothering affair that we were wrapped in down by Buana, but exquisitely delicate. The difference it makes to the beauty of

the forest is just the same difference you would get if you put a
delicate veil over a pretty woman's face or a sack over her head.
In fact, the mist here was exceedingly becoming to the forest's
beauty. Now and again growls of thunder roll out from, and
quiver in, the earth beneath our feet. Mungo is making a big
tornado, and is stirring and simmering it softly so as to make it
strong. I only hope he will not overdo it, as he does six times
in seven, and make it too heavy to get out on to the Atlantic,
where all tornadoes ought to go. If he does the thing will go and
burst on us in this forest tonight.

The forest now grows less luxuriant though still close—we
have left the begonias and the tree-ferns, and are in another
zone. The trees now, instead of being clothed in rich, dark-
green moss, are heavily festooned with long, greenish-white
lichen. It pours with rain.

At last we reach the place where the sergeant says we ought
to camp for the night. I have been feeling the time for camping
was very ripe for the past hour, and Kefalla openly said as much
an hour and a half ago, but he got such scathing things said to
him about civilians' legs by the sergeant that I did not air my
own opinion.

We are now right at the very edge of the timber belt. My
head man and three boys are done to a turn. If I had had a bull
behind me or Mr Fildes in front, I might have done another
five or seven miles, but not more.

The rain comes down with extra virulence as soon as we set
to work to start the fire and open the loads. I and Peter have
great times getting out the military camp-bed from its tight,
bolster-like case, while Kefalla gives advice, until, being irritated
by the bed's behaviour, I blow up Kefalla and send him to chop
firewood. However, we get the thing out and put up after cutting
a place clear to set it on: owing to the world being on a stiff
slant hereabouts, it takes time to make it stand straight. I get
four stakes cut, and drive them in at the four corners of the bed,
and then stretch over it Herr von Lucke's waterproof ground-
sheet, guy the ends out to pegs with string, feel profoundly grateful to both Herr Liebert for the bed and Herr von Lucke for the
sheet, and place the baggage under the protection of the German
Government's two belongings. Then I find the boys have not got
a fire with all their fuss, and I have to demonstrate to them the
lessons I have learnt among the Fans regarding fire-making. We
build a fire-house and then all goes well. I notice they do not
make a fire Fan fashion, but build it in a circle.

I dine luxuriously off tinned fat pork and hot tea, and then feeling still hungry go on to tinned herring. Excellent thing tinned herring, but I have to hurry because I know I must go up through the edge of the forest on to the grass land, and see how the country is made during the brief period of clearness that almost always comes just before nightfall. So leaving my boys comfortably seated round the fire having their evening chop, I pass up through the heavily lichen-tasselled fringe of the forest-belt into deep jungle grass, and up a steep and slippery mound.

In front the mountain-face rises like a wall from behind a set of hillocks, similar to the one I am at present on. The face of the wall to the right and left has two dark clefts in it. The peak itself is not visible from where I am; it rises behind and beyond the wall. I stay taking compass bearings and look for an easy way up for tomorrow. My men, by now, have missed their 'ma' and are yelling for her dismally, and the night comes down with great rapidity for we are in the shadow of the great mountain mass, so I go back into camp.

Alas! how vain are often our most energetic efforts to remove our fellow creatures from temptation. I knew a Sunday down among the soldiers would be bad for my men, and so came up here, and now, if you please, these men have been at the rum, because Bum, the head man, has been too done up to do anything but lie in his blanket and feed. Kefella is laying down the law with great detail and unction. Cook who has been very low in his mind all day, is now weirdly cheerful, and sings incoherently. The other boys, who want to go to sleep, threaten to 'burst him' if he 'no finish'. It's no good—cook carols on, and soon succumbing to the irresistible charm of music, the other men have to join in the choruses. The performance goes on for an hour, growing woollier and woollier in tone, and then dying out in sleep.

I write by the light of an insect-haunted lantern, sitting on the bed, which is tucked in among the trees some twenty yards away from the boys' fire. There is a bird whistling in a deep rich note that I have never heard before.

Next morning—23 September 1895—they make their assault on the 3,760-ft peak of the mountain.

We clamber up into the long jungle grass region and go on our way across a series of steep-sided, rounded grass hillocks, each

of which is separated from the others by dry, rocky water-courses. The effects produced by the seed-ears of the long grass round us are very beautiful; they look a golden brown, and each ear and leaf is gemmed with dewdrops, and those of the grass on the sides of the hillocks at a little distance off show a soft brown-pink.

After half an hour's climb, when we are close at the base of the [mountain's south-east] wall, I observe the men ahead halting, and coming up with them find Monrovia Boy down a hole; a little deep blow-hole, in which, I am informed, water is supposed to be. But Monrovia soon reports 'No live'.

I now find we have not a drop of water, either with us or in camp, and now this hole has proved dry. There is, says the sergeant, no chance of getting any more water on this side of the mountain, save down at the river at Buea.

This means failure unless tackled, and it is evidently a trick played on me by the boys, who intentionally failed to let me know of this want of water before leaving Buea. Had I known, of course I should have brought up a sufficient supply. Now they evidently think that there is nothing to be done but to return to Buea, and go down to Victoria, and get their pay, and live happily ever after, without having to face the horror of the upper regions of the mountain. They have worked their oracle with other white folk, I find, for they quote the other white folk's docile conduct as an example to me. I express my opinion of them and of their victims in four words—send Monrovia Boy, who I know is to be trusted, back to Buea with a scribbled note to Herr Liebert asking him to send me up two demijohns of water. I send Cook with him as far as the camp in the forest we have just left with orders to bring up three bottles of soda water I have left there, and to instruct the men there that as soon as the water arrives from Buea they are to bring it on up to the camp I mean to make at the top of the wall.

The men are sulky, and Sasu, Peter, Kefalla and head man say they will wait and come on as soon as Cook brings the soda water, and I go on, and presently see Xenia and Black Boy are following me. We get on to the intervening hillocks and commence to ascend the face of the wall.

The angle of this wall is great, and its appearance from below is impressive from its enormous breadth, and its abrupt rise without bend or droop for a good 2,000 feet into the air. It is covered with short, yellowish grass through which the burnt-up, scoriaceous lava rock protrudes in rough masses.

I got on up the wall, which when you are on it is not so perpendicular as it looks from below, my desire being to see what
sort of country there was on the top of it, between it and the
final peak. Sasu had reported to Herr Liebert that it was a
wilderness of rock, in which it would be impossible to fix a tent,
and spoke vaguely of caves. Here and there on the way up I
come to holes, similar to the one my men had been down for
water. I suppose these holes have been caused by gases from
an under hot layer of lava bursting up through the upper cool
layer. As I get higher, the grass becomes shorter and more
sparse, and the rocks more ostentatiously displayed. Here and
there among them are sadly tried bushes, bearing a beautiful
yellow flower, like a large yellow wild rose, only scentless. It is
not a rose at all, I may remark.

The ground, where there is any basin made by the rocks, grows
a great sedum, with a grand head of whity-pink flower, also a
tall herb, with soft downy leaves silver grey in colour, and having a very pleasant aromatic scent, and here and there patches
of good honest parsley. Bright blue, flannelly-looking flowers
stud the grass in sheltered places and a very pretty large green
orchid is plentiful. Above us is a bright blue sky with white
cloud rushing hurriedly across it to the N.E. and a fierce sun.
When I am about half-way up, I think of those boys, and,
wanting rest, sit down by an inviting-looking rock grotto, with
a patch of the yellow flowered shrub growing on its top. Inside
it grow little ferns and mosses, all damp; but alas! no water
pool, and very badly I want water by this time.

Below me a belt of white cloud had now formed, so that I
could see neither the foot-hillocks nor the forest, and presently
out of this mist came Xenia toiling up, carrying my black bag.
'Where them Black Boy live?' said I. 'Black Boy say him foot be
tire too much,' said Xenia, as he threw himself down in the
little shade the rock could give. I took a cupful of sour claret out
of the bottle in the bag, and told Xenia to come on up as soon as
he was rested, and meanwhile to yell to the others down below
and tell them to come on. Xenia did, but sadly observed,
'softly softly still hurts the snail', and I left him and went on up
the mountain.

When I had got to the top of the rock under which I had
sheltered from the blazing sun, the mist opened a little, and I
saw my men looking like as many little dolls. They were still
sitting on the hillock where I had left them. Buea showed from
this elevation well. The guard house and the mission house, like

little houses in a picture, and the make of the ground on which
Buea station stands, came out distinctly as a ledge or terrace,
extending for miles N.N.E. and S.S.W. This ledge is a strange-
looking piece of country, covered with low bush, out of which
rise great, isolated, white-stemmed cotton trees.

After taking some careful compass bearings for future use
regarding the Rumby and Omon range of mountains, which were
clearly visible and which look fascinatingly like my beloved
Sierra del Cristal, I turned my face to the wall of Mungo, and
continued the ascent. The sun, which was blazing, was reflected
back from the rocks in scorching rays. But it was more bearable
now, because its heat was tempered by a bitter wind.

The slope becoming steeper, I gradually made my way towards the left until I came to a great lane, as neatly walled with
rock as if it had been made with human hands. It runs down the
mountain face, nearly vertically in places and at stiff angles
always, but it was easier going up this lane than on the outside
rough rock, because the rocks in it had been smoothed by mountain torrents during thousands of wet seasons, and the walls
protected one from the biting wind, a wind that went through
me, for I had been stewing for nine months and more in tropic
and equatorial swamps.

Up this lane I went to the very top of the mountain wall,
and then, to my surprise, found myself facing a great, hillocky,
rock-encumbered plain, across the other side of which rose
the mass of the peak itself, not as a single cone, but as a wall
surmounted by several, three being evidently the highest
among them.

I started along the ridge of my wall, and went to its highest
part, that to the S.W., intending to see what I could of the
view towards the sea, and then to choose a place for camping
in for the night.

When I reached the S.W. end, looking westwards I saw the
South Atlantic down below, like a plain of frosted silver. Out of
it, barely twenty miles away, rose Fernando Po to its 10,190
feet with that majestic grace peculiar to a volcanic island. Immediately below me, some 10,000 feet or so, lay Victoria with the
forested foot-hills of Mungo Mah Lobeh encircling it as a dia-
dem, and Ambas Bay gemmed with rocky islands lying before it.
On my left away S.E. was the glorious stretch of the Cameroon
estuary, with a line of white cloud lying very neatly along the
course of Cameroon River.

In one of the chasms of the mountain wall that I had come

up—in the one furthest to the north—there was a thunderstorm brewing, seemingly hanging on to, or streaming out of the
mountain side, a soft billowy mass of dense cream-coloured
cloud, with flashes of golden lightnings playing about in it with
soft growls of thunder. Surely Mungo Mah Lobeh himself, of all
the thousands he annually turns out, never made one more
lovely than this.

Soon the white mists rose from the mangrove-swamp, and
grew rose-colour in the light of the setting sun, as they swept
upwards over the now purple high forests. In the heavens, to
the north, there was a rainbow, vivid in colour, one arch of it
going behind the peak, the other sinking into the mist sea below,
and this mist sea rose and rose towards me, turning from pale
rose-colour to lavender, and where the shadow of the Mungo
lay across it, to a dull leaden grey. It was soon at my feet, blotting the underworld out, and soon came flowing over the wall
top at its lowest parts, stretching in great spreading rivers over
the crater plain, and then these coalescing everything was shut
out save the two summits: that of Cameroon close to me, and
that of Clarence away on Fernando Po. These two stood out
alone, like great island masses made of iron rising from a formless, silken sea.

The space around seemed boundless, and there was in it
neither sound nor colour, nor anything with form, save those
two terrific things. It was like a vision, and it held me spell-
bound, as I stood shivering on the rocks with the white mist
round my knees until into my wool-gathering mind came the
memory of those anything but sublime men of mine; and I
turned and scuttled off along the rocks like an agitated ant left
alone in a dead universe.

I soon found the place where I had come up into the crater
plain and went down over the wall, descending with twice
the rapidity, but ten times the scratches and grazes, of the
ascent.

I picked up the place where I had left Xenia, but no Xenia
was there, nor came there any answer to my bush call for him,
so on I went down towards the place where, hours ago, I had
left the men. The mist was denser down below, but to my joy
it was warmer than on the summit of the wind-swept wall.

I had nearly reached the foot of this wall and made my mind
up to turn in for the night under a rock, when I heard a melancholy croak away in the mist to the left. I went towards it and
found Xenia lost on his own account, and distinctly quaint in

manner, and then I recollected that I had been warned Xenia is slightly crazy. Nice situation this: a madman on a mountain in the mist. Xenia, I found, had no longer got my black bag, but in its place a lid of a saucepan and an empty lantern.

In a homicidal state of mind, I made tracks for the missing ones followed by Xenia. I thought mayhap they had grown on to the rocks they had sat upon so long, but presently, just before it became quite dark, we picked up the place we had left them in and found there only an empty soda-water bottle. Xenia poured out a muddled mass of observations to the effect that 'they got fright too much about them water palaver'.

Finding our own particular hole in the forest wall was about as easy as finding 'our particular rabbit hole in an unknown hay-field in the dark', and the attempt to do so afforded us a great deal of varied exercise. I am obliged to be guarded in my language, because my feelings now are only down to one degree below boiling point. The rain now began to fall, thank goodness, and I drew the thick ears of grass through my parched lips as I stumbled along over the rugged lumps of rock hidden under the now waist-high jungle grass.

Our camp hole was pretty easily distinguishable by daylight, for it was on the left-hand side of one of the forest tongues, the grass land running down like a lane between two tongues here, and just over the entrance three conspicuously high trees showed. But we could not see these 'picking-up' points in the darkness, so I had to keep getting Xenia to strike matches, and hold them in his hat while I looked at the compass. Presently we came full tilt up against a belt of trees which I knew from these compass observations was our tongue of forest belt, and I fired a couple of revolver shots into it, whereabouts I judged our camp to be.

This was instantly answered by a yell from human voices in chorus, and towards that yell in a slightly amiable—a very slightly amiable—state of mind I went.

I will draw a veil over the scene, particularly over my observations to those men. They did not attempt to deny their desertion, but they attempted to explain it, each one saying that it was not he but the other boy who 'got fright too much'.

As the black sergeant was nominally our guide, I asked him for his views on the situation. He said that when he got back to the camp the boys were drunk, which I daresay was true, but left the explanation of why he went back out of the affair. I pointed this out, and Bum, the head man, charged into the gap

with the statement that Black Boy had got 'sick in him tummick, he done got fever bad bad too much', and so he and the rest had to escort Black Boy back to camp. This statement, though a contribution to the knowledge of the reason of the return, was manifestly untrue; because Black Boy, who did not know English, sat laughing and talking at the fire during this moving recital of his woes. Those men should have rehearsed their explanations, and then Black Boy could have done a good rousing writhe to support poor Bum's statement.

I closed the palaver promptly with a brief but lurid sketch of my opinion on the situation, and ordered food, for not having had a thing since 6.30 AM, and it being now 11 PM, I felt sinkings. Then arose another beautiful situation before me. It seems when Cook and Monrovia got back into camp this morning Master Cook was seized with one of those attacks of a desire to manage things that produce such awful results in the African servant, and sent all the beef and rice down to Buea to be cooked, because there was no water here to cook it. Therefore the men have got nothing to eat. I had a few tins of my own food and so gave them some, and they became as happy as kings in a few minutes, listening and shouting over the terrible adventures of Xenia, who is posing as the Hero of the Great Cameroon. I get some soda-water from the two bottles left and some tinned herring, and then write out two notes to Herr Liebert asking him to send me three more demijohns of water, and some beef and rice from the store, promising faithfully to pay for them on my return.

I would not prevent those men of mine from going up that peak above me after their touching conduct today. Oh! no; not for worlds, dear things.

CHAPTER THIRTEEN

Ascent of Cameroon Mountain

Next morning five of the party are sent back, leaving Mary Kingsley in the forest camp with the remaining three, awaiting the arrival of water.

There are an abominable lot of bees about; they do not give one a moment's peace, getting beneath the waterproof sheets over the bed, and pretending they can't get out and forthwith losing their tempers, which is imbecile, because the whole four sides of the affair are broad open.

The ground, bestrewn with leaves and dried wood, is a mass of large flies rather like our common house-fly, but both butter-flies and beetles seem scarce; but I confess I do not feel up to hunting much after yesterday's work, and deem it advisable to rest.

My face and particularly my lips are a misery to me, having been blistered all over by yesterday's sun, and last night I inadvertently whipped the skin all off one cheek with the blanket, and it keeps on bleeding, and, horror of horrors, there is no tea until that water comes.

About 8.30, to our delight, the gallant Monrovia Boy comes through the bush with a demijohn of water, and I get my tea, and give the men the only half-pound of rice I have and a tin of meat, and they eat, become merry, and chat over their absent companions in a scornful, scandalous way. Who cares for hotels now? When one is in a delightful place like this, one must work, so off I go to the north into the forest, after giving the rest of the demijohn of water into the Monrovia Boy's charge with strict orders it is not to be opened till my return. Quantities of beetles.

A little after two o'clock I return to camp, after having wandered about in the forest and found three very deep holes, down which I heaved rocks and in no case heard a splash. The other demijohns of water have not arrived yet, and we are get-ting anxious again because the men's food has not come up, and they have been so exceedingly thirsty that they have drunk most of the water—not, however, since it has been in Monrovia's

charge; but at 3.15 another boy comes through the bush with another demijohn of water. We receive him gladly, and ask him about the chop. He knows nothing about it. At 3.45 another boy comes through the bush with another demijohn of water; we receive him kindly; *he* does not know anything about the chop. At 4.10 another boy comes through the bush with another demijohn of water, and knowing nothing about the chop, we are civil to him, and that's all.

A terrific tornado which has been lurking growling about then sits down in the forest and bursts, wrapping us up in a lively kind of fog, with its thunder, lightning and rain. It was impossible to hear, or make one's self heard at the distance of even a few paces, because of the shrill squeal of the wind, the roar of the thunder, and the rush of the rain on the trees round us. It was not like having a storm burst over you in the least; you felt you were in the middle of its engine-room when it had broken down badly. After half an hour or so the thunder seemed to lift itself off the ground, and the lightning came in sheets, instead of in great forks that flew like flights of spears among the forest trees. The thunder, however, had not settled things amicably with the mountain; it roared its rage at Mungo, and Mungo answered back, quivering with a rage as great, under our feet.

As soon as we saw what we were in for, we had thrown dry wood on to the fire, and it blazed just as the rain came down, so with our assistance it fought a good fight with its fellow elements, spitting and hissing like a wild cat. It could have managed the water fairly well, but the wind came, very nearly putting an end to it by carrying away its protecting bough house, which settled on 'Professor' Kefalla, who burst out in a lecture on the foolishness of mountaineering and the quantity of devils in this region.

Just in the midst of these joys another boy came through the bush with another demijohn of water. We did not receive him even civilly; I burst out laughing, and the boys went off in a roar, and we shouted at him, 'Where them chop?' 'He live for come,' said the boy, and we then gave him a hearty welcome and a tot of rum, and an hour afterwards two more boys appear, one carrying a sack of rice and beef for the men, and the other a box for me from Herr Liebert, containing a luxurious supply of biscuits, candles, tinned meats and a bottle of wine and one of beer.

We are now all happy, though exceeding damp, and the boys sit round the fire, with their big iron pot full of beef and rice,

busy cooking while they talk. The worst of it is those tiresome bees, as soon as the rain is over, come in hundreds after the rum, and frighten me continually. The worthless wretches get intoxicated on what they can suck from round the cork, and then they stagger about on the ground buzzing malevolently. When the boys have had the chop and a good smoke, we turn to and make up the loads for tomorrow's start up the mountain, and then, after more hot tea, I turn in on my camp bed—listening to the soft sweet murmur of the trees and the pleasant, laughing chatter of the men.

There were quantities of large longicorn beetles about during the night—the sort with spiny backs; they kept on getting themselves hitched on to my blankets and when I wanted civilly to remove them they made a horrid fizzing noise and showed fight—cocking their horns in a defiant way. I awake finally about 5 AM soaked through to the skin. The waterproof sheet has had a label sewn to it, so is not waterproof, and it has been raining softly but amply for hours.

About seven we are off again, with Xenia, head man, Cook, Monrovia Boy and a labourer from Buea—the watercarriers have gone home after having had their morning chop.

We make for the face of the wall by a route to the left of that I took on Monday, and when we are clambering up it, some 600 feet above the hillocks, swish comes a terrific rainstorm at us accompanied by a squealing, bitter cold wind. We can hear the roar of the rain on the forest below, and hoping to get above it we keep on; hoping, however, is vain. The dense mist that comes with it prevents our seeing more than two yards in front, and we get too far to the left. I am behind the band today, severely bringing up the rear, and about 1 o'clock I hear shouts from the vanguard, and when I get up to them I find them sitting on the edge of one of the clefts or scars in the mountain face.

We keep on up a steep grass-covered slope, and finally reach the top of the wall. The immense old crater floor before us is to-day the site of a seething storm, and the peak itself quite invisible. My boys are quite demoralised by the cold. I find most of them have sold the blankets I gave them out at Buana; and those who have not sold them have left them behind at Buea, from laziness perhaps, but more possibly from a confidence in their powers to prevent us getting so far.

I believe if I had collapsed too—the cold tempted me to do so as nothing else can—they would have lain down and died in the cold sleety rain.

I sight a clump of gnarled sparsely-foliaged trees bedraped heavily with lichen, growing in a hollow among the rocks; thither I urge the men for shelter and they go like storm-bewildered sheep. My bones are shaking in my skin and my teeth in my head, for after the experience I had had of the heat here on Monday I dared not clothe myself heavily.

The men stand helpless under the trees, and I hastily take the load of blankets Herr Liebert lent us off a boy's back and undo it, throwing one blanket round each man, and opening my umbrella and spreading it over the other blankets. Then I give them a tot of rum apiece, as they sit huddled in their blankets, and tear up a lot of the brittle, rotten wood from the trees and shrubs, getting horrid thorns into my hands the while, and set to work getting a fire with it and the driest of the moss from beneath the rocks. By the aid of it and Xenia, who soon revived, and a carefully scraped up candle and a box of matches, the fire soon blazes, Xenia holding a blanket to shelter it, while I, with a cutlass, chop stakes to fix the blankets on, so as to make a fire tent.

The other boys now revive, and I hustle them about to make more fires, no easy work in the drenching rain, but work that has got to be done. We soon get three well alight, and then I clutch a blanket—a wringing wet blanket, but a comfort—and wrapping myself round in it, issue orders for wood to be gathered and stored round each fire to dry, and then stand over Cook while he makes the men's already cooked chop hot over our first fire, when this is done getting him to make me tea, or as it more truly should be called, soup, for it contains bits of rice and beef, and the general taste of the affair is wood smoke.

Kefalla by this time is in lecturing form again, so my mind is relieved about him, although he says, 'Oh ma! It be cold, cold too much. Too much cold kill we black man, all same for one as too much sun kill you white man. Oh ma! . . .,' &c. I tell him they have only got themselves to blame; if they had come up with me on Monday we should have been hot enough, and missed this storm of rain.

The bitter wind and swishing rain keep on. We are to a certain extent sheltered from the former, but the latter is of that insinuating sort that nothing but a granite wall would keep off.

Just at sundown, however, as is usual in this country, the rain ceases for a while, and I take this opportunity to get out my seaman's jersey, and retire up over the rocks to have my fight into it unobserved. It is a mighty fight to get that thing on, or

off, at the best of times, but today it is worse than usual, because I have to get it on over my saturated cotton blouse, and verily at one time I fear I shall have to shout for assistance or be suffocated, so firmly does it get jammed over my head. But I fight my way unaided into it, and then turn to survey our position, and find I have been carrying on my battle on the brink of an abysmal hole whose mouth is concealed among the rocks and scraggly shrubs just above our camp. I heave rocks down it, as we in Fanland would offer rocks to an Ombwiri, and hear them go 'knickity-knock, like a pebble in Carisbrook well'. I think I detect a far away splash, but it was an awesome way down.

The men are now quite happy; over each fire they have made a tent with four sticks with a blanket on, a blanket that is too wet to burn, though I have to make them brace the blankets to windward for fear of their scorching.

The wood from the shrubs here is of an aromatic and a resinous nature, which sounds nice, but it isn't; for the volumes of smoke it gives off when burning are suffocating, and the boys, who sit almost on the fire, are every few moments scrambling to their feet and going apart to cough out smoke, like so many novices in training for the profession of fire-eaters. However, they soon find that if they roll themselves in their blankets, and lie on the ground to windward they escape most of the smoke. They have divided up into three parties: Kefalla and Xenia, who have struck up a great friendship, take the lower, the most exposed fire. Head man, Cook, and Monrovia Boy have the upper fire, and the labourer has the middle one—he being an outcast for medical reasons. They are all steaming away and smoking comfortably.

I form the noble resolution to keep awake, and rouse up any gentleman who may catch on fire during the night, a catastrophe which is inevitable, and see to wood being put on the fires, so elaborately settle myself on my wooden chop-box, wherein I have got all the lucifers which are not in the soapbox. The very address on that chop-box, ought to keep its inside dry and up to duty, for it is 'An den Hochwohlgebornen Freiherrn von Stettin', &c. Owing to there not being a piece of ground the size of a sixpenny piece level in this place, the arrangement of my box camp takes time, but at last it is done to my complete satisfaction, close to a tree trunk, and I think, as I wrap myself up in my two wet blankets and lean against my tree, what a good thing it is to know how to make one's self comfortable in a place like this. This tree stem is perfection,

just the right angle to be restful to one's back, and one can rely all the time on Nature hereabouts not to let one get thoroughly effete from luxurious comfort, so I lazily watch and listen to Xenia and Kefalla at their fire hard by.

There seem but few insects here. I have only got two moths tonight—one pretty one with white wings with little red spots on, like an old-fashioned petticoat such as an early Victorian-age lady would have worn—the other a sweet thing in silver.

Then a horrid smell of burning Negro interrupts my writing and I have to get up and hunt it down. After some trouble I find it is a spark in cook's hair, he sleeping the while sweetly. I rouse him, *via* his shins, and tell him to put himself out, and he is grateful.

My face is a misery to me, as soon as it dries it sets into a mask, and when I move it, it splits and bleeds.

(Later, *i.e.* 2.15 AM). I have been asleep against that abominable vegetable of a tree. It had its trunk covered with a soft cushion of moss, and pretended to be a comfort—a right angle to lean against, and a softly padded protection to the spine from wind, and all that sort of thing; whereas the whole mortal time it was nothing in this wretched world but a water-pipe, to conduct an extra supply of water down my back. The water has simply streamed down it, and formed a nice little pool in a rocky hollow where I keep my feet, and I am chilled to the innermost bone, so have to scramble up and drag my box to the side of Kefalla and Xenia's fire, feeling sure I have contracted a fatal chill this time.

I scrape the ashes out of the fire into a heap, and put my sodden boots into them, and they hiss merrily, and I resolve not to go to sleep again. 5 AM—Have been to sleep twice, and have fallen off my box bodily into the fire in my wet blankets, and should for sure have put it out like a bucket of cold water had not Xenia and Kefalla been roused up by the smother I occasioned and rescued me—or the fire. It is not raining now, but it is bitter cold and Cook is getting my tea. I give the boys a lot of hot tea with a big handful of sugar in, and they then get their own food hot.

The weather is undecided and so am I, for I feel doubtful about going on in this weather, but I do not like to give up the peak after going through so much for it. The boys being dry and warm with the fires have forgotten their troubles. However, I settle in my mind to keep on, and ask for volunteers to come with me,

and Bum, the head man, and Xenia announce their willingness.
I put two tins of meat and a bottle of Herr Liebert's beer into
the little wooden box, and insist on both men taking a blanket
apiece, much to their disgust, and before six o'clock we are off
over the crater plain. It is a broken bit of country with rock
mounds sparsely overgrown with tufts of grass, and here and
there are patches of boggy land, not real bog, but damp places
where grow little clumps of rushes, and here and there among the
rocks sorely-afflicted shrubs of broom, and the yellow-flowered
shrub I have mentioned before, and quantities of very sticky
heather, feeling when you catch hold of it as if it had been
covered with syrup.

It is evil going, but perhaps not quite so evil as the lower
hillocks of the great wall where the rocks are hidden beneath
long slippery grass. We wind our way in between the mounds,
or clamber over them, or scramble along their sides impartially.

We keep as straight as we can, but get driven at an angle
by the strange ribs of rock which come straight down. These are
most tiresome to deal with, getting worse the higher we go, and
so rotten and weather-eaten are they, that they crumble into
dust and fragments under our feet. Head man gets half a dozen
falls, and when we are about three parts of the way up Xenia
gives in. The cold and the climbing are too much for him, so I
make him wrap himself up in his blanket, which he is glad
enough of now, and shelter in a depression under one of the
many rock ridges, and head man and I go on.

When we are some 600 feet higher the iron-grey mist comes
curling and waving round the rocks above us, like some savage
monster defending them from intruders, and I again debate
whether I was justified in risking the men, for it is a risk for
for them at this low temperature, with the evil weather I know,
and they do not know, is coming on. But still we have food and
blankets with us enough for them, and the camp in the plain
below they can reach all right, if the worst comes to the worst;
and for myself—well—that's my own affair, and no one will be
a ha'porth the worse if I am dead in an hour.

So I hitch myself on to the rocks, and take bearings, particularly bearings of Xenia's position, who, I should say, has got a
tin of meat and a flask of rum with him, and then turn and face
the threatening mist. It rises and falls, and sends out arm-like
streams towards us, and then Bum, the head man, decides to
fail for the third time to reach the peak, and I leave him
wrapped in his blanket with the bag of provisions and go on

alone into the wild, grey, shifting, whirling mist above, and soon find myself at the head of a rock ridge in a narrowish depression, walled by massive black walls which show fitfully but firmly through the mist.

I can see three distinctly high cones before me; and then the mist, finding it cannot drive me back easily, proceeds to desperate methods, and lashes out with a burst of bitter wind, and a sheet of blinding, stinging rain. I make my way up through it towards a peak which I soon see through a tear in the mist is not the highest, so I angle off and go up the one to the left, and after a desperate fight reach the cairn—only, alas! to find a hurricane raging and a fog in full possession, and not a ten yards' view to be had in any direction.

Near the cairn on the ground are several bottles, some of which the energetic German officers, I suppose, had emptied in honour of their achievement, an achievement I bow down before, for their pluck and strength had taken them here in a shorter time by far than mine. I do not meddle with anything, save to take a few specimens and to put a few more rocks on the cairn, and to put in among them my card, merely as a civility to Mungo, a civility his Majesty will soon turn into pulp. Not that it matters—what is done is done.

The weather grows worse every minute, and no sign of any clearing shows in the indigo sky or the wind-reft mist. The rain lashes so fiercely I cannot turn my face to it and breathe, the wind is all I can do to stand up against.

Verily I am no mountaineer, for there is in me no exultation, but only a deep disgust because the weather has robbed me of my main object in coming here, namely to get a good view and an idea of the way the unexplored mountain range behind Calabar trends.

My only consolation is that my failure to do this bit of work is not only my own fault, save as regards my coming here at the wrong season, which matter was also beyond my control. Moreover there was just the chance, as this is the tornado season, and not the real wet, that I might have had a clear day on the peak. I took my chance and it failed, so there's nothing to complain about.

Comforting myself with these reflections, I start down to find Bum, and do so neatly, and then together we scramble down carefully among the rotten black rocks, intent on finding Xenia. The scene is very grand. At one minute we can see nothing save the black rocks and cinders under foot; the next the wind-torn

mist separates now in one direction, now in another, showing us always the same wild scene of great black cliffs, rising in jagged peaks and walls around and above us. I think this walled caldron we had just left is really the highest crater on Mungo.

We soon become anxious about Xenia, for this is a fearfully easy place to lose a man in such weather, but just as we get below the thickest part of the pall of mist, I observe a doll-sized figure, standing on one leg taking on or off its trousers—our lost Xenia, beyond a shadow of a doubt, and we go down direct to him.

When we reach him we halt, and I give the two men one of the tins of meat, and take another and the bottle of beer myself, and then make a hasty sketch of the great crater plain below us. At the further edge of the plain a great white cloud is coming up from below, which argues badly for our trip down the great wall to the forest camp, which I am anxious to reach before nightfall after our experience of the accommodation afforded by our camp in the crater plain last night.

While I am sitting waiting for the men to finish their meal, I feel a chill at my back, as if some cold thing had settled there, and turning round, see the mist from the summit above coming in a wall down towards us. These mists up here, as far as my experience goes, are always preceded by a strange breath of ice-cold air—not necessarily a wind.

We start off down the mountain as rapidly as we can. Xenia is very done up, and head man comes perilously near breaking his neck by frequent falls among the rocks; my unlucky boots are cut through and through by the latter. When we get down towards the big crater plain, it is a race between us and the pursuing mist as to who shall reach the camp first, and the mist wins, but we have just time to make out the camp's exact position before it closes round us, so we reach it without any real difficulty. When we get there, about one o'clock, I find the men have kept the fires alight and Cook is asleep before one of them with another conflagration smouldering in his hair. I get him to make me tea, while the others pack up as quickly as possible, and by two we are all off on our way down to the forest camp.

Just as we reach the high jungle grass, down comes the rain and up comes the mist, and we have the worst time we have had during our whole trip, in our endeavours to find the hole in the forest that leads to our old camp.

Unfortunately, I must needs go in for acrobatic performances

on the top of one of the highest, rockiest hillocks. Poising myself on one leg I take a rapid slide sideways, ending in a very showy leap backwards which lands me on top of the lantern I am carrying today, among miscellaneous rocks. There being fifteen feet or so of jungle grass above me, all the dash and beauty of my performance are as much thrown away as I am, for my boys are too busy on their own accounts in the mist to miss me.

After resting some little time as I fell, and making and unmaking the idea in my mind that I am killed, I get up, clamber elaborately to the top of the next hillock, and shout for the boys, and 'Ma', 'Ma', comes back from my flock from various points out of the fog. I find Bum and Monrovia Boy, and learn that during my absence Xenia, who always fancies himself as a path-finder, has taken the lead, and gone off somewhere with the rest. We shout and the others answer, and we join them, and it soon becomes evident to the meanest intelligence that Xenia had better have spent his time attending to those things of his instead of going in for guiding, for we are now right off the track we made through the grass on our up journey, and we proceed to have a cheerful hour or so in the wet jungle, ploughing hither and thither, trying to find our way.

At last we pick up the top of a tongue of forest that we all feel is ours, but we—that is to say, Xenia and I, for the others go like lambs to the slaughter wherever they are led—disagree as to the path. He wants to go down one side of the tongue, I to go down the other, and I have my way, and we wade along, skirting the bushes that fringe it, trying to find our hole. I own I soon begin to feel shaky about having been right in the affair, but soon Xenia, who is leading, shouts he has got it, and we limp in, our feet sore with rugged rocks, and everything we have on, or in the loads, wringing wet, save the matches, which providentially I had put into my soap box.

Anything more dismal than the look of that desired camp when we reach it, I never saw. Pools of water everywhere. The fire-house a limp ruin, the camp bed I have been thinking fondly of for the past hour a water cistern. I tilt the water out of it, and say a few words to it regarding its hide-bound idiocy in obeying its military instructions to be waterproof; and then, while the others are putting up the fire-house, head man and I get out the hidden demijohn of rum, and the beef and rice, and I serve out a tot of rum each to the boys, who are shivering dreadfully, waiting for Cook to get the fire. He soon does this,

and then I have my hot tea and the men their hot food, for now we have returned to the luxury of two cooking pots.

Their education in bush is evidently progressing, for they make themselves a big screen with boughs and spare blankets, between the wind and the fire-house, and I get Xenia to cut some branches, and place them on the top of my waterproof sheet shelter, and we are fairly comfortable again, and the boys quite merry and very well satisfied with themselves.

There is a very peculiar look on the rotten wood on the ground round here; tonight it has patches and flecks of irides-cence like one sees on herrings or mackerel that have been kept too long. The appearance of this strange eerie light in among the bush is very weird and charming. I have seen it before in dark forests at night, but never so much of it.

By 10 o'clock next morning [27 September 1895] we are off down to Buea. At 10.15 it pours as it can here; by 10.17 we are all in our normal condition of bedraggled saturation, and plod-ding down carefully and cheerfully among the rocks and roots of the forest, following the path we have beaten and cut for our-selves on our way up. It is dangerously slippery, particularly that part of it through the amomums, and stumps of the cut amomums are very likely to spike your legs badly—and, my friend, never, never, step on one of the amomum stems lying straight in front of you, particularly when they are soaking wet. Ice slides are nothing to them, and when you fall, as you inevit-ably must, because all the things you grab hold of are either rotten, or as brittle as Salviati glass-ware vases, you hurt your-self in no end of places, on those aforesaid cut amomum stumps. I am speaking from sad experiences of my own, amplified by observations on the experiences of my men.

The path, when we get down again into the tree-fern region, is inches deep in mud and water, and several places where we have a drop of five feet or so over lumps of rock are worse work going down than we found them going up, especially when we have to drop down on to amomum stems. One abominable place, a V-shaped hollow, mud-lined, and with an immense tree right across it—a tree one of our tornadoes has thrown down since we passed—bothers the men badly, as they slip and scramble down, and then crawl under the tree and slip and scramble up with their loads. I say nothing about myself. I just take a flying slide of twenty feet or so and shoot flump under the tree on my back, and then deliberate whether it is worth while getting up again to go on with such a world; but vanity forbids my

dying like a dog in a ditch, and I scramble up, rejoining the others.

We then pass through a clump of those lovely great tree-ferns. The way their young fronds come up with a graceful curl, like the top of a bishop's staff, is a poem; but being at present fractious, I will observe that they are covered with horrid spines, as most young vegetables are in Africa. But talking about spines, I should remark that nothing save that precious climbing palm —I never like to say what I feel about climbing palms, because one once saved my life—equals the strong bush rope which abounds here. It is covered with short, strong, curved thorns. It creeps along concealed by decorative vegetation, and you get your legs twined in it, and of course injured. It festoons itself from tree to tree, and when your mind is set on other things, catches you under the chin, and gives you the appearance of having made a determined but ineffectual attempt to cut your throat with a saw. It whisks your hat off and grabs your clothes, and commits other iniquities too numerous to catalogue here. Years and years that bush rope will wait for a man's blood, and when he comes within reach it will have it.

We are well down now among the tree-stems grown over with rich soft green moss and delicate filmy-ferns. I should think that for a botanist these south-eastern slopes of Mungo Mah Lobeh would be the happiest hunting grounds in all West Africa.

The vegetation here is at the point of its supreme luxuriance, owing to the richness of the soil; the leaves of trees and plants I recognise as having seen elsewhere are here far larger, and the undergrowth particularly is more rich and varied, far and away. Ferns seem to find here a veritable paradise. Everything, in fact, is growing at its best. I dare say a friend of mine who told me that near Victoria he had struck his umbrella into the ground one evening, and found in the morning it was growing leaves all up its stick, was overstating the facts of the case; still, if the incident could happen anywhere it would be in this region.

We come to another fallen tree over another hole; this tree we recognise as an old acquaintance near Buea, and I feel disgusted, for I had put on a clean blouse, and washed my hands in a tea-cupful of water in a cooking pot before leaving the forest camp, so as to look presentable on reaching Buea; and all I have got to show for my exertion that is clean or anything like dry is one cuff over which I have been carrying a shawl.

We double round a corner by the stockade of the station's

plantation, and are at the top of the mud glissade—the new Government path, I should say—that leads down into the barrack-yard.

Our arrival brings Herr Liebert promptly on the scene, as kindly helpful and energetic as ever, and again anxious for me to have a bath. The men bring our saturated loads into my room, and after giving them their food and plenty of tobacco, I get my hot tea and change into the clothes I had left behind at Buea, and feeling once more fit for polite society, go out and find his Imperial and Royal Majesty's representative making a door, tightening the boards up with wedges in a very artful and professional way. We discourse on things in general and the mountain in particular. The great south-east face is now showing clear before us, the clearness that usually comes before nightfall. It looks again a vast wall, and I wish I were going up it again tomorrow.

The last reported eruption was in 1852, when signs of volcanic activity were observed by a captain who was passing at sea. The lava from this eruption must have gone down the western side, for I have come across no fresh lava beds in my wanderings on the other face. Herr Liebert has no confidence in the mountain whatsoever, and announces his intention of leaving Buea with the army on the first symptom of renewed volcanic activity. I attempt to discourage him from this energetic plan, pointing out to him the beauty of that Roman soldier at Pompeii who was found, centuries after that eruption, still at his post; and if he regards that as merely mechanical virtue, why not pursue the plan of the elder Pliny? Herr Liebert planes away at his door, and says it's not in his orders to make scientific ovservations on volcanoes in a state of eruption. When it is he'll do so—until it is, he most decidely will not. He adds Pliny was an admiral and sailors are always as curious as cats.

Buea seems a sporting place for weather even without volcanic eruptions; during the whole tornado season (there are two a year), over-charged tornadoes burst in the barrack yard. From the 14th of June till the 27th of August you never see the sun, because of the terrific and continuous wet season downpour. At the beginning and end of this cheerful period occurs a month's tornado season, and the rest of the year is dry, hot by day and cold by night.

On the following day Mary Kingsley and her carriers tramp back to Victoria in torrential rain.

My boots are a dreadful nuisance today. I got them dried last night for the first time since I left Victoria, and they are like boards. Xenia brought them to me this morning and I congratulated him on being able to do without boots, but he proudly pointed to his distorted toe-joints, and informed me that once he always wore boots, better boots than mine, and boots that were 'all shiny'.

The old chief at Buana was very nice today when we were coming through his territory. He came out to meet us with some of his wives. Both men and women among these Bakwiri are tattooed, or rather painted, on the body, face and arms, but as far as I have seen not on the legs. The patterns are handsome, and more elaborate than any such that I have seen. One man who came with the party had two figures of men tattooed on the region where his waistcoat should have been. I gave the chief some tobacco though he never begged for anything. He accepted it thankfully, and handing it to his wives preceded us on our path for about a mile and a half and then having reached the end of his district, we shook hands and parted.

After all the rain we have had, the road was of course worse than ever, and as we were going through the forest towards the war hedge, I noticed a strange sound, a dull roar which made the light friable earth quiver under our feet, and I remembered with alarm the accounts Herr Liebert has given me of the strange ways of rivers on this mountain; how by Buea, about 200 metres below where you cross it, the river goes bodily down a hole. How there is a waterfall on the south face of the mountain that falls right into another hole, and is never seen again, any more than the Buea River is. How there are in certain places underground rivers, which though never seen can be heard roaring, and felt in the quivering earth under foot in the wet season, and so on. So I judged our present roar arose from some such phenomenon, and with feminine nervousness began to fear that the rotten water-logged earth we were on might give way, and engulf the whole of us, and we should never be seen again.

But when we got down into our next ravine, the one where I got the fish and water-spiders on our way up, things explained themselves. The bed of this ravine was occupied by a raging torrent of great beauty, but alarming appearance to a person desirous of getting across to the other side of it. On our right hand was a waterfall of tons of water thirty feet high or so. The brown water wreathed with foam dashed down into the

swirling pool we faced, and at the other edge of the pool, striking a ridge of higher rock, it flew up in a lovely flange some
twelve feet or so high, before making another and a deeper
spring to form a second waterfall. My men shouted to me above
the roar that it was 'a bad place'. They never give me half the
credit I deserve for seeing danger, and they said, 'Water all go
for hole down there, we fit to go too suppose we fall.' 'Don't fall,'
I yelled, which was the only good advice I could think of to give
them just then.

Each small load had to be carried across by two men along
a submerged ridge in the pool, where the water was only breast
high. I had all I could do to get through it, though assisted by
my invaluable Bakwiri staff. But no harm befell. Indeed we
were all the better for it, or at all events cleaner. We met five
torrents that had to be waded during the day; none so bad as
the first, but all superbly beautiful.

When we turned our faces westwards just above the wood
we had to pass through before getting into the great road, the
view of Victoria, among its hills, and fronted by its bay, was
divinely lovely and glorious with colour. I left the boys here, as
they wanted to rest, and to hunt up water, &c., among the little
cluster of huts that are here on the right-hand side of the path,
and I went on alone down through the wood, and out on to the
road, where I found my friend, the Alsatian engineer, still
flourishing and busy with his cheery gang of wood-cutters. I
made a brief halt here, getting some soda water. I was not
anxious to reach Victoria before nightfall, but yet to reach it
before dinner, and while I was chatting, my boys came through
the wood and the engineer most kindly gave them a tot of brandy
apiece, to which I owe their arrival in Victoria. I left them again
resting, fearing I had overdone my arrangements for arriving
just after nightfall and went on down that road which was more
terrible than ever now to my bruised, weary feet, but even more
lovely than ever in the dying light of the crimson sunset, with all
its dark shadows among the trees begemmed with countless fire-
flies—and so safe into Victoria—sneaking up the Government
House hill by the private path through the Botanical Gardens.

Idabea, the steward, turned up, and I asked him to let me
have some tea and bread and butter, for I was dreadfully hungry.
He rushed off, and I heard tremendous operations going on in the
room above. In a few seconds water poured freely down through
the dining-room ceiling. It was bath palaver again. The excellent Idabea evidently thought it was severely wanted, more

wanted than such vanities as tea. Fortunately, Herr von Lucke was away down in town, looking after duty as usual, so I was tidy before he returned to dinner. When he returned he had the satisfaction a prophet should feel. I had got half-drowned, and I had got an awful cold, the most awful cold in the head of modern times, I believe, but he was not artistically exultant over my afflictions.

My men having all reported themselves safe I went to my comfortable rooms, but could not turn in, so fascinating was the warmth and beauty down here; and as I sat on the verandah overlooking Victoria and the sea, in the dim soft light of the stars, with the fire-flies round me, and the lights of Victoria away below, and heard the soft rush of the Lukola River, and the sound of the sea-surf on the rocks, and the tom-tomming and singing of the natives, all matching and mingling together, 'Why did I come to Africa?' thought I. Why! who would not come to its twin brother hell itself for all the beauty and the charm of it!

POETRY
IN EVERYMAN

A SELECTION

Silver Poets of the Sixteenth Century

EDITED BY
DOUGLAS BROOKS-DAVIES
A new edition of this famous
Everyman collection **£6.99**

Complete Poems

JOHN DONNE
The father of metaphysical verse in
this highly-acclaimed edition **£4.99**

Complete English Poems, Of Education, Areopagitica

JOHN MILTON
An excellent introduction to
Milton's poetry and prose **£6.99**

Selected Poems

JOHN DRYDEN
A poet's portrait of Restoration
England **£4.99**

Selected Poems

PERCY BYSSHE SHELLEY
'The essential Shelley' in one
volume **£3.50**

Women Romantic Poets 1780-1830: An Anthology

Hidden talent from the Romantic era,
rediscovered for the first time **£5.99**

Poems in Scots and English

ROBERT BURNS
The best of Scotland's greatest lyric
poet **£4.99**

Selected Poems

D. H. LAWRENCE
A newly-edited selection spanning
the whole of Lawrence's literary
career **£4.99**

The Poems

W. B. YEATS
Ireland's greatest lyric poet
surveyed in this ground-breaking
edition **£6.50**

£5.99

£4.99

£3.50

AVAILABILITY

All books are available from your local bookshop or direct from
Littlehampton Book Services Cash Sales, 14 Eldon Way, LinesideEstate,
Littlehampton, West Sussex BN17 7HE. PRICES ARE SUBJECT TO CHANGE.

To order any of the books, please enclose a cheque (in £ sterling) made payable to
Littlehampton Book Services, or phone your order through with credit card details (Access,
Visa or Mastercard) on 0903 721596 (24 hour answering service) stating card number and
expiry date. Please add £1.25 for package and postage to the total value of your order.

DRAMA
IN EVERYMAN

A SELECTION

Everyman and Medieval Miracle Plays

EDITED BY A. C. CAWLEY
A selection of the most popular medieval plays **£3.99**

Complete Plays and Poems

CHRISTOPHER MARLOWE
The complete works of this fascinating Elizabethan in one volume **£5.99**

Complete Poems and Plays

ROCHESTER
The most sexually explicit – and strikingly modern – writing of the seventeenth century **£5.99**

Restoration Plays

Five comedies and two tragedies representing the best of the Restoration stage **£7.99**

Female Playwrights of the Restoration: Five Comedies

Rediscovered literary treasures in a unique selection **£5.99**

Poems and Plays

OLIVER GOLDSMITH
The most complete edition of Goldsmith available **£4.99**

Plays, Poems and Prose

J. M. SYNGE
The most complete edition of Synge available **£6.99**

Plays, Prose Writings and Poems

OSCAR WILDE
The full force of Wilde's wit in one volume **£4.99**

A Doll's House/The Lady from the Sea/The Wild Duck

HENRIK IBSEN
A popular selection of Ibsen's major plays **£3.99**

£2.99

£2.99

£2.99

AVAILABILITY

All books are available from your local bookshop or direct from
Littlehampton Book Services Cash Sales, 14 Eldon Way, LinesideEstate, Littlehampton, West Sussex BN17 7HE. PRICES ARE SUBJECT TO CHANGE.

To order any of the books, please enclose a cheque (in £ sterling) made payable to Littlehampton Book Services, or phone your order through with credit card details (Access, Visa or Mastercard) on 0903 721596 (24 hour answering service) stating card number and expiry date. Please add £1.25 for package and postage to the total value of your order.

SHORT STORY COLLECTIONS
IN EVERYMAN

A SELECTION

The Secret Self
Short Stories by Women
'A superb collection' *Guardian* **£4.99**

Selected Short Stories
and Poems
THOMAS HARDY
The best of Hardy's Wessex in a
unique selection **£4.99**

The Best of
Sherlock Holmes
ARTHUR CONAN DOYLE
All the favourite adventures in one
volume **£4.99**

Great Tales of Detection
Nineteen Stories
Chosen by Dorothy L. Sayers **£3.99**

Short Stories
KATHERINE MANSFIELD
A selection displaying the
remarkable range of Mansfield's
writing **£3.99**

Selected Stories
RUDYARD KIPLING
Includes stories chosen to reveal the
'other' Kipling **£4.50**

The Strange Case of
Dr Jekyll and Mr Hyde
and Other Stories
R. L. STEVENSON
An exciting selection of gripping
tales from a master of suspense **£3.99**

Modern Short Stories 2:
1940-1980
Thirty-one stories from the greatest
modern writers **£3.50**

The Day of Silence and
Other Stories
GEORGE GISSING
Gissing's finest stories, available for
the first time in one volume **£4.99**

Selected Tales
HENRY JAMES
Stories portraying the tensions
between private life and the outside
world **£5.99**

£4.99

£6.99

CLASSIC NOVELS
IN EVERYMAN

A SELECTION

The Way of All Flesh
SAMUEL BUTLER
A savagely funny odyssey from joy-less duty to unbridled liberalism **£4.99**

Born in Exile
GEORGE GISSING
A rationalist's progress towards love and compromise in class-ridden Victorian England **£4.99**

David Copperfield
CHARLES DICKENS
One of Dickens' best-loved novels, brimming with humour **£3.99**

The Last Chronicle of Barset
ANTHONY TROLLOPE
Trollope's magnificent conclusion to his Barsetshire novels **£4.99**

He Knew He Was Right
ANTHONY TROLLOPE
Sexual jealousy, money and women's rights within marriage – a novel ahead of its time **£6.99**

Tess of the D'Urbervilles
THOMAS HARDY
The powerful, poetic classic of wronged innocence **£3.99**

Wuthering Heights
and Poems
EMILY BRONTE
A powerful work of genius – one of the great masterpieces of literature **£3.50**

Tom Jones
HENRY FIELDING
The wayward adventures of one of literatures most likable heroes **£5.99**

The Master of Ballantrae
and Weir of Hermiston
R. L. STEVENSON
Together in one volume, two great novels of high adventure and family conflict **£4.99**

£3.99

£2.99

£3.99

AVAILABILITY

All books are available from your local bookshop or direct from
**Littlehampton Book Services Cash Sales, 14 Eldon Way, LinesideEstate,
Littlehampton, West Sussex BN17 7HE.** PRICES ARE SUBJECT TO CHANGE.

To order any of the books, please enclose a cheque (in £ sterling) made payable to Littlehampton Book Services, or phone your order through with credit card details (Access, Visa or Mastercard) on 0903 721596 (24 hour answering service) stating card number and expiry date. Please add £1.25 for package and postage to the total value of your order.

ESSAYS, CRITICISM AND HISTORY IN EVERYMAN

A SELECTION

The Embassy to Constantinople and Other Writings
LIUDPRAND OF CREMONA
An insider's view of political machinations in medieval Europe
£5.99

The Rights of Man
THOMAS PAINE
One of the great masterpieces of English radicalism **£4.99**

Speeches and Letters
ABRAHAM LINCOLN
A key document of the American Civil War **£4.99**

Essays
FRANCIS BACON
An excellent introduction to Bacon's incisive wit and moral outlook **£3.99**

Puritanism and Liberty: Being the Army Debates (1647-49) from the Clarke Manuscripts
A fascinating revelation of Puritan minds in action **£7.99**

History of His Own Time
BISHOP GILBERT BURNET
A highly readable contemporary account of the Glorious Revolution of 1688 **£7.99**

Biographia Literaria
SAMUEL TAYLOR COLERIDGE
A masterpiece of criticism, marrying the study of literature with philosophy **£4.99**

Essays on Literature and Art
WALTER PATER
Insights on culture and literature from a major voice of the 1890s **£3.99**

Chesterton on Dickens: Criticisms and Appreciations
A landmark in Dickens criticism, rarely surpassed **£4.99**

Essays and Poems
R. L. STEVENSON
Stevenson's hidden treasures in a new selection **£4.99**

£3.99

£4.99

AVAILABILITY

All books are available from your local bookshop or direct from
Littlehampton Book Services Cash Sales, 14 Eldon Way, LinesideEstate, Littlehampton, West Sussex BN17 7HE. PRICES ARE SUBJECT TO CHANGE.

To order any of the books, please enclose a cheque (in £ sterling) made payable to Littlehampton Book Services, or phone your order through with credit card details (Access, Visa or Mastercard) on 0903 721596 (24 hour answering service) stating card number and expiry date. Please add £1.25 for package and postage to the total value of your order.

WOMEN'S WRITING
IN EVERYMAN

A SELECTION

Female Playwrights of the Restoration
FIVE COMEDIES
Rediscovered literary treasures in a unique selection **£5.99**

The Secret Self
SHORT STORIES BY WOMEN
'A superb collection' *Guardian* **£4.99**

Short Stories
KATHERINE MANSFIELD
An excellent selection displaying the remarkable range of Mansfield's talent **£3.99**

Women Romantic Poets 1780-1830: An Anthology
Hidden talent from the Romantic era, rediscovered for the first time **£5.99**

Selected Poems
ELIZABETH BARRETT BROWNING
A major contribution to our appreciation of this inspiring and innovative poet **£5.99**

Frankenstein
MARY SHELLEY
A masterpiece of Gothic terror in its original 1818 version **£3.99**

The Life of Charlotte Brontë
MRS GASKELL
A moving and perceptive tribute by one writer to another **£4.99**

Vindication of the Rights of Woman and The Subjection of Women
MARY WOLLSTONECRAFT
AND J. S. MILL
Two pioneering works of early feminist thought **£4.99**

The Pastor's Wife
ELIZABETH VON ARNIM
A funny and accomplished novel by the author of *Elizabeth and Her German Garden* **£5.99**

£4.99

£2.99

£5.99

AVAILABILITY

All books are available from your local bookshop or direct from
Littlehampton Book Services Cash Sales, 14 Eldon Way, LinesideEstate, Littlehampton, West Sussex BN17 7HE. PRICES ARE SUBJECT TO CHANGE.

To order any of the books, please enclose a cheque (in £ sterling) made payable to Littlehampton Book Services, or phone your order through with credit card details (Access, Visa or Mastercard) on 0903 721596 (24 hour answering service) stating card number and expiry date. Please add £1.25 for package and postage to the total value of your order.

gloom fell over the whole ship from the death of the purser, Mr Crompton. It was one of those terribly, sudden, hopeless cases of Coast fever, so common on the West Coast, where no man knows from day to day whether he or those round him will not, before a few hours are over, be in the grip of malarial fever, on his way to the grave.

honour in the field of colonial enterprise with Germany; and so, as Mr Pepys would say, home to Victoria, in the lovely late afternoon. There was just a doubt, however, for half-an-hour or so, whether we should succeed in rounding the rocky promontory that separates Ambas from Man-o'-War Bay, for the sea had got rough in the mysterious way seas do down here, without any weather reason, and the wind, what there was of it, was dead against us. But although my dress was nearly reduced to the dead level of my other dresses, the thing was done.

The next few days I spent expecting the *Nachtigal*. Of course I had unpacked all my things again and most of them were at the wash, when Idabea rushes into my room saying, '*Nachtigal* kommt', and I packed furiously, and stood by to go aboard, having been well educated by my chief tutor Captain Murray, on the iniquity of detaining the ship. When, however, I was packed, I found that it was not the *Nachtigal* which had come in, but the *Hyæna*—the guard-ship of Cameroons River—out for an airing, and as her commander Captain Baham, kindly asked me on board to lunch, I had to unpack again.

At lunch I had the honour of meeting the two officers who had first ascended the peak of Cameroon from the south-east face, and I learnt from them many things which would have been of great help to me had I had this honour before I went up, but which were none the less good to know; and during the whole of their stay in Ambas Bay I received from the *Hyæna* an immense amount of pleasure, courtesy and kindness, adding to the already great debt in these things I owe to Cameroons—a debt which I shall never forget, although I can never repay it.

The third announcement of the *Nachtigal* proved true, and with my dilapidated baggage I went round in her, under the charge of Herr von Besser, into Old Calabar, where I received every hospitality from Mr Moore and Mr Wall, for my good friends Sir Claude and Lady MacDonald had left for England some months previously—for the last time as it turned out, for shortly after his arrival in England Sir Claude was sent as British Minister to Pekin.

When I reached Calabar I found that the *Bakana*, commanded by Captain Porter and having for her chief engineer Mr Peter Campbell, was expected to come in daily, and being a sister ship to the *Batanga* and so one of the finest boats in the service, I decided to wait for her, going up to say good-bye to Miss Slessor at Okÿon during the few days at my disposal.

We had a comfortable voyage up to Sierra Leone, where a

considerable fuss and left the bay without a word of apology to
the Governor.

The *Nachtigal* left Victoria the next day, it being held too
unhealthy a place for the Governor to stay in after a severe illness, and went round to Man-o'-War Bay. And the day after
Herr von Lucke took me round to the plantation in Man-o'-War
Bay, whereat the Governor was staying for a few days.

Man-o'-War Bay is a very peculiar and charming bay to the
south of Ambas, having a narrower inlet and not quite so great
a depth as the latter, from which it is separated by a high rocky
promontory of hills. I do not think it has been carefully sounded,
but there is deep water close alongside its shores, which rise very
steeply in densely wooded mountains. The main peculiarity of
it is that through a rock wall at its eastern end there is a natural
tunnel in the rock, and you can row through this in a boat and
then find yourself on another sheet of water which has no other
inlet or outlet, and is, if possible, more beautiful than Man-o'-
War Bay itself, though much smaller. It would be an exquisite
place for smuggling.

*Mary Kingsley is shown round a plantation on the southern shore
of the bay where coffee, having been attacked by a disease, is being
replaced by cacao.*

Just as we reached the nursery, and my education was flowing
on in a peaceful, pleasant stream, forty-eight burning hot
pinchers were inserted into me and I knew 'joy's short life was
overpast' for that afternoon, in other words that I had got into
a train of drivers. Resolving to suffer and be strong, I said
nothing, and seeing that there were no more of the enemy on the
ground immediately round me, I lived my tormentors down, and
did my best to keep up an appearance of interest in cacao, but
really the only thing that did interest me just then was whether
either of my companions had got drivers on them.

They never mentioned drivers. They had a little difference
of opinion over coffee disease, and a lengthy discussion on the
relative value of white and blue kokos as food-supply for
labourers, and one of them talked a little wildly, for him, at
moments. But there was no headlong dash for water, surrounded
in blue flames of bad language, such as I am accustomed to when
a lord of creation gets drivers on him, and I proudly thought
that to me alone belonged the glory of quietly living down driver
ants, but I subsequently learnt that England had to share this

his great chance of recovery, namely, getting out to sea. The true sanatorium for the Coast would be a hospital vessel attached to each district, but as this is practically impossible, the next best thing would be for the indefatigable Mr A. L. Jones and Messrs Elder Dempster to have a special hospital cabin on every one of their vessels.

The Governor of Cameroon, Herr von Puttkamer, arrives in the bay in his yacht the Nachtigal.

Herr von Puttkamer kindly asked me to breakfast on board the *Nachtigal,* and confirmed Herr von Lucke's statement about my being welcome to go round in her to Calabar. He said as soon as he got back to Cameroons he should be sending her round with the Commissioner.

I had a very pleasant afternoon, and got a good deal of material for a work on the Natural History of Governors which I do not intend to publish, but I will just state that all the West Coast Governors, whatever may be the nation they represent, are exceedingly good society. The Governor of Cameroons I consider the best; he is the most experienced, for one thing. But for fear there should be a rush of people out from home to enjoy the charms of the society of West African Governors, I will remark that they have their faults. They are awfully bad for your clothes. It is this way: after being in West Africa some little time, particularly if you have been away in the bush, your wardrobe is always in a rarefied state. For example, when in Cameroons I had one dress, and one only, that I regarded as fit to support the dignity of a representative of England, so of course when going to call on the representative of another Power I had to put that dress on, and then go out in open boats to war-ships or for bush walks in it, and equally of course down came tornadoes and rain by the ton. I did not care for the thunder, lightning, or wind. What worried me was the conviction that that precious rain would take the colour out of my costume.

Governor von Puttkamer has a peculiarity not shared by any other Governor on the Coast. He likes the sea, so during breakfast the *Nachtigal* was ordered to steam about the bay, which she energetically did. Fortunately, I like the sea too, or—well! as it was, the only inconvenience we suffered was getting a heavy shock in the middle of the meal. We thought we had discovered a new rock, but found we had only struck a sleeping whale. What the whale thought I do not know, but it made a

could to aid the mission work of the United Presbyterians in
Calabar, came out and did his best to establish a sanatorium
where the fever-stricken missionaries from Calabar could come
and recruit their health without having to make the voyage
home to England. The station he established upon the mountain
at the elevation of 3,000 feet is now occupied by a Roman
Catholic mission, and their health has been little, if at all, better
than that of other Roman Catholics at a lower level.

I say other Roman Catholics advisedly, because these missionaries live, as a rule, in a more healthy way than members of
other missions in West Africa. The reasons why the upper slopes
of Mungo do not afford the healthiness expected of them are
many. Chief among them is the exceedingly heavy rainfall. At
Babundi, I am told, there was a panic a short time ago among
the natives because there was no rain for an entire week, and
this extraordinary phenomenon gave rise to the idea that something serious had gone wrong with Nature and that something
was going to happen, but a calm business man told me this story
must be without foundation, because it has never been dry for a
week at Babundi.

The reason of the heavy rainfall and drenching mists which
fall on the mountain is that it is surrounded by enormous steaming swamps: to the north by those of the Rio del Rey and
Calabar, to the south by those of the Cameroon, Mungo, and
Bimbia Rivers, while its superior height catches the heavy,
water-laden clouds floating in from the Atlantic. In addition to
this, the cold air rushes down its sides in draughts that condense
the water in the hot overladen lower layers of the atmosphere.

One hears a great deal in West Africa of the 3,000 feet line as
being the limit of the region of malarial fever, but I do not think
this is anything more than a theoretical idea, and indeed there
are few situations in West Africa besides Mungo, where the
theory could be put to the test. Buea and De Buncha, Mr
Thomson's sanatorium site, are at about this elevation. Buea
has not yet had sufficient trial as a health resort to speak of it
finally, but the great prevalence there of phagedænic ulcers
does not lead one to regard the air as healthy.

I regard this idea of the possibility of finding an elevated
situation in West Africa suitable for a sanatorium, as one of the
most dangerous the governmental authorities suffer from, for it
induces them to build houses in out-of-the-way places, and send
men suffering from fever to them to die, robbing the sick man of

work would be suspended for the next hour or so, and finally, after giving good sport, the pig would be brought back squealing by triumphant and heated stewards.

When I got back to Victoria one of my first inquiries was after that Bobia pig. I instantly saw I had aroused sad memories, and learnt that the cook—its most responsible custodian—was under arrest, though out on bail—on its behalf. It seems it got adrift as usual, and when the hunt was started no pig was to be found, so cook, fearing the ire of Germany, posts off into the town and gets hold of the first pig there he can lay hands on. Now this pig was the property of a lady—a woman of spirit, and she clouted cook and swore cook clouted her. But anyhow cook bore off his prize, and tied it up in place of the Bobia pig, trusting that his busy master would not notice the difference in the two pigs, and would not hear of his raid.

His hopes were vain. Herr von Lucke saw that this succulent little porker was not the offering from Bobia, and with a truly Roman sense of duty, handed his own cook over to be tried by the native court, presided over by the Baptist minister and two local chiefs. The case took nearly all day, and all the Government House staff had to be absent from their work, giving evidence as to the character of the cook, and the pig, and so on. The case went against cook in the end, and he had to pay damages to the injured lady and return his capture. What became of the original Bobia pig I do not know, for it had not been found up to the time of my leaving Victoria.

An account follows of the founding of Victoria, capital of Cameroon, by Baptists driven from the Spanish-held island of Fernando Po by a proclamation in 1858 that no religious profession other than that of the Roman Catholic Church would be tolerated. Mary Kingsley rejects a prevailing belief in the healthy nature of the country surrounding Ambas Bay.

The idea that a sanatorium might be built high on the mountain, above the so-called fever line—a line that is merely an imaginative figment, for local conditions alter it in every separate place —at first seemed reasonable, but a closer knowledge of the peculiar meteorological conditions of the great mountain has proved this idea also to be an erroneous one.

A very noble and devoted Scotch gentleman named Thomson, possessed of considerable wealth and anxious to do what he

slightly bigger than its neighbours, and it is called sometimes Pirate Island. Its sides are strictly perpendicular, and you can get to the top by a projecting rock ridge which runs up the cliff on the northern side. I did not go up, for the day I was taken round it the weather was too rough for us to get to the ledge of rock on which you land. Strangely enough, this rocky and least fertile of all the islands in Ambas Bay is densely inhabited by a quantity of fisher-folk and their wives, families, pigs and goats, all living together in a village on the top, facing seawards. Facing landwards they have made on the top of a sheer cliff a long bench, on which the fishermen sit in a row most of the day, watching Victoria, while their wives look after the rest of the inhabitants and do odd jobs generally, and I should imagine these good ladies must lead anxious lives for fear of either the children or the live stock falling out of the village into the sea.

At night Ambas Bay is dotted all over with the torches of these fishermen, as they seem to do most of their fishing by spearing, and they are obliged to be industrious at their profession because among other inconveniences Bobia has no water, and all the water has to be bought and brought from the mainland and there is no room for a plantation. Besides, the pig population is too heavy to allow of agriculture. I deeply regret not having been able to bring home a Bobia pig. One would have caused a profound sensation at the Royal Agricultural Show.

These interesting animals are black in colour, as indeed is common in African pigs, two-thirds head, and after a very small and very flat bit of body, end in an inordinately long tail. Their mental dispositions are lively, frolicsome and extremely nomadic and predatory. The Chief of Bobia, in a burst of affection, gave Herr von Lucke one just before I arrived in Victoria, and a good deal of my time while waiting to start up Mungo, was spent in assisting Idabea and the steward boys in chivying this pig. Herr von Lucke had given strict orders it was to be kept tied up, and solemnly warned his retainers they were responsible for its safe keeping. But somehow or another it was always slipping its cable and getting away, and I used to meet it away in the Botanical Gardens, and in fact in so many unexpected places that I should not have been surprised to have met it anywhere. After my first few days' experience of it, whenever I met it I used first to try and secure it, and then failing brilliantly, post off uphill and report its iniquities. All household

CHAPTER FOURTEEN

Cameroon to Calabar

and so Home

*On the day after Mary Kingsley's return to Victoria, Herr von
Lucke takes her in a boat to see the islands in the bay.*

This Bay of Amboises, commonly called Ambas Bay, is without
doubt both the most lovely and the most fertile spot on the
whole of the western side of the continent of Africa; and
experienced mariners who have wandered far and wide say that
it has few rivals in either quality in any other region of the
world. To me with my experience of the world strictly limited to
England and West Africa, it is an unthinkable thing that there
can be any place more perfect in loveliness, majesty, colour and
charm, with its circumambient mountains to landward—mountains that rise out of its dark, clear waters to heights from 3,000
to 13,760 feet. At their feet is just one narrow strip of flat shore,
on which, nestling among the mango trees, is the pretty, long,
ribbon-like town of Victoria—a soft brown native town, here
and there speckled with a few white European buildings, while
in the bay itself are three islands—Ambas, Mondoleh and
Bobia—and several pinnacle rocks with energetic acrobats of
trees growing in among their clefts and crevices.

Ambas Island is the outermost island in the bay. It is smaller
and lower than Mondoleh and but little forested. Indeed most of
it is only covered with brushwood and grass, for there is not
much soil among its rocks. It now belongs to an officer of the
Hyæna, who won it in a raffle for 500 marks. But although
Ambas Island is very beautiful, and so on, I do not think the
returns on the invested capital will be high for some years to
come. It has no human habitation or inhabitants yet on it,
and its population consists of goats and pigs. The most
noticeable thing about Ambas Island is the fact that both the
English and the Germans have got it arranged wrong on their
charts.

Bobia is the most interesting of all the three islands. It is on
a line with the Pirate rocks. Indeed it is really one of them, only